The Schooling of Girls in Britain and Ireland, 1800–1900

Routledge Research in Gender and History

The Schooling of Girls in Britain and Ireland, 1800–1900

Jane McDermid

Routledge
Taylor & Francis Group

NEW YORK   LONDON

First published 2012
by Routledge
711 Third Avenue, New York, NY 10017

Simultaneously published in the UK
by Routledge
2 Park Square, Milton Park, Abingdon, Oxon OX14 4RN

*Routledge is an imprint of the Taylor & Francis Group,
an informa business*

Library of Congress Cataloging-in-Publication Data
McDermid, Jane.
   The schooling of girls in Britain and Ireland, 1800–1900 / Jane
McDermid.
      pages cm. — (Routledge research in gender and history)
Includes bibliographical references and index.
   1. Girls—Education—Great Britain—History—19th
century.   2. Girls—Education—Ireland—History—19th
century.   I. Title.
   LC2047.M34 2012
   371.822094109034—dc23
   2011044786

ISBN13: 978-0-415-18196-9 (hbk)
ISBN13: 978-0-203-12004-0 (ebk)

Typeset in Sabon
by IBT Global.

This book is dedicated to the memory of Auriel Samuelsen, 1936–2011

Contents

Acknowledgments

In the research and writing of this book I have incurred many debts, enough to fill a companion volume. For the sake of brevity and to spare blushes, I will simply acknowledge key organizations and associated individuals. The Women's History Network (particularly Sue Morgan and June Purvis) and Women's History Scotland (especially Esther Breitenbach) have been constant sources of support and advice. The History of Education Society (notably Richard Aldrich and Ruth Watts) and its journal, *History of Education*, as well as the Centre for the History of Women's Education at the University of Winchester (especially Joyce Goodman and Stephanie Spencer) have been generous in accepting me as a relatively late arrival to the history of education. I also benefited from the two joint conferences held between the History of Education Society and the Australia and New Zealand History of Education Society (in Swansea in 2003 and Sydney in 2008). All these organizations have provided opportunities to present my research in its early stages; their conferences and seminar series have helped me develop ideas and pointed me in directions I might otherwise have missed. I learned a lot from papers presented by, as well as participating on panels with, other scholars, including Lynn Abrams, Maria Luddy, Jane Martin, Lindy Moore, Deirdre Raftery, Jane Rendall, Wendy Robinson and Marjorie Theobald. I have received much needed help from archivists and librarians, notably Nick Graffy at Hartley Library, Southampton University. Colleagues in History at Southampton have also offered encouragement and made editorial suggestions (in particular John Oldfield and Adrian Smith). On a personal level I am grateful to Frank and Mimi Cogliano who generously let me 'borrow' their flat in Edinburgh each July for successive years, which has been so conducive to relaxation as well as research and writing.

1   Introduction

This book is an attempt to compare and contrast the formal education of the majority of girls in the UK of Britain and Ireland in the nineteenth century. Previous studies of female education have generally been concerned with one of the countries which make up the UK, the majority being on England. Books about 'Britain' also invariably centre on England with occasional references to Scotland and little noted specifically about Wales. Such 'British' studies tend not to include Ireland despite its incorporation into the Union in 1801.[1] Building on these works as well as an earlier study of the schooling of working-class girls in Victorian Scotland, the aim here is to present a comparative synthesis of the formal education of working- and middle-class girls in the same period with the emphasis on the interaction of gender, social class, religion and nationality across the UK.[2] In the following chapters, similarities as well as differences between both the social classes and the constituent parts of the Union will be examined.[3]

The opportunity in 2005 to participate in the Economic and Social Research Council (ESRC) seminar series on social change in the history of education in the UK since 1800, and in particular to work with Deirdre Raftery and Gareth Elwyn Jones, convinced me of the gains which such a comparison between the education of girls in the constituent parts of the Union would offer.[4] This is the case as much for what they had in common as for what distinguished them. For example, across the UK there were strikingly similar concerns about whether working-class girls could fulfil their domestic responsibilities, either in their own home or employed in someone else's, though as will be shown in Chapter 2, there was disagreement over where such skills should best or more appropriately be taught.

My study of working-class girls' education in nineteenth-century Scotland questioned whether the educational tradition, summed up in the phrase 'democratic intellect', had any relevance for girls since it was an essentially masculine construct, represented by the 'lad of parts' or talented boy whose poverty should not bar him from university.[5] Lindy Moore had already shown that girls in the mixed-sex parish schools might be taught the 'university' subjects of classics and mathematics.[6] I found that what girls and boys were taught in the parish schools before 1872 and in the board schools thereafter depended very much on local circumstances. For example, since the early nineteenth century, Aberdeenshire's parish schools had benefited from the Dick (1833) and Milne (1846) bequests which encouraged the teaching of higher or university subjects.[7] These bequests ensured that a higher proportion of university-educated masters were employed in the region's parish schools than elsewhere in Scotland, highlighting the other masculine figure at the heart of the national tradition in education, the dominie, who as will be seen in Chapter 4 continued to dominate the teaching profession even when outnumbered by women.[8] For Helen Corr, this is a reflection of the later development of feminism in Scotland, at least within the teaching profession, compared to England.[9] The implication is that compared again to England, Scotland was a deeply, even peculiarly, patriarchal society, and yet a study of Presbyterianism in Scotland found no concerted campaign by the churches against higher education for women.[10] Such complications led me to look at the place of women teachers within the board schools after 1872 and compare it with the situation in England, which is developed here in Chapter 4.[11]

This book approaches education in the narrow sense of formal and systematic instruction, though especially in the case of middle-class girls, there was little in the way of either aspect at least until the end of the period. Whereas the focus is on girls, the analysis rests heavily on gender as a social and cultural determinant of what, where, why and how girls were educated. Gender, of course, was not the only factor influencing their education, nor was it always the primary one, though it was almost always in the mix with social class, family values and needs, religion and politics.

The perspective is that of observer. The primary sources used, such as the reports of government commissions into education and pamphlets written by educational and feminist reformers, do not tell us much about how the taught experienced schooling, as distinct from what the teachers, educationalists, clergy, feminists and politicians thought about the state of their education, how it might be improved and the parameters within which they should be educated. Again, this is especially the case for working-class girls whose schooling is examined in Chapter 2. Very few working-class women in this period wrote autobiographies, though as Jonathan Rose has observed whatever their social class 'memoirists are not entirely representative'.[12] Most of the evidence used here consists of observations of and judgments about them presented by their social superiors who were rarely flattering though often sympathetic, if condescending, in their views. They were certainly not neutral: they brought their own assumptions and values to bear in their reports on education—and more generally in the case of the lower classes also on their lives and morals—as well as on the questions they asked and the decisions they made on what to record or omit. Still, such reports provide a mass of material which, whatever the prejudices, can be revealing about both the expectations and the reality of female education, highlighting gaps, if not contradictions, between the ideology of domesticity and the ideal of separate spheres, on the one hand, and, on the other, the underlying realities of most Victorian women's lives.

The main subjects of this study are the majority of girls of the working and middle classes who were educated in the standard ways and not those who were regarded as outside the norm, whether ideologically, socially or morally. Thus, for example, ideas of radicals on education, particularly of girls and women, are not included here, though previous studies have pointed out that even the Owenite call for intellectual equality was not intended primarily for women's personal development: in line with the ideas discussed in this study it was more for the good of their families.[13]

The focus here is also on day schools and in particular on state intervention in the education of the poor. Indeed, the question of the role of the state in education was another mark of social class distinction. Thus in 1864 Harriet Martineau (1802–1876) declared that 'there is nobody in England who for a moment dreams of asking the state to undertake . . . the education of the daughters of the most active, practical, and domestic class of English citizens'.[14] Yet while she believed that the best place for educating girls of her own social class was the home, she held that the state had a role to play in the education of the working class. Moreover, middle-class women saw themselves as having a duty of philanthropy towards the poor, especially girls and women, for example, through Sunday and charity schools, which state intervention could not replace but rather would facilitate.

State intervention in the formal schooling of working-class children came at different times in the constituent parts of the UK. It was seen first in Ireland in 1831 and nearly four decades later in England and Wales (1870) and Scotland (1872). Before state intervention, the education of girls in charity, dame and other private (or adventure) schools had always been weighted towards the domestic, with poor girls more likely to be taught sewing and knitting than reading and writing, related to both the domestic tasks expected of females and the more restricted range of wage-earning occupations open to women of the lower classes.[15] The curriculum in such establishments was very limited, though some organisers of Sunday schools for working-class children and adults offered supplementary evening classes in secular subjects during the week, while in the latter part of the nineteenth century, school boards also ran evening continuation classes for girls and boys. Both concentrated on elementary and vocational subjects, and neither challenged contemporary understandings of women's role. Some Mechanics' Institutes (established by middle-class male philanthropists for working-class men) set up day schools for members' children, girls and boys, for example, in Liverpool and Leeds, but these were for a tiny minority and not for the poorest, while the curriculum for girls emphasised their domestic duties. Moreover, the more radical Owenites and Chartists were suspicious of the education offered by the Institutes as 'so many traps to catch the people' set by the rich and powerful.[16]

There were some female Chartist speakers, and a few women gave lectures in the Institutes as they did in the Owenite Halls of Science, but it was more common for the Institutes either to bar women or to admit them only as onlookers.[17] Moreover, despite the rivalry between the Owenite Halls and the Mechanics' Institutes, both tended to see the need to educate women primarily for their wifely duties.[18] June Purvis has highlighted the significance of both Mechanics' Institutes and Working Men's Colleges in helping to shape 'patterns of provision that reinforced patriarchal and familial ideologies as well as the divisions between the social classes and between men and women'.[19] Like both movements, though to a more limited degree and with the general aim of social control, government legislation on the education of the Victorian poor aimed to raise their cultural standards, while in keeping with all the efforts directed at educating the working class, it continued to place great emphasis on domestic subjects in the curriculum for girls. Indeed, the late nineteenth and early twentieth centuries saw an even greater part of the girls' curriculum taken up with domestic subjects under the influence of social Darwinism and eugenics.

This chapter will now set the context—political, social, economic, cultural and ideological—for the education of girls in the Victorian period. The next five sections will focus on the UK as a whole, while the sixth, 'Home rule for women', records a significant difference between Britain and Ireland in the role of Protestant lay women in the management of the schooling of the poor after the educational legislation of 1870 for England and Wales and 1872 for Scotland established local school boards to which women who met the property requirements could both vote in and stand for election. In Ireland, the intention behind the 1831 legislation to establish non-denominational schooling had been thwarted by the 1860s, with national schools run locally by the churches with, as will be seen in Chapter 2, religious orders dominant in the schooling of the Catholic poor.

POLITICS, SOCIETY AND EDUCATION

The 'long' nineteenth century (from the 1780s until the early 1900s) was a period of considerable interest in and anxiety about education across the UK. This was partly reaction to perceived social and political problems in the wake of the unrest caused by or related to the French Revolution of 1789 and the subsequent revolutionary wars, not least the Irish Rebellion of 1798 which was brutally suppressed and led to the incorporation of Ireland into the British state in 1801. There was also radical politics within Britain, from the Corresponding Societies to Owenism and from the Chartists with their petitions for universal male suffrage to the middle-class campaigns for limited electoral reform as well as calls for constitutional change—again notably the movement for Home Rule in Ireland—which forced the ruling elite to consider the need for popular education through government intervention.[20] That in turn brought concerns in Ireland, Scotland and Wales, often related to religious differences, over increasing centralization and the potential for Anglicization. Churches of all denominations tended to resist state control of education even as they increasingly needed state funding to subsidize their own efforts. Outside of the north, Ireland was predominantly Catholic but subject to a minority Protestant Anglo-Irish Ascendancy even after the Act of 1869 disestablished the Church in Ireland. Similarly in Wales, the Anglican elite was deeply resented by the Nonconformist majority which led to stiff resistance among the latter to state interference in the education of the poor. In contrast to both Ireland and Wales, Scotland's Established Church was that of the majority, but the century after 1750 had been one of increasing turbulence within Presbyterianism, culminating in the Disruption of 1843.[21] After that, the Presbyterian churches welcomed state intervention as a means to ensure the continuation of a national system of education, borrowing ideas and practices from the English, not least in the domestic education of girls, but also preserving aspects of the Scottish educational tradition which privileged boys.

Another factor underpinning the focus on perceived educational problems was the process of industrialization, though that was experienced rather differently across the British Isles. In addition, there was pressure from rapid urbanization, related to the growth in migration from rural to urban areas and between the constituent parts of the UK, most notably from Ireland to Britain which grew dramatically with the impact of the Great Famine in the second half of the 1840s. Whereas Irish Catholics were peripheral to Victorian Wales, they were the most significant minority in Scotland: by 1910, they made up ten per cent of the population in the latter but 17.6 per cent of Glasgow's population.[22] England was the largest, wealthiest and the dominant member of the Union, with political power concentrated at Westminster.[23] By 1901 over 30 million people lived in England compared to just below four million in Ireland, whose population had halved since the Famine, and 4.5 million in Scotland; and though there was a higher birth rate in Scotland than in England, there was also a higher rate of emigration. Indeed, the rate of emigration from Scotland was one of the highest in nineteenth-century Europe after Ireland and then Norway.[24] The population of Wales exceeded two million by 1911, but while it was considerably smaller than the other parts of the UK, the rate of Welsh emigration to the colonies was also much lower than that of either the Irish or the Scots.[25]

There had always been a certain suspicion among the upper classes in England about education potentially giving the poor ideas above their station: as late as 1861 the educationalist and penal reformer Mary Carpenter (1807–1877) counselled the National Association for the Promotion of Social Science (NAPSS) that in the education of the children of the poor 'there must be nothing to pamper self-indulgence, to raise the child in his own estimation above his natural position in society'. That advice was in a long passage on boarding institutions (including orphanages, industrial and reformatory schools), but Carpenter was considering more generally 'those children who are destined to earn their living by manual labour'. She was deeply sympathetic toward labouring people, especially pauper children, and aware of the structural factors underlying poverty; yet she also accepted that women's primary role was domestic and that pauper or delinquent girls could be reformed through training for a domestic future: 'The girl is especially adapted by nature for a *home*.'[26] That was a widespread view, whereas more generally poverty was blamed on the moral failings of the poor rather than economic causes. Hence, the social and political unrest between the 1780s and the 1840s had led to a change in attitude: schooling the poor came to be seen as a necessary means of maintaining political and social stability.

Perhaps the first reflection of this was the national education system designed for Ireland in 1831. Fifteen years later the Welsh-speaking Member of Parliament (M.P.) for Coventry, William Williams (1788–1865), demanded a royal commission to look into the state of education in Wales. Williams was impressed by the national system in Ireland as well as by the tradition of parish schools in Scotland which dated back to the Reformation. In both systems, teaching was in English, regarded in Ireland as the language of politics and commerce but associated in Scotland with the Reformation and their national image as a moral and orderly people.[27] Yet whereas the Scots saw their educational tradition as a mark of their national identity, Williams reflected the 'crisis of identity' in early Victorian Wales when he declared: 'If the Welsh had the same advantage for education as the Scotch, they would, instead of appearing a distinct people, in no respect differ from the English: could it therefore not be wisdom and sound policy to send the English schoolmaster among them?'[28] The subsequent parliamentary inquiry into the state of education in Wales is discussed in Chapter 2. The report of the commissioners, published in 1847 and dubbed the 'Blue Books' because of the colour of its binding, was extremely controversial in Wales, not least because of the damning indictment of the morals of the Welsh poor, particularly the women.[29]

Education throughout the UK in the Victorian period was profoundly affected by social class as well as religion, but there was less prejudice against teaching the children of the poor in Ireland (in hedge schools), Scotland (parish schools) and Wales (circulating and Sunday schools where the teaching was in Welsh) compared to England, which was partly related to the respect accorded to the schoolmaster in the smaller parts of the Union. Still, even in Scotland where the parish school was meant to be 'democratic' in the sense of being open to children of all social classes, it was most commonly attended by the working and lower middle classes and more likely to be by boys than girls. Though the parish school was built around the meritocratic ideal the much vaunted 'democratic intellect' was, as noted above, a masculine construct.[30] Yet while there were criticisms of the parochial system by the end of the eighteenth century, there was considerable anxiety that any changes would dilute what was peculiarly Scottish about education by the imposition of ideas and practices from England which, though the dominant partner in the Union, was perceived to be inferior in both. Such concern intensified in the early 1860s with Robert Lowe's (1811–1892) 'payment by results' (the Revised Code of 1862): the emphasis on elementary schooling threatened the treasured link between parish school and university in Scotland. More generally, Lowe's aim as Vice President of the Committee of Council on Education was both to increase 'efficiency' and cut costs, leading to the educational impoverishment of the already poor and their teachers.[31]

Still, despite fears of centralization, reflected in growing standardization of female education across the UK, there was room for local initiatives. Whereas Wales was included in the 1870 Elementary Education Act, it went significantly beyond English practices with the 1889 Intermediate Education Act, as had Ireland a decade earlier.[32] England still viewed the proper education of the lower orders to be elementary, though John Roach has established that by 1890 there had been some success in opening up opportunities for secondary education for the poor but able boy at least, while he believes that for middle-class girls their education was 'more radically transformed in the second half of the nineteenth century than the education of boys', though it was still for the minority.[33] There was not the same concern with secondary education in Scotland as there was in Wales due to its prized link between parish school and university, which was to the disadvantage of girls until the end of the century. In intermediate education, though for different reasons, Scotland was more like England in that what secondary schooling there was for working-class children was developed by the larger boards through the establishment of higher departments or higher grade schools in the later nineteenth century. Still, in Scotland there was little organic connection to Westminster politics, which was particularly the case on issues related to education and poor relief.[34] Indeed, outside of the English 'home' counties, it was local politics which played the biggest part in the lives of most people in the nineteenth century.[35] The result was the dominance of local elites, which differed according to the economic and social makeup of the regions.

RELIGION, UNIONISM AND EDUCATION

On the eve of Victoria's coronation, two Edinburgh writers, James Simpson (1781–1853) and George Combe (1788–1858), had advocated non-sectarian education. Whereas Simpson called for the same education for all classes and both sexes up to the age of 14 in the belief that the faculties of the female were the same as those of the male, more common was Combe's insistence on the need for instruction in the domestic skills to be included in the female curriculum.

I regard the great secular business of female life to be the producing, nurture, and rearing of children; the due management of domestic affairs; and the cultivation of those graces, virtues and affections which shed happiness on the family circle. These occupations are equally important to women as professions are to men; and under a proper system of education, women should be taught every species of knowledge, and instructed in every accomplishment which may directly contribute to the proper discharge of their duties.[36]

As will be shown in Chapter 3, however, Combe also insisted that women needed a broad education, including science and philosophy, if they were to be properly equipped for promoting the physical and mental development of their children.[37]

Both Simpson and Combe were harshly criticized for their stance on religion which was deemed atheistic. Britain was a Protestant state, and as Linda Colley has pointed out, 'intolerant Protestantism . . . served as a powerful cement between the English, the Welsh and the Scots, particularly lower down the social scale'.[38] Further up that scale there was the 'co-optation' of the Welsh and Scottish elites by the late eighteenth century, though this was not simply a matter of domination and exploitation but often one of reciprocity.[39] Colley has written with insight about the 'forging of a nation' from the Act of Union which incorporated Scotland until Victoria's accession to the throne, highlighting the role played by (mainly middle-class) women and their 'place in the nation'.[40] This study suggests that ideas about gender especially as reflected in the education of girls could be seen as a unifying thread in a union of multiple identities: although each nation and national minority was defensive of the reputation of *their* women, they all held essentially to the same ideal of womanhood.

Since Benedict Anderson published *Imagined Communities,* it is almost a truism to say that all national identities are invented and that people come to imagine a shared experience of identification with an extended community.[41] From 1801 the UK was a constitutional union of four nations in which England was clearly dominant, Ireland reluctant and Wales resentful, while Scotland regarded itself as the junior partner in the imperial project.[42] Whereas both Scotland and Wales accepted the Union, the Catholic majority in Ireland saw its status as more a subservient colony than a willing partner: effectively forced into the UK, the majority of Irish did not conceive of themselves as part of the British 'nation'.[43] Moreover, Anderson's definition of the nation was as an imagined *political* community, whereas the nineteenth-century British 'nation' excluded the majority of women as well as substantial numbers of men. He overlooked the fact that national identities are also gendered, and certainly female figures were prominent in national allegories in each of the constituent parts of the UK. The following chapters will show, however, that in education agreement on gender roles, particularly on the role of women, served to knit the constituent parts of the UK together, notably through links between Protestant middle-class feminists.

Yet each of those constituent parts also had its own tensions: in Ireland between Ulster (the most industrialized part of the country) and the three other provinces; in Wales between the agricultural north and industrial south; in Scotland between Highlands and Lowlands. England itself experienced regional tensions, for example, between London and the Midlands and north, reflected in the campaigns over electoral reform. All parts of the Union also had divisions between urban and rural. From the middle of the century, however, the British state, and particularly education, was subject to increasing centralization, which brought additional fears of Anglicization among the three smaller parts of the Union. In Wales, determination to maintain the national culture was reflected in resistance to the domination of education by the Anglican Church; in Scotland, concern over the loss of national identity led to efforts to maintain elements of the educational tradition. In both countries acceptance of the Union for economic and political reasons was balanced by determination to remain culturally distinct. In Ireland, Unionism was strong only in the north; in most of the country, it was politically as well as culturally resented and resisted, though being governed from Westminster meant that English influences could not be entirely excluded. Those influences could be seen above all in female education.

Whereas the Irish, Catholic as well as Protestant, engaged in the imperial project in large numbers, widespread and persistent anti-Catholicism within the UK made it very difficult for Catholics in Ireland to join the feminist campaigns for the reform of middle-class girls' education. These reformers were above all Protestant; indeed it has been argued that nineteenth-century feminism was 'a creed of the Protestant middle classes'.[44] The Catholic Emancipation Act of 1829 did not put an end to anti-Catholic sentiments nor prevent Catholics in Britain from feeling a beleaguered minority. The Anglican Evangelical writer on female education, Hannah More (1745–1833), for example, was profoundly anti-Catholic, reflected in her opposition to the Catholic Emancipation Act, while Dublin-born Frances Power Cobbe (1822–1904) was prejudiced against Irish Catholics even as she spent many years in Italy where she viewed the pomp and ceremony of the papal mass as a pantomime.[45] Indeed, as Margaret Ward has pointed out, those middle-class women who participated in the feminist campaigns shared what Antoinette Burton defined as 'national-imperial identification'; into the twentieth century 'those most prominent within Irish feminist circles were associated with efforts to retain the imperial link'.[46] Unionism could tolerate a range of identities as long as they served the national-imperial cause.[47]

As Chapters 2 and 3 will show, the public role of middle-class Catholic lay women was further constricted by the key part played by female religious orders in girls' education in Ireland. At the same time, the Catholic Church in Britain developed strategies, notably through education, to incorporate, though not to assimilate, the Irish poor into the British state.[48] Whereas Paul O'Leary sees the Catholic Church in Wales as concerned not just with the predominance of Protestantism within the school board system but also with the loss of Irish identity which joining it might entail, Karly Kehoe's study of the Church in Scotland focuses on the tensions (social class and cultural, but also reflecting an east-west divide) between Irish and Scottish Catholics, with the Church hierarchy determined, notably by means of education, to dilute the Irishness of both the migrants to and the Church in Scotland.[49]

Perhaps the condition of Catholic schools in Britain, especially with the Church's decision to remain outside the school systems set up by the legislation of 1870 and 1872, was the starkest reflection of the fears of the authorities concerning the impact of industrialization and urbanization on the working class. Given the widespread poverty of the migrant communities, constructing and maintaining an education system was a huge challenge. For example, Catholic schools in Glasgow, which housed the majority of Irish Catholics who lived in Scotland, were overcrowded and plagued by irregular attendance and lack of punctuality, the standard of teaching was lower, most Catholic teachers did not possess certificates and there was a heavier reliance on pupil teachers than in the board schools.[50] In general, the widespread poverty among the Victorian Catholic population meant that children were expected to earn as soon as possible, resulting in very irregular attendance. Remaining outside the board system, however, did not mean that Catholic schools were uninfluenced either by government policy or by reforming ideas on education. Indeed, as will be shown in Chapters 2 and 3, Catholics and Protestants agreed that female education was crucial, for both the family and society and women, especially of the middle class, had a crucial role to play in this.

Thus, whatever the denomination, girls' education in the nineteenth century was subject to the ideal of female domesticity. Social class, moreover, also meant that this common ideal would be inculcated by different means, notably through a segregation of the classes in different types of schools with socially appropriate curricula. Indeed, as the following chapters will show, Victorian feminists championed gender differences in education as a means of providing middle-class women with a legitimate public role and the spinsters among them with career opportunities which men could not claim and which would bring the female teacher both status and influence in public life as the headmistress of girls' schools and as the domestic science teacher.

FEMALE EDUCATION AND THE MORAL COMMUNITY

A key question, whatever the region or social class, was what were girls to be educated for?[51] While formal schooling of the poor was now recognised as a means of ensuring a stable, ordered society and basic literacy and numeracy became increasingly relevant skills for paid employment, ladies were not expected to have to work for a living, and the choices for those who did were even more circumscribed than they were for the daughters of the poor. As Chapter 4 will show, even when a young lady was likely to have to support herself, she was not to be (or seen to be) prepared by education for such an eventuality. Harriet Martineau wrote as late as 1860: 'There are still wives of merchants and manufacturers who, pondering the prospects of their daughters, say, "The truth is, no woman who has been engaged in education ever can obtain the position of one who has not". There is still a reluctance in men to refer to the fact that their mothers or sisters have kept school.' She went on

> Wherever we go among parents of the middle class, we find the one gnawing anxiety which abides in their hearts is the dread of their daughters 'having to go out as governesses'. 'Anything but that!' says the father, when talking confidentially after his day's work at the office, or the mill, or in the counting-house, or in going the rounds of his patients. 'Anything but that!' sighs the mother, as she thinks of her own girls placed and treated as she has seen so many.[52]

Vocational education was not for ladies: it would signal the failure of the father to provide for his daughter and her failure to compete in the marriage stakes. At the same time, women generally, it was felt, were the key to a harmonious society. On the one hand, a clear demarcation of gender roles was seen to be 'natural'; on the other, it was believed that the ideology of domesticity had to be inculcated. For the daughters of the poor, this was reflected in the concerns of the Evangelical revival of the late eighteenth century, with its focus on Sunday and charity schools.[53] But Evangelicals were also very concerned that the education which ladies received did not prepare them for such a role: as will be seen in Chapter 3, Evangelical writers were severely critical of the superficiality of what was taught to young ladies of the upper and middle classes and of the frivolous, even immoral, behaviour of 'society'.

Another influence on late eighteenth-century writings on female education were works on moral philosophy, political economy, social mores and history by authors based in Scotland, particularly Edinburgh, who took a keen interest in the role that the feminine character could play in a moral community, perceiving a correlation between motherhood and nationhood.[54] They were both influential for and influenced by the bluestockings around Elizabeth Montagu in London.[55] Such writers and intellectual circles generally agreed that the position of women in society, and indeed men's treatment of them, was an indication of the level of civilization and so was historically constructed. Since it had changed over time, there was the possibility of further improvement. The institution of the family and the role of women within it were deemed to be of profound significance for civil society, thus also holding out the possibility of a public role for women though still within limited areas which could be identified as connected to the domestic sphere.

The emphasis, then, was not on equality between women and men—indeed, some Enlightenment philosophers such as David Hume (1711–1776) insisted men were by nature both physically and intellectually superior. Nevertheless, there was a sense of women in partnership (albeit unequal) with men, both in the family and in civil society.[56] There was still a notion of different spheres for the sexes, which it has been argued was heightened in the late eighteenth and early nineteenth centuries.[57] But the public/ private spheres were not entirely separate or impermeable, and nor was there only one public: propertied men still laid claim to the political sphere, but their female counterparts increasingly claimed a place in civil society.[58] Whatever their political and religious views, women writers in the late eighteenth century not only did not accept that their sphere was inferior to the male sphere, but also as William Stafford has explained, they saw the domestic as the 'best space'. Moreover, it was: 'best for men as well as for women. It can be best in this way, because it undergoes considerable expansion at their hands, into the "social", into activity and usefulness in the community.'[59]

This claim that women, at least those of the upper and middle classes, could have a public role—indeed, that they had a public duty—in developing society and laying the foundations for a patriotic 'nation' was a theme of writings, both radical and conservative, which called for improvements in female education.[60] While these ideas had much in common, not least as will be seen in Chapter 3 in the severe critique of an education based on the showy 'accomplishments' and recommendation of a serious schooling for young ladies, conservative Evangelicals like Hannah More still saw the home as woman's proper sphere.[61] Her writings were certainly influential. Indeed it has been claimed that she 'had scotched the ideas of Mary Wollstonecraft and scotched them so successfully that it was to take even longer to secure the rights of women than to establish the rights of free men'.[62] Yet More's criticisms of female education were not far removed from the more radical ideas of Nonconformists, notably the Quakers and Unitarians, two small sects which were disproportionately influential both for improvements in female education, especially of the middle classes, and in the development of feminism, particularly in England.[63] As Sue Morgan has pointed out, on the one hand, the pronouncements on female education by women with strong religious beliefs may have sharpened social differences between women: many such women were convinced of racial and class hierarchies and of their own (superior) place in these.[64] On the other hand, while education sought to inculcate certain roles, it also gave some women at least opportunities to take on new roles and responsibilities in the public sphere.[65] At the same time as these women wanted to preserve the hierarchies, they also sought to transform the lives of individuals within the established order.[66] Indeed, as Mary Hilton has observed, by the late eighteenth century:

> Women writers had crowded into the educational market where they expressed their views in a range of popular texts. Configuring themselves as the nation's teachers, they had reached out from the literary world to construct a variety of intellectual and pedagogical practices, propagating them through educational treatises, conduct books, popular guides, stories and handbooks.[67]

As will be shown in Chapter 4, such writings tapped into the desire of governesses and mistresses in boarding schools both to improve their own education and to professionalize their teaching.

Chapter 4 will also examine the social class division between education (for ladies) and training (for the daughters of the poor): the ideology of domesticity was to be applied in quite different ways according to social status. Thus, advocates of the domestic schooling of lower-class girls rejected such a vocational curriculum in the education of women of their own social standing. They were influenced by the ideas discussed above and saw education as a means of preparing middle-class women for a public role based on their domestic virtues and duties. Victorian feminists insisted that only a serious academic education, one as rigorous as that provided in the best schools available to middle-class boys, could ensure ladies were equipped for such a role. Whereas the starting point in improving the schooling of the poor was and remained at the elementary stage, reformers of middle-class girls' education began with secondary and quickly moved on to higher education. As Chapter 3 will show England, swiftly followed by Ireland, led the way in reforms of middle-class girls' schools, while Wales developed a system of secondary (intermediate) schools which by the end of the century covered most of the country and reached further down the social scale, opening up opportunities for children, girls as well as boys, of lower middle-class and upper working-class parents.[68] Scotland appeared to lag behind here, held back by the traditional link between parish schools and the universities which favoured boys and by the continuing preference for university-educated schoolmasters, even in schools for young ladies which were run by women. Indeed, there was a general belief in Scotland that education for middle-class girls was sound so that reform was not perceived as such a pressing issue as in the rest of the UK. Moreover, in contrast to the rest of the UK, the most prestigious private girls' schools in Scotland were run by men who were interested in educational reform.

While it is debatable whether the education of middle-class girls in Scotland suffered as a result, the reforms, especially in England and Ireland, point to the prominence of feminists among the campaigners and pioneering headmistresses. Feminists wanted to ensure that girls received as thorough an education as their brothers, which meant an education out-side of the home, both of the family and the substitute domestic space of the small private boarding establishments. As will be seen in Chapter 3, government inspectors as well as educational reformers were very critical of the lack of thoroughness in the curriculum of such schools: it was not only the teaching of the accomplishments which was deemed superficial but also the broad range of subjects offered, compared to the supposed depth of the male curriculum's focus on the classics. Still, whereas the reformed schools for girls pioneered in England sought to emulate the academic strengths of the best schools for boys, Michèle Cohen has pointed out that it did not include adopting such a narrow classical curriculum: emulation did not mean slavishly copying.[69] Moreover, as will be shown in Chapter 3, there was still room for the accomplishments.

Yet although it had become 'acceptable—even advisable' for girls to receive a formal education at the end of the Victorian period, most mid-dle-class girls received their education outside of the new high schools.[70] Indeed, Carol Dyhouse has shown that as late as 1920 most girls in Eng-land received a significant part of their education in the home.[71] While boys as well as girls learned gender roles and expectations in the fam-ily home, Susan Williams argues that a 'female knowledge' was imparted down the generations of women in the home which included both the ide-ology of domesticity and lessons in the practicalities of domestic work (either how to carry it out or how to oversee it being done).[72] Mothers would instil moral and religious values in both sons and daughters, as well as the gendered expectations of both; they would also be responsible for the early education of their infants, but middle-class boys were more likely to be placed in an institutional setting at a much younger age than girls who continued to receive most of their education through home school-ing. The gendering of middle-class education not only entailed differences between the schooling of girls and boys (for example, in curriculum) but reinforced sexual inequalities (for example, in opportunities for secondary and university education). Regional differences seem to have had less of an impact on middle-class than on working-class girls' education, though there were more opportunities in the major cities across the UK than in small towns. Thus, while middle-class girls received much of their educa-tion in their own home, they were also likely to be sent away from their family, sometimes at a considerable distance, to be 'finished' or 'polished' in boarding schools.[73]

Whereas in contrast to their working-class counterparts (to whom the next section turns), young ladies were not expected to add to the family income, Georgina Brewis has shown that they were expected to continue their mothers' philanthropic tradition through voluntary work with or for their working-class counterparts which was often organised by their schools.[74] Of course, middle-class girls' education was also susceptible to economic crisis if, for example, the father died or was made bankrupt or otherwise incapable of supporting his family: for example, Mary Woll-stonecraft (1759–1797) and even more her sisters Eliza and Everina—the latter 'found themselves blown from post to post, in a desperate search for families who would employ them'—had to find work as governesses.[75] As Chapter 4 shows this led to considerable anxiety over the plight of the governess.

FAMILY, WORK AND EDUCATION OF THE POOR

By the end of the Victorian period, literacy rates across the UK were over 90 per cent and almost equal between the sexes, but absenteeism from schools for the poor remained a serious concern. Throughout the century the atten-dance of both sexes was dictated by the needs of the family, often frequently interrupted by paid employment and when help was needed at home. As Chapter 2 will show, however, gender was always a factor, though again not always the most prominent one, in school attendance whatever the region. In addition, Chapter 4 will confirm that the practical realization of the ideal of female domesticity not only profoundly influenced the school-ing of working-class girls, but also both that and the demand for teachers drew more women from the upper working and lower middle classes into the teaching profession until they came to be numerically dominant across the British Isles.

Compulsory attendance at board schools (in Scotland from 1872 and in England and Wales from 1880, though it was another decade before fees were abolished) generally narrowed the gap between boys and girls, while the poorer attendance rates of girls in the middle age range were evened out by the late nineteenth century when they were staying on longer in school.[76] However, boys in rural areas were still more likely to finish their education by returning in the winter, while girls were more likely to be kept at home to help with housework and childcare.

This was especially the case if mothers worked outside of the home or experienced what Jane Humphries terms a 'surge in sweated homework'. She has observed from contemporary working-class autobiographies that child labour declined from the middle of the century and by the last quarter of the century children under nine years old had 'practically disappeared' from the British economy, while there was a significant fall in the paid employment of those aged between ten and 14.[77] The half-time system of schooling, however, did not end until 1921. It was more prevalent in Eng-land and Wales, while it was also a regional phenomenon. For example, the 1851 census revealed that Bedfordshire was the county in England with the highest rate of enrolment in Sunday schools, which was an indication of significant rates of child labour.[78] According to the census, 11.9 per cent of boys but 21.5 per cent of girls aged five to nine were employed, while among the next age range (ten to 14), it was almost equal: 49.6 per cent of boys and 50.6 per cent of girls.[79] Indeed, Richard Aldrich has shown that in Bedfordshire, with its economic focus on straw plaiting and lace making, even the full-time employment of 'very young children in establishments known as plait and lace schools, continued well after the supposed regulation of lace and plait by the Factory Workshops Act of 1867'. In addition, many children in that county were half-timers, most of the girls employed in these industries and the boys in agriculture. Whereas decline in the local industries of lace (by the 1870s) and straw plaiting (by the 1890s) greatly reduced the numbers of female half-timers, even in 1901 Bedfordshire had the highest percentage (13.3) of boys under 14 years of age in paid employment in England and Wales, where the average was 10.3 per cent.[80]

While lace-making was not particularly widespread in Scotland and Wales compared to England or Ireland, the example of Bedfordshire reveals gender sanctioning female labour in industries which were already established as women's work before industrialization. As Pamela Sharpe has observed, straw plaiting in the countryside fulfilled several roles, including as a traditional cottage industry like spinning, a local philanthropic venture, a commercial enterprise and a prescriptive ideal underlining the belief that woman's place was in the home not the factory or workshop. Moreover, it 'appealed to a sense of the rural world as it ought to be'.[81] In contrast, in mining areas, notably the Rhondda valleys, gender (reflected in government legislation) acted to exclude women and to limit them to a very narrow range of employment thought appropriate to their sex, notably teaching and domestic service.[82]

It has also been suggested that by the end of the Victorian period children were more likely to attend school on a full-time basis and then enter paid employment, especially in the bigger cities.[83] Family responsibilities, however, still took children out of school. Although girls were more likely than boys to be removed to help with domestic chores and childcare, both sons and daughters ran errands for mothers or, as noted above, assisted them in piecework in the home. Where boys were kept from school for domestic reasons, it was usually because there were no elder daughters and parents who depended on older children to help in the home were more likely to return their sons to school when possible, whereas daughters were more likely to be withdrawn completely.

Yet while attendance of the children of the poor was interrupted by the family's need for them to contribute either directly or indirectly to the household income, opportunities for paid employment particularly for girls and women differed markedly across the British Isles, not only between rural and urban areas but also within these. As noted above, the mining industry offered more chances to boys, especially after women were banned from working underground in 1842. Whether girls were employed after that depended on the structure of the local economy: thus there was female labour ('pit brow lasses') in the Wigan coalfield (though some mines would not employ married women), but by the 1870s no women were employed in the newly opened Rhondda Valley mines.[84] Similarly, whereas fewer women were employed in agriculture in England by the later nineteenth century, it remained a significant sector for female employment in Ireland, Scotland and Wales.[85] For example, in farming areas across Scotland, there was heavy seasonal demand for child labour, resulting in a pattern of a brief period of full-time schooling, followed by several years of winter attendance.[86]

Thus, across the British Isles, girls and women who were in paid employment were in a much more restricted range of occupations, and even single female adults were more likely to be employed part time than men. Again, there were regional differences. Whereas women in Wales had fewer opportunities for paid work than women in England—the 1911 census recorded that one in ten married women in England were employed compared to one in 20 in Wales—there were even fewer in the urban than in the rural areas of Wales.[87] For example, each census from 1861 to the end of the Victorian period shows that between six and ten per cent more of the total female population over the age of ten was in paid employment in the rural county of Cardigan than in the industrial county of Glamorgan, while female participation rates in the Welsh labour force declined in the later Victorian period.[88] Another example from the 1871 census shows that in textile towns, such as Dundee and Paisley, where most child and youth employment was for girls, boys were more likely to stay on at school, whereas in big cities and in areas of heavy industry and mining (such as Glasgow, Lanarkshire and Lothian), it was girls.[89]

The jobs open to women in the early part of the century demanded little in the way of skill, but at the same time women's paid work, and especially that of wives, was both frowned upon and under-reported for much of the century.[90] Indeed, while girls' attendance rates improved with state intervention and in some areas overtook those of boys by the end of the century, this was not simply a reflection of more educational opportunities but also (like the Bedfordshire example noted above) of a decline in the female participation rate in the market economy.[91]

Industrialization, then, took different forms across the British Isles, with one historian querying whether Victorian Wales, with its heavy dependence on extractive industries, was an industrialized economy.[92] In Scotland the Argyll Commission which reported on the state of education in the late 1860s was accused of taking the situation in Glasgow as the norm for the country as a whole when in fact that city and the surrounding region had a very particular form of industrialization.[93] Certainly, across the UK by the end of the century, the same basic standards of literacy and numeracy prevailed, but the experience of education among the poor was not uniform, reflecting the very regional nature of the economy. Yet whereas local employment opportunities influenced the experience of schooling for working-class children everywhere, there were also similarities between regions: for example, in Scotland there was the continuing importance of agricultural labour even in heavily urbanized and industrialized regions. At the end of Victorian period, the great majority of Scotland's population lived in towns in the western Lowlands centred on Glasgow, which contained 44.2 per cent of the population; but still, seasonal work in agriculture was an important source of family income even in Scotland's largest city, and in contrast to England such employment was for girls as well as boys.[94] Children in the city's outlying areas were kept off at harvest time, either to pick potatoes or to stay at home, while their mothers worked in the fields, though it was more often that girls would substitute for the mother at home.

Thus, it was not only in agricultural regions of Ireland and Wales but also throughout urban Scotland that schools had to cope with the demands of their rural hinterland for child and adult female labour well into the twentieth century.[95] Generally, in country districts throughout the UK, prolonged absences meant that teachers had to revise what had been taught months earlier. As a result, the curriculum tended to be limited to the basics, which implies a certain equality in the experience of girls and boys. A particular concern of the middle class was that field work, whether by mothers and daughters, meant that the latter could not learn what were deemed the necessary domestic skills in the home. Though there was a gendered division of labour among the adults, middle-class observers worried about what they deemed the promiscuous mingling of the sexes in field work, particularly as boys and girls worked mostly at the same tasks though some jobs were restricted to the boys: in Perthshire, for example, boys and girls picked fruit, but only the former served as beaters for the gamekeeper and caddied for golfers.[96]

Perth was a magnet for Highland labour: by the end of the century, 40 per cent of the town's population of 30,000 had come from the surrounding counties.[97] Highland parishes covered huge tracts of land where poverty and the continuing importance of agriculture meant that older girls and boys shared a common experience of outdoor labour (including on the family croft) for much of the year and only a brief winter season in school, though generally before the 1872 Act boys were more likely to return than girls.[98] There was similarly a very heavy demand for seasonal child labour in rural Ireland where the interests of farming was a factor in thwarting efforts to impose compulsory education.[99] The main opposition, however, came from the Catholic Church and its deep suspicion of state intervention behind which the Church saw the ultimate intention of imposing a compulsory secular education.[100]

Across the UK, the service sector, and especially domestic service, was a key employer of girls. Yet that too was not uniform: for example, it was a more significant employer of girls and women in Ireland, England and Wales than in Scotland; moreover, in Wales there were at least ten per cent more women in service than in England between 1871 and 1901.[101] There were also regional differences: domestic service, for example, was more prominent in Edinburgh and Aberdeen than in Glasgow and Dundee. The female employment rate in Dundee, with its reliance on a single industry (textiles) and within that industry on jute, was exceptionally high within the UK as a whole.[102] Even in sectors such as fishing where the main demand for labour was for males, for example, in Aberdeenshire and on the Western Isles, it also employed women resulting in absenteeism among older girls whose mothers were engaged 'at the herring', notably as gutters and packers. Paul Thompson has pointed to the 'spectacular' scale of this labour migration:

> Each year the herring season would open in late May off the Western Isles and gradually move clockwise round the northern and eastern coasts, culminating in the East Anglian season from October to December. At the industry's peak just before World War 1 there were altogether some 12,000 Scottish herring gutters alone, 3,500 of them from the Western Isles, and 5,000 who would travel south for the English season.[103]

Yet education in Aberdeenshire was seen as superior to the rest of Scotland, especially for boys. As noted above, this county benefited from educational bequests which subsidized the teaching of university subjects, making it virtually impossible for a non-graduate, and so female, to be appointed to Aberdeenshire parish schools. This continued after 1872 but as will be seen in Chapter 4 even in this region the trend was for women to predominate among school board teachers though men still monopolized the promoted posts.

As the British economy developed, parents began to see benefits, in terms of job opportunities, to be gained from educating their daughters, particularly from the middle of the century with the employment of pupil teachers and female assistants in schools for the poor which increased significantly after the 1870 Elementary Education Act for England and Wales and the 1872 Education (Scotland) Act. The attendance of girls at schools in Ireland also grew, but for different reasons: the impact of the Great Famine saw decreased employment rates of girls and women in agriculture and an increased rate of female emigration so that schools offered skills which would make them attractive workers, notably in domestic service.[104] Still, it remained a basic education for the most part due to the Catholic Church's insistence on separating the sexes even in areas where enrolments were low, contributing to a situation in which 'the majority of national schools remained very small, inadequately furnished and poorly equipped'.[105]

DOMESTICITY AND DOMESTIC SUBJECTS

The education of girls, then, was heavily influenced by the Victorian ideal of female domesticity, with the emphasis on practical skills in the schooling of poor girls. However, as suggested above the evidence for rural areas qualifies that generalization. In country districts, sewing, knitting, and less frequently domestic economy were taught but often not regularly and sometimes to boys as well as girls due to the demands of teaching in a mixed-sex school which had a single female teacher. Whereas sewing was often resented by parents (and by the class teacher in mixed-sex schools), knitting generally was not: stocking-knitting had been a predominantly female handicraft, and though it no longer attracted the high rate of wages which it had done in the eighteenth century, it was a skill still useful within the family. If boys were taught sewing and knitting, it might be due to the local economy: for example, in fishing regions where boys and men spent long periods at sea and in regions such as Dundee where boys could earn money sewing sacks.

Generally, urban schools were in a better position than rural ones to provide domestic subjects, and because there were fewer resources in the latter, there was less emphasis on domestic subjects than in the cities. Certainly, the ideology of separate spheres helped shape the curriculum of and attitudes towards female and male pupils, but few children could expect their experience of school to have much influence on their future job prospects. Nevertheless, education in remote rural areas still 'privileged' boys who were seen as the principal migrant contributor to the family income, although in practice women were at least as mobile as men. Indeed, Highland to Lowland migration patterns in Scotland and emigration from Ireland in the later Victorian period both show a predominance of single women.[106]

The Victorian upper and middle classes were in favour of domestic education for their social inferiors, which they believed would improve working-class living standards as well as the skills of domestic servants. Those who championed the teaching of cooking argued that the great aim was to help wives of labouring men provide thoroughly good and nutritious food for their families at the smallest possible cost, which would also anchor the husband to the domestic sphere and keep him away from the temptations of the street and the public house.[107] Thus, for Victorian reformers schooling the daughters of the poor for a domestic role was not confined to the skills of housekeeping; it was also concerned with the morality of the lower classes. Both concerns continued into the early twentieth century, to which were added fears for the health and fitness of the imperial nation, resulting in renewed emphasis on motherhood and female education.[108]

Hence, whereas the emphasis was on sewing in the mid-nineteenth century, that shifted to cookery and laundry in the later decades. The number of girls studying domestic economy increased in the 1880s and 1890s with government grants. As will be seen in Chapter 2, boards throughout Britain established higher grade schools for the minority of pupils, mainly from the lower middle and upper working classes, studying at least three years post-elementary. They offered girls who stayed on a wider curriculum geared to external examination and suitable for future employment in the expanding commercial sector. While even at the end of the Victorian period, Wales had the most restricted employment opportunities for girls, they faced limitations across the UK: for example, the Edinburgh School Board Minutes for June 1877 listed the jobs open to girls with a basic education as domestic service, messengers, shop assistants, dressmakers, book-folders, relief stampers, pupil teachers, and compositors.[109] Yet even in a city where domestic service remained a significant occupational group for women, by the beginning of the twentieth century, the most common sector of female employment was industrial work.[110] Moreover, whereas Edinburgh's economic history might be seen as confirming the importance of sewing in the female curriculum—in eighteenth-century Edinburgh sewing had been a trade with specialisms—commercial development in the nineteenth century, particularly the growth of retail establishments, made it more difficult for women to set up a business, not least because they had less access to finance than men.[111]

Although there was concern about the plight of the seamstress, those 'slaves of the needle', reflected in the popularity of Thomas Hood's 1843 poem *The Song of the Shirt*, generally sewing in schools was seen not so much as a preparation for a trade but more as a foundation for domesticity.[112] Hence, such domestic subjects retained an important place in the curriculum for girls. Even when specific (or higher) subjects had been introduced into the elementary school curriculum in the later nineteenth century to broaden the education of working-class children who stayed on to the later standards, girls had to take domestic economy as one so that those who also wanted to take cookery had to do so at the expense of more 'academic' subjects. There was no similar restriction on boys; moreover, whereas specific subjects had three levels, giving a sense of progression, the three topics of the domestic economy syllabus were each rather basic.[113]

As will be seen in Chapter 2, this emphasis on domestic subjects in the female curriculum was differently received by poor parents across the UK. It was more positively received in Ireland and Wales and also by the Catholic Church which saw it as a means to raise the cultural and moral standing of its community within a hostile environment. Parents in England and Scotland were more likely to resist, though again there were regional differences, according to the local economy and the domestic demands made on wives and daughters, notably in mining areas.[114] It nevertheless appears that parental resistance to daughters being taught domestic subjects was strongest in Scotland where parents tended not to distinguish between a curriculum intended to instruct girls as housewives and one intended to train them as servants.

Despite the heavy emphasis on domestic subjects in the education of working-class girls, it was primarily at endowed institutions and at industrial or ragged schools, established as reformatories or to provide for potential vagrants, that girls were prepared for domestic service.[115] Elementary schooling would 'rescue' children from the streets; indeed it would make the streets safe from idle and potentially delinquent children. Thus the context for Industrial Schools and corrective institutions was a perceived need to protect 'at risk' girls and young women, reflecting a sentimentalization of childhood which was linked to the dual notion of girls and women as being both sexually innocent and threatening. The social difference in virtue was particularly explicit in reformatory and industrial schools: the pupils were working class, their rescuers the lady 'child-savers' and the education girls perceived to be vulnerable received in these institutions was particularly basic, with the emphasis on discipline and domesticity.[116]

Yet while the curriculum for girls under the school boards was broader than in those institutions, it was also gendered and based on similar concerns for the morals and manners of the working-class female: hence the prominence of domestic subjects. Similarly, in the national schools in Ireland, cookery, laundry work and needlework dominated the female curriculum by the late nineteenth century.[117] In Scotland, however, to include such vocational subjects in board schools went against the parochial tradition. Lindy Moore cites a number of reasons for opposition to domestic subjects in Scotland: a belief that intellectual discipline was the best means of developing an intelligent, moral and cultured individual; the tradition of mixed schooling and higher subjects; the opposition of teachers; the dominance of men as schoolmasters in parish schools before the 1872 Act and as headmasters of board schools after that; and the attendance of a proportion of middle-class girls.[118] As the following chapter will show, however, such resistance proved futile in the face of government policy and educational campaigners.

This sustained campaign to introduce domestic economy into the curriculum of working-class girls as well as the establishment of cookery schools in key urban centres across the UK from the 1870s highlighted ways in which gender roles were mediated by social class. Initially aimed at working-class women, the failure of cookery schools to attract them in significant numbers led to a shift in focus to their daughters, with the aim of providing trained cookery teachers for elementary schools. By the end of the century, cookery schools had become domestic science colleges, providing post-school education—regarded as a form of further or even higher education, not vocational training—to middle-class women and preparing them for suitably respectable professional employment opportunities, not only in teaching but also in public health. In addition, teachers from cookery schools offered day and evening classes aimed at both working and middle-class women, with the fees paid by the latter subsidizing the former and efforts to defray costs by selling the cooked food. Thus, not only did philanthropic efforts to provide domestic education to poor women continue after formal schooling was made compulsory but they did so in collaboration with school boards and with cookery schools in the larger cities.[119]

This emphasis on the centrality of domestic subjects in working-class girls' schooling was ideological, accepted and even championed by feminists. Certainly, many schools could not afford either the facilities or the specialist teachers, provision in rural, especially remote, areas was particularly limited, and many schoolmistresses who were also expected to teach across the curriculum were resentful of the space taken up by domestic subjects, but the trend was for their place in the girls' curriculum to expand: such subjects as laundry, housewifery and infant care were all added to the curriculum.[120] As will be seen in the following chapters, such an explicitly gendered curriculum for working-class girls reinforced social class divisions as well as gender roles throughout the UK. It also, as the following section shows, empowered middle-class women to make a significant contribution to the schooling of the poor, demonstrating those links between feminine domestic virtues and civic duties.

HOME RULE FOR WOMEN

Helen Corr sees the campaign for domestic subjects in later nineteenth-century Scotland under the banner 'Home Rule for Women' as essentially an urban phenomenon which was not confined to Scotland and was linked to female representation on school boards.[121] Across the UK the ideology of separate spheres for the sexes informed the expansion of the boundaries of the public sphere for women in the Victorian period, 'counteracting the tendency to prefer narrow private ends to the public good'.[122] Middle-class women in particular 'mobilised the idea of themselves as a moral vanguard to justify their entry into public campaigns'.[123] The management of the education of the poor, however, differed between Ireland and the rest of the UK. Ireland had a National Board (a government-appointed board of prominent mixed-denominational men) from the 1831 Act, intended to oversee a non-denominational system. This was less centralized in practice than it appears. National schools were funded by the National Board in Dublin but managed at local level, while by the middle of the century the schools under the Board were effectively denominational and the Catholic schools were mostly run by religious orders.[124] Lay women in Victorian Ireland, both Protestant and Catholic, did not have the opportunity to develop a role in education through school boards. In addition, while Catholic middle-class women in Ireland also dedicated themselves to philanthropic work, Maria Luddy has shown that the growth of religious orders pushed out lay women. Some of the latter continued to run charities outside of the fields of education, nursing the poor and refuges for young girls and prostitutes; but generally they were 'relegated' to raising funds, unable to compete with the organisational power of religious orders 'whose members committed their whole lives to charity work'.[125]

In contrast, elsewhere in the UK it was Protestant lay women who played a significant role in the governance of working-class education. Education was deemed part of the domestic sphere, reflected in the fact that before the state intervened in education many upper- and middle-class women had been involved in the management of schools for the poor as part of their philanthropic role.[126] Female managers had focused on the girls' domestic skills, as there were restrictions on what women could do until reform to property law in the later Victorian period.[127] Patricia Hollis records that a fifth of managers of schools under the London board were female in the 1880s and that in 1893 there was a requirement that a third of the managers be women.[128] Women's role was extended by the education acts of 1870 for England and Wales and 1872 for Scotland. These established elected school boards to manage education locally, and as noted above, women, whether married or single, who met the electoral qualifications could both vote and stand for membership. Although always a small minority of those who served on the boards, many of the female members both supported women's entry to the universities and devoted themselves to public service. School board women did not challenge the notion of separate spheres for the sexes, but their assertion that women's duty was to act for the public good challenged the artificial divisions between them.

Thus, as Jane Martin has shown for London, although school board women generally did not contest assumptions about femininity, they altered them through their public work.[129] In their view, the interaction of the public and private, so long as it was guided and managed by virtuous public-spirited women and men of their class, would promote the good of both spheres. They believed that in general local communities needed women in public service and in particular children needed women on school boards; but while they saw education as a local responsibility with a specific niche for women, it was also one which had national and indeed imperial significance.[130] In addition, the Welsh came to see education which was not under the control of the established church as a means to safeguard their national culture from the suffocating embrace of Westminster, while there was a common belief among Scots that their separate education system was central to a sense of Scottish identity and of their worth within the Empire.

Thus, throughout Britain education was a key area where women could achieve a measure of status and authority, and the work of women on school boards set an important precedent for women to hold public office. Women who sat on school boards had to have not just the time but the financial security to be able to do so: as Patricia Hollis has pointed out, school board women were rarely in waged work so that in the case of Annie Besant who was elected to the Tower Hamlets board in 1889 but needed to support herself, her allies provided her with a wage of £150 a year.[131] Still, this example shows that while the numbers of women on school boards remained very small, by the end of the Victorian period, they were no longer limited to the upper middle class. Some were or had been working women, while a significant number had been schoolmistresses.[132] Further, whereas most early women members were supporters of the two main political parties, by the turn of the century, a few were socialists.[133] Whatever their political persuasion, most school board women were supporters of the female franchise, while those in Wales and Scotland tended to be Unionists who were also keenly aware of and protective towards their national identity. They reflected the 'union of multiple identities': Britain as a civic rather than an ethnic state.[134] Moreover, many school board women were not only involved in a number of local public bodies but were committed imperialists, some having engaged in foreign missionary work and now turning their attention to the home mission.[135]

Generally, however, women's work on the boards went beyond charity into what has been termed 'civic maternalism'.[136] In effect, women became the moral guardians of civic virtue. Their role in the family meant that they could—indeed, should—influence society, while their notion of 'women's mission' confirmed gender differences mediated by social class. A large majority championed the domestic education of working-class girls and insisted on the need for ladies to oversee it.

There was never equal representation with men on the boards: women were always in the minority, and many boards never had a female member. Indeed, most small boards did not even have a committee for industrial work which in the bigger boards was regarded as the main sphere of women's competence. Even on the relatively large board of Dundee, which was regarded as a 'woman's town' due to the high proportion of female workers in the dominant textile industry and where there had been calls for female representation on the school board since the 1872 Act, a woman was not returned until 1894.[137] On the largest of all boards, London, only 29 of the 326 people elected during its existence were women; indeed, while numbers on Scottish boards were also small, they were proportionately slightly more women members than in England and Wales.[138] It took longer for women to break through in the smaller cities and towns where they generally relied on the support of local individuals (usually businessmen and professionals) rather than organised ladies' platforms. The churches tended to dominate small boards, and although their religious beliefs often led them into the public arena, female candidates were seen as representing their gender rather than their denomination.[139]

Most school board women focused on the girls' industrial work (i.e., sewing), overseeing their domestic education; and if the board boasted an industrial committee, it was often chaired by a female member. Few, however, were elected to chair either the finance committee or the board itself. There were exceptions: one was Mrs Rose Crawshay who was elected to the Merthyr Tydfil country Vaynor school board in 1871 which she chaired for the next eight years.[140] Another was Flora Stevenson in Edinburgh who chaired the finance committee and was elected unanimously to chair the board itself after her tenth successive (and successful) campaign in 1900. Elected again in 1903 (she died in service two years later), Stevenson was a spinster whose work on the board was highly respected. Indeed, whereas at least half of the female members included in a study of school boards in Scotland never married, contemporary accounts show that they were not considered 'redundant' or 'surplus women'.[141] And while many women served only one or two terms—Peter Gordon has found that only half the female members of the London school board served for more than one term of three years—a significant number served several consecutive terms.[142]

Of course, women's status as board members was 'special' in that they were seen as representing a particular interest, but although women standing for the first time tended to emphasize their commitment to the domestic training of girls, it subsequently became one of a number of policies on which they campaigned. Grace Paterson's 21-year career on the Glasgow school board reveals the scope of women's activities in the general working of the board was much wider than that.[143] This was not only the case on the larger boards. For example, in 1897 when Jessie Moffat stood for a fourth term on the small Ardrossan (Ayrshire) school board, she pointed to her proven experience over nine years in the general work of the board and a 'willingness to grasp the question of higher education and deal with it in a broad and liberal way'.[144] Thus, however narrow their declared specialism in domestic education appears, in practice school board women took a more comprehensive approach to the syllabus. They supported the introduction of physical education for girls as well as boys, while they considered that talented girls should have the opportunity to advance their education as their male counterparts did, reflected in their campaigns for the development of secondary education within the board system as well as the opening up of the universities to women. As Rose Crawshay wrote in the *Cardiff and Merthyr Guardian* in June 1870, 'we want as thorough an education for girls as is given to boys'.[145]

There was some concern about the heavy emphasis in the curriculum on domestic subjects for girls, expressed for example by Flora Stevenson and Mary Burton in Edinburgh, Elizabeth Garrett and Emily Davies in London, Helena Richardson in Bristol and Lydia Becker in Manchester.[146] As will be seen in Chapter 2, a few also considered that both the practical skills and supposed moral benefits derived from this subject could apply to boys as well, to make them better fathers and to equip them for life in the armed forces and in fishing. Still, they constituted a minority and one which was careful to refute the charge that a board school education rendered girls unfit or unwilling to enter domestic service. The majority felt that since working-class women had little time for their daughters' domestic education, school board women should devote themselves to it because the male-dominated boards were apathetic about the subject and relied on untrained teachers.

Furthermore, school board women conceived the aim of domestic education as more than making competent housewives: their concern was wider, taking in public health and well-being. They were influenced by the late nineteenth-century fears for the imperial race's health and fitness, while they shared concerns about the increase in infant mortality rates at the same time that birth rates in Britain were falling: as Neil Daglish has pointed out, by the 1880s fewer children were being born at a time when there were fewer chances of survival into adulthood.[147] These anxieties were reflected in the aim of school board women to develop a domestic curriculum which went beyond the basics of cleaning, cooking and sewing to cover hygiene, nutrition, health and welfare. While they accepted that domestic duties were above all female responsibilities, they insisted that the domestic sphere was not simply a private affair: it had public consequences and value. They saw a schooling for girls which included domestic subjects as essential for enabling them as adults to make a positive contribution to civic society, whether from their own homes or in paid employment.

Domestic education, then, was not only for the family but for the community, for the public as well as the private good. School board women recognised that the subordination of women in the private sphere constrained their participation in the public; they spoke the language of separate spheres, while they sought to extend the boundaries of the domestic for both middle- and working-class women, though in their different and unequal social spheres and in a considerably more limited way for the latter. While school board women accepted both the gendered division of labour and the social hierarchy, in Scotland and Wales they disagreed with what they saw as the English notion of an elementary education for the working class. For the Welsh, as will be seen in Chapter 2, this was related to the criticisms of the working class and especially of its women in the infamous Blue Books of 1847 which stimulated Welsh national consciousness, with Nonconformity playing a significant role in educational campaigns for improvements in provision in Wales at all levels.[148] In Scotland, school board women interpreted their 'democratic tradition' as encouraging a meritocracy which should include talented poor girls as well as boys. As Robert Anderson has noted, Scottish women adapted the classic 'lad of parts to dominie' route both to improve their own education and to become respectably self-supporting.[149]

Many of the women who sat on the boards also declared themselves to be guardians of the interests of schoolmistresses who were generally from a lower social stratum than they occupied. In addition, they sought to develop a specialism for middle-class women as qualified teachers of cookery. Thus, Grace Paterson—honorary secretary (that is, unpaid principal) of the Glasgow School of Cookery (1875–1907)—strove to have the training received in cookery schools and later domestic science colleges accepted as a form of higher education, opening up to middle-class women an increasing number of 'caring' professions related to public health as well as education.[150] Like most school board women, Paterson insisted on the employment by boards of professionally trained cookery teachers and campaigned for the appointment of qualified female inspectors of domestic subjects.

Of course, lady visitors had inspected the needlework done in a variety of schools for the poor, including charity, ragged and industrial schools, and had continued to do so in the early years of the board schools; indeed,

one board, Exeter, incorporated the lady visitors through a ladies' committee which reported directly to the board.[151] That arrangement continued
for the lifetime of the board, but soon many of the larger school boards in
England were employing qualified women to inspect the domestic subjects.
Thus, some boards, for example, Liverpool's, built on the philanthropic
experience of lady visitors to appoint women as inspectors of needlework
and of the infants' departments from the 1870s.[152] By the early 1880s Her
Majesty's Inspectorate (HMI) had followed suit: a 'Directress' of Needlework was appointed in 1883 and an 'Inspectress' of Cookery and Laundry
in 1890.[153] It was 1902 before there was a similar appointment in Scotland,
reflecting the resistance of the male educational authorities if not to the
inclusion of domestic economy in the girls' curriculum, then to its recognition as a subject suitable for inspection.[154]

It is, of course, difficult to assess the influence of so few women on public
life. They were indeed exceptional, 'perceived and grouped in terms of gender and allocated responsibilities accordingly'.[155] Nevertheless, as Patricia
Hollis has demonstrated, although school board women began by establishing their credentials in 'womanly work', they were very soon contributing to the full range of educational policy.[156] The ladies' platform in school
board elections may well have reinforced traditional notions of women's
place, but their work through the committee structures brought what were
considered private concerns into the public sphere.

Female board members across Britain pursued similar goals by similar
means, working within a patriarchal system to enlarge the opportunities for
women. School boards in England and Wales were replaced by unelected
local education authorities with the 1902 Education Act, but they continued in Scotland for another 16 years, while for the following decade the
authorities which replaced them were also elected, allowing women a continuing role in Scottish school governance based on the legitimacy of the
ballot box over a period of nearly six decades.

Moreover, while school board women in Scotland had much in common with their counterparts in England, the former also believed that their
country was distinguished by its national tradition in education. That tradition was patriarchal, but whereas in England the schooling of the poor
was held in low social esteem, in Scotland as in Wales (and Ireland), it was
seen as a key means of cementing the national community and preserving
its identity within the Union. In contrast to Wales (and indeed Ireland),
Scotland had a degree of autonomy within the Union in the form of what
Lindsay Paterson terms 'domestic sovereignty'. He sees middle-class women
contributing to the development of a national system of education after the
1872 Education Act by championing domestic economy in the schooling of
working-class girls, thereby attaching educational value to women's traditional activities.[157]

That could also be said of the board system in England and Wales. While
continuing, even reinforcing, both the social hierarchy and the ideology of

separate spheres, the actions of female board members led to some positive benefits for lower-class women through improvements in their education and incorporation into the teaching profession, albeit in a junior role and within gendered parameters. Although the Educational Institute for Scotland (established in 1847) had only admitted women as members in the wake of the 1872 Education Act and was not in favour of school boards, preferring education to be under local government, it nevertheless welcomed the elected women as allies of the profession and made a number of them honorary fellows. The Institute acknowledged, in terms which would have been acceptable to school board women, 'the right of women to receive an education essentially and substantially equal to that of men (however one may differ from the other in subordinate details)'.[158] There is a whiff of paternalism in this statement, as well as the implicit assumption that the women would support the masters in what would remain a male-dominated system: schoolmistresses as the handmaidens to a patriarchal ideal. Indeed, Victorian schoolmistresses throughout the UK, particularly in elementary schools, tend to be depicted as complicit in defending and reproducing patriarchy, whether conscious of doing so or not, and as adopting the traditional mothering role in the classroom: teachers as 'mothers-made conscious'.[159]

When the functions of the school boards in Scotland were finally absorbed into local government in 1929, the Scottish situation resembled that in England and Wales: a few women continued to have a role in the governance of local schooling through being co-opted to the appointed education committees of local councils, but it was a substantially diminished one.[160] Still, for over 30 years in England and Wales and over half a century in Scotland, school board women participated in public debates on education, communicating their ideas to a wide audience at public meetings and through the local press, not only during the triennial election campaigns but in the regular reports of board meetings. In the process, these women helped shape public opinion and established women's right to an active role within civic society.[161]

ORGANISATION

The following three chapters examine aspects of female education in the Victorian period by focusing first on the schooling of working-class girls, second on the education of their middle-class counterparts and finally on the education or training considered appropriate to the women who taught them. The distinction between 'schooling' and 'education' of the girls and 'education' and 'training' of their mistresses points to the centrality of social class and the hierarchies—of class as well as gender—to which they were groomed to conform. The expectation of knowing and accepting one's place, however, did not mean that society was static: as the wider context discussed in this chapter has shown, there were many pressures on those hierarchies to which they had to adapt and which, in turn, allowed room for manoeuvre, reflected in the work of school board women. There is irony in the fact that successful manoeuvring by middle-class women to improve their education and widen their sphere of action also reinforced the ideology of domesticity in general and in particular placed significant constraints on the lives of working-class women. Even those among the latter who experienced limited social mobility by, in the words of Frances Widdowson, 'going up into the next class' found they were being crowded out by the lower middle class in the later decades of the Victorian period, though she adds that the impact of the latter on the training colleges was a liberalizing one.[162]

As Chapter 2 will show, pressure from campaigners, including feminists, and educational legislation from the 1860s ensured that the curriculum in schools in receipt of government funding across the UK was gendered. Victorian educational reformers, however, were not only concerned with the children of the poor. Chapter 3 considers the evidence in government reviews of the education of the daughters of the middle class, the feminist campaigns to improve their formal schooling and the related campaign to gain entry into higher education. In contrast to the daughters of the poor, even at the end of the Victorian period, many middle-class girls received the bulk of their education at home. The result, according to Dorothea Beale (1831–1906) was that the daughters of the middle class were 'more igno-rant and untrained than the children of the national schools'.[163] Chapter 3 examines the efforts of such campaigners to establish formal schooling for these girls not only appropriate to their social class but also on a par with the best education available to their brothers.

Middle-class women in the Victorian period had a variety of ways of improving their education outside of the home, for example, through attend-ing (albeit it not on equal terms with and often apart from men) public lec-tures, scientific and cultural societies, Mechanics' Institutes, Working Men's Colleges, the Young Women's Christian Association and, from the 1860s, various university extension courses, all of which offered 'adult' rather than higher education.[164] Still, the most respectable paid position open to them remained teaching, though again this was limited by the constraints of social class: those who taught the poor tended to come from the upper working or lower middle class. Chapter 4, then, considers the working- and middle-class women who taught in the various schools for girls, examining their own education and in particular their training: women of the middle classes who went into teaching received an education at secondary and, for a minority by the end of the century, at university level, whereas those who became elementary schoolmistresses had a basic, or elementary, schooling and voca-tional training limited to the subjects they were to impart. Still, by the end of the Victorian period a tiny minority of the latter, notably in Scotland, were encouraged to take courses at university.

Campaigns to reform middle-class girls' education were related to the perceived need to improve the employment opportunities for ladies who had to support themselves and, perhaps, their families. They remained aloof from elementary schools until the early twentieth century, except for specialist posts such as cookery teaching; moreover, though ladies who did not have to work still had a philanthropic role as unpaid visitors in schools of the poor by the end of the century, it had become acceptable for middle-class women to take paid work as inspectors of domestic subjects.

This movement of women into teaching in large numbers is examined in Chapter 4 which begins with the criticisms of the education of, and that given by, the governess, a paid position regarded as the most appropriate for impoverished single ladies at the start of the century. It was still an option, and for a small elite a much better paid and more prestigious one, at the end of the century.[165] The focus then shifts to the social class and educational distinctions between the teachers in the new high schools for girls which developed from the 1860s and those in elementary schools established the following decade. Whereas in England, it had been the Anglican clergyman who was the figure symbolising authority and respect, in Ireland, Scotland and Wales, it was the schoolmaster.[166] The Victorian period, however, saw a decline in the status of the latter at a time when middle-class women were claiming education as a domestic mission. Of course, this notion of a special female influence was conservative, and patriarchal control of education persisted: the examination of female teachers in Chapter 4 together with the above discussion of women on school boards reveal ways in which the incorporation of women into both areas was to strengthen the established order. It was an order which feminists and educational reformers for the most part accepted: as Dorothea Beale conceded to the NAPSS in 1865:

> And here let me at once say that I desire to institute no comparison between the mental abilities of boys and girls, but simply to say what seems to be the right means of training girls, so that they may best perform that subordinate part in the world, to which I believe they have been called.[167]

Thus, while women's very presence subverted the patriarchal ideal, it did not overturn it. Further, as the next chapter shows, the curriculum imposed on working-class girls may well have reinforced that ideal in their homes since it concentrated so heavily on educating them for a much narrower conception of the woman's sphere.

2 Gender and Social Control in the Education of Working-Class Girls

The Victorian period saw major inquiries into the education of the working classes in the UK, notably in 1824 in Ireland, 1847 in Wales, 1861 in England and 1866 in Scotland. The reasons were generally the same: worries over the impact of industrialization and urbanization on the social and moral conditions of the unlettered and un-churched poor, perceptions of a rising crime rate, especially among juveniles, and a growing need for an educated workforce. Yet it was in Ireland, incorporated into the Union only in 1801, that the government at Westminster first established a system of popular education (1831). The question of why the government was more willing to intervene so early in Ireland is seen by historians of Irish education to rest on the different treatment of a country which was formally part of the UK but was in practice still considered a colony.[1] Certainly, the issues affecting the schooling of the poor in Ireland were similar to Wales and the Scottish Highlands: religious, social and linguistic differences and a perception on the part of government and moral reformers that the lower orders were in urgent need of civilizing and social control. A similarity which reformers in Ireland shared with Wales and England was the intention that the schooling of the labouring/dangerous classes would remain separate from that of their social superiors: the aim was to make the former worthy subjects of the crown who accepted their subordinate place in society. The situation was seen to be different in Scotland with its 'democratic' tradition and preference for mixed-sex schooling, but that was subject to increasing criticism by the 1830s. Indeed, within the socialization process at the heart of educational reform throughout the British Isles, the ideology of separate spheres for the sexes was to play a fundamental part: women were the key to an ordered society.

RELIGION AND LANGUAGE IN THE SCHOOLING OF WORKING-CLASS GIRLS BEFORE 1870

Religion was a key factor in the schooling of the poor throughout the UK, and it was integral to the resistance to state control in Wales and Ireland in particular. In the case of the former, it has been pointed out that while education in Ireland and Scotland have histories which are distinct from, though still influenced by, developments in England, it is much more difficult to separate the history of Welsh education.[2] This is partly because England and Wales were treated legally as inseparable, and partly because the Welsh upper class had become Anglicized by the eighteenth century, while there was an influx of English entrepreneurs to Wales during the process of industrialization. Indeed, in the early decades of the nineteenth century the Anglican National Society provided more schools than any other voluntary organisation, though most of these were in north Wales where the smallest number of Welsh people lived. In the teaching of girls, the Society saw its role as to train them to be useful servants and good wives and mothers: in 1814, it stated the need to wean girls away from 'prevailing low vices'.[3]

Nevertheless, by the early nineteenth century, the strength of Nonconformity and of the Sunday school movement served to set Welsh education apart from the English experience. Here, the Welsh Sunday school movement was particularly successful.[4] Although the non-denominational British and Foreign School Society (BFSS) also had to deal with denominational variety and rivalry, notably in the south of Wales where there was resistance among dissenters to state aid, those in north Wales who were concerned about the loss of Welsh identity and in particular of the Welsh language saw the BFSS as a means of counteracting Anglican control in education. Educational reformers such as Hugh Owen (1804–1881) who was instrumental in persuading the BFSS to become involved in Wales also saw the need for Welsh children to master English, though his emphasis was more on the professional and imperial opportunities for boys of the middle class.[5] The importance of these related developments was recognised in the Report of the Commission of Inquiry into the State of Education in Wales, published in 1847. The combination of the predominance of dissent and the teaching in their Sunday schools being in Welsh led to the caution that too heavy a reliance on such schools could result in 'fanaticism' and political unrest, especially in view of the recent Chartist agitation.[6]

This was also the case in Ireland, incorporated into the Union after the 1798 Rebellion. From the start of the 1801 Union, there were calls for educational reform. These reflected both the particular situation in Ireland and concerns, notably related to gender, religion and social class, shared with the rest of the UK, as well as an assumption that English was the language of a superior (Protestant) culture, one essential for a burgeoning economy. A report of the Board of Education in Ireland noted in 1809 that Protestant charter schools had since 1733 aimed to 'convert and civilize the native (Popish) Irish': both masters and mistresses were to instruct the children in English, in the principles of the Protestant (Anglican) religion, in virtue and industry, husbandry and housewifery, and manual occupations appropriate to their sex, which would enable them to support themselves. In addition, the girls were to be taught domestic skills (such as plain sewing, knitting and washing) and were expected not only to make and mend their own clothes but also to produce and maintain all the stockings of the charter school pupils.[7] It was generally observed that the proof of deficient domestic skills lay in the ragged appearance of poor women and their children.[8] Still, while the commissioners appeared to pay particular attention to the domestic training of poor girls, they insisted that 'the education of boys should be fully attended to'.[9] They acknowledged that the gendered division of training and occupation was not rigid: boys in some charter schools were taught to knit stockings and repair their own clothes and shoes. Indeed, the commissioners even considered that it would be 'most desirable' they should do so in all charter schools.[10] Unlike the girls, however, boys were not expected to take turns in the kitchen.

By the 1820s, charter schools were subject to severe criticism of their poor accommodation, teaching and management, while there was now disapproval of their proselytism and their method of separating the children from their parents. One fear was for female morality: the charter schools lost control once the girls were apprenticed, and either they left their place or were 'turned without protection on the world'.[11] By the 1820s the preference was for day schools, which were not only cheaper than boarding but, it was hoped, left the children with parents as both 'authority and love figures'. This was deemed especially important for girls in preventing them from slipping into prostitution.[12]

Generally, it was felt that the existing schools for the poor did not suit the 'peculiar situation and circumstances' of Ireland. This conclusion was made despite praise for the 'nunnery schools' where the sisters displayed 'great order and regularity' as well as 'unwearied assiduity and attention' in their education of the poor.[13] A similar judgment was made by the Argyll Commission into Scottish education 40 years later: in particular it was felt that the religious orders 'refined and tempered' those girls who attended school. [14] The low opinion of charter schools reflected the influence of the Society for Promoting the Education of the Poor in Ireland (usually known as the Kildare Place Society) which was active from 1811, campaigning for state-funded non-denominational schooling. It did not establish schools of its own, and while it offered support to local initiatives, the management of these non-denominational schools was often religious. Although a minority of local managers was made up of Catholic priests, in practice both the Society and the schools it supported were dominated by Protestants, particularly evangelicals. Thus the champion of Catholic Emancipation, Daniel O'Connell, who had originally been a member of the Society, left it in 1819 to form the Irish National Society for Promoting the Education of the Poor. One result of the work of these societies was that two royal commissions were set up, one in 1824 and the other in 1828. As in England and Wales, the preference was for single-sex schools for older children, though it was acknowledged without comment that children were not separated by sex in the parochial schools of Scotland.[15]

The churches were central to the education of the poor across the British Isles, but whereas Westminster preferred to avoid direct state intervention in England and Wales, by the late 1820s there was a call for the establishment of a state-funded national, non-denominational system of education for Ireland. As in Wales, the majority of the poor in Ireland were not members of the established church. The latter resented the implicit loss of control in a state-inspected system and resisted the recommendations. The Church of England was deeply suspicious of Catholic clergy and their hold over their 'ignorant' flock. Thus one pamphlet of 1826 complained of the 'domineering influence' exerted by the clergy over Catholics: the priest, it was alleged, would always be in control unless the 'stupidity of soul and want of powers of reflection and discernment in their people, as if they were born to be irredeemable slaves of superstition' be overcome. The Catholic Emancipation Act of 1829 convinced the government that concessions on schooling to the Catholics in Ireland were unavoidable, and from 1831 state-funded schooling for the poor was overseen by a National Board of Commissioners, with representatives from the main religions (Anglican, Catholic and Presbyterian). However, the pamphleteer of 1826 added a postscript which was critical of the proposed exemption of Catholic children in national schools from reading the scriptures and reiterated fears of ecclesiastical dominance and concern for the future of Protestantism in Ireland.[16]

Throughout the UK, churches resisted non-denominational schooling for the poor. In Ireland, too, some of the Catholic hierarchy and religious orders, notably the Christian Brothers, were suspicious of integrated schooling, while the Presbyterians as well as the Church of Ireland were hostile to the national system from the start. A majority of Anglican clergy tried to avoid regulation by the board through setting up the Church Education Society in 1839 to run its own schools. This had considerable success until the Church of Ireland was disestablished by an act of parliament in 1869 (effective in 1871), after which most of the society's schools affiliated to the national system. However reluctantly, Presbyterians opted to work within this system but lobbied for control to be decentralized. The Board ceded a great deal of its authority to the school managers in 1840, a concession which undermined the original aim of non-denominationalism. Outside of Ulster, the demographic profile meant that few national schools would have a balance between Catholics and Protestants, partly because the former were in the majority and partly because the very much smaller number of poor Anglicans went to the Church Education Society schools.[17] For its part, the Catholic Church accepted the national system at first, but by the middle of the century emulated the Presbyterians in seeking denominational control of the schools. This was largely because of the fear that mixed denominational schools were a cover for Protestant proselytising, a suspicion reinforced by the impact of the Great Famine in the late 1840s and also because the Church Education Society schools were attracting poor Catholics in considerable numbers.[18] The solution was for the state to finance a denominational system. Hence, within less than 20 years, the national system in Ireland was marked by religious segregation.

While anti-Catholic sentiment in the UK saw the majority of the Irish as 'priest-ridden', religion generally played a central role in nineteenth-century education.[19] Indeed, it has been claimed that 'religion probably exercised a greater influence on the lives of Welsh people during [the nineteenth] century than was the case in England or in any other Protestant country'. Nonconformity was dominant in working-class communities in Wales:

> Socially and culturally, and often politically, their lives were centred on the chapel, and class differences in outlook coincided with religious differences, and this cleavage was intensified by a language barrier. In the industrial areas the workers were mainly Welsh in speech and strongly Nonconformist in religion, while the works proprietors and officials were predominantly English-speaking and members of the Established Church.[20]

One result was that before the 1870 Elementary Education Act Welsh working-class parents were hostile to secular education, with high rates of absenteeism and early withdrawal of sons as well as daughters from school. These characteristics were noted in the various educational inquiries after 1833, which also insisted on the need for more schools, especially in the industrial regions where the population was increasingly concentrated. It was recognised that Sunday schools, where teaching focused on the Bible and was in Welsh, were more popular than day schools, especially it seems because attendance meant no loss of wages for young boys who in the mid-nineteenth century could find work from the age of ten. Hence there was a high rate of illiteracy among young men (aged 18 to 22).

This might be taken as an indication that in those regions of heavy and extractive industries where there were more employment opportunities for boys than girls, the former were more likely to be kept from day school. Certainly, the examples of Ireland and Wales reflect the fact that by the early Victorian period, the majority of boys and girls in the British Isles had brief and irregular experiences of schooling. Thus in Wales, attendance averaged as little as two years in total. The 1846–1847 Commission into the state of education in Wales was very critical of most schools for the poor and more generally of the lack of secular education throughout Wales, citing poor buildings, inadequate equipment, unqualified and often poorly educated teachers. Such criticisms were not unique to Wales: indeed, they echoed the complaints against the Irish charter schools. However, the report on Wales implied they pertained even more to girls' education than to boys'. Welsh parents, it was claimed, generally set more store by the benefits of a son attending day school than a daughter, while in practice, throughout the UK in the early and mid-nineteenth century, poor parents saw daughters as more useful at home than sons, though they expected the latter to add to the family income as soon as possible: hence the irregular attendance of both sexes. Indeed, this was also the case in England and Scotland. Thus throughout the UK until the educational reforms of the mid-nineteenth and late nineteenth century, poor attendance was even more likely for girls than boys. For example, in his evidence on attendance in the manufacturing districts of Rochdale and Bradford to the Newcastle Commission into the state of popular education in England and Wales in 1861, Mr. Winder reported that 'When the washing or baking day comes round, the mother must put the younger children in charge of their elder brothers or sisters. It is this cause which makes the percentages for the girls lower than for the boys.'[21]

Yet the report also revealed that attendance generally was higher in these two industrialized textile manufacturing towns than it was in the southern agricultural counties of Devon, Somerset and Hertfordshire and, notably, in Wales. There, the daughters of the poor who wished to improve their reading skills were expected to do so by going to Sunday school, since the presumption was that the skill would improve their religious observance and female virtue. Dissenting Sunday schools had by far the biggest attendance of adult women, with instances of some even in their 80s seeking, and delighting in, literacy.[22] As noted above, these schools tended to teach in Welsh, which was the first language of the majority of the working class. It was classified by one of the 1846–1847 commissioners, Robert Lingen (1819–1905) who succeeded James Kay-Shuttleworth (1804–1877) as Secretary of the Committee of the Privy Council on Education two years after the publication of the report, as 'a language of old-fashioned agriculture, of theology, and of simple rustic life'. In his view, it served to isolate the Welsh people in an empire dominated by the English language. He regarded Welsh as a barrier to 'the moral progress and commercial prosperity of the people'.[23] Without schooling in English, Welsh children would remain 'helplessly local as they might have done a thousand years ago'.[24] What is particularly interesting about the report of 1847 on Wales is that when it wrote of 'children', it differentiated between the aims of an education in English for boys and girls in terms which might have included Ireland and the Scottish Highlands and Islands: education was to make the boys aware of the 'limits, capabilities, general history . . . of that empire in which he is born a citizen'. Whereas education would liberate boys from the burden of an uncivilized past, it was to contain girls to the domestic sphere: boys would serve the empire, girls the nation.

> When it is considered how influential is the mind of the mother in moulding the conduct and determining the character of her offspring, it appears doubly essential that girls should be well and carefully educated.[25]

This was still recognised as a problem in the early 1860s when concern was again expressed that 'at the very threshold of the difficulties in the way of educational extension among the Welsh people is the fact that the great bulk of the population are ignorant of the English language'. The Welsh language, it was believed, was 'of the past not the present', and would, indeed should, gradually die out.[26]

Similar views of the Irish language and of Scottish Gaelic were prevalent, of the latter notably in the Scottish Lowlands where, since the Reformation, literacy in English had been seen as central to the Scottish national character: indeed, at the beginning of the century proficiency in the English language was believed to set the Scots apart as a moral, orderly people, in striking contrast to the Irish.[27] In Ireland the hedge schools, which had been an attempt to subvert the penal legislation (at least until the Relief Act of 1782) and resist English cultural assimilation, had proved much more popular with Catholic parents than the charter schools and schools of the Protestant education societies.[28] Yet while the Irish language was taught, English had become central even in the hedge schools by the early eighteenth century: the hedge schoolmasters, of whom there were harsh criticisms in the Inquiry of 1824, focused on imparting literacy in English. Not only were they responding to the emerging Catholic middle class who saw English as essential for business and trade but to the demands of poor parents who believed that English would provide their children with more employment opportunities. Moreover, hedge schools did not simply disappear with the advent of the national school system in 1831 as the better hedge schools, like the parish schools in Scotland, combined elements of intermediate (or secondary) with elementary education, though also as in Scotland the focus was on men, both as pupils and teachers.[29]

It was generally believed that girls' education was particularly neglected throughout non-English speaking regions of the UK. Yet whereas the Commissioners of 1847 implied that the poor in Wales were indifferent to education, the Scottish Presbyterian emphasis on a literate population encouraged a belief that poor females in the Highlands and Islands aspired to schooling, partly out of shame over illiteracy within a predominantly literate society and partly to improve their occupational opportunities.[30] Certainly, Gaelic-speaking girls were even less likely to attend parish schools than their brothers. Indeed, in Scotland as a whole by the 1840s, only a third of all boys and a quarter of girls attended the publicly funded schools within the state-church system.[31] Although by the 1840s the debate over whether or not the parochial school system was in general decline was focused on the impact of industrialization and urbanization, especially around Glasgow and the west-central belt of the country, it had long been recognised that across the Highlands and Islands parish schools were few and not easily accessible to a scattered population. The concern expressed at the start of the Victorian period over whether Scotland had been reduced to that status of a 'half-educated nation' revolved around the notion of a democratic tradition in education in which both men and women should be literate, but whereas the condition of the parish school was the focus for concern in the Lowlands by the early nineteenth century, in the Highlands and Islands charitable individuals and organisations had concentrated on establishing female schools of industry. This indicated a belief in the need for a literate population but with differing vocational schooling for boys and girls, including a specific emphasis on domestic skills for the latter which was increasingly common throughout the British Isles.

Moreover, besides the demand for child labour, the needs of the family being put before the education of the child and the usefulness of girls in helping with housework and childcare as reasons for irregular attendance at schools across the UK, the Argyll Commission reported in 1866 that the parish school system was not working in the Highlands. To fill the gaps, schools were run by charitable and missionary societies, such as the Society in Scotland for Propagating Christian Knowledge (SSPCK), the Church of Scotland Ladies' Gaelic School Association and the Free Church Ladies' Association. All agreed with the reports on Wales in 1847 and England in 1861 that the poor, male and female, of the Highlands and Islands needed to be 'civilized', and looked on girls as the key to raising the moral standards of the lower orders.[32] Nevertheless, Assistant Commissioner Alexander Nicolson was very critical of schools for girls in the Highlands and Islands.[33] Here, there were similarities with the Welsh situation in that the Gaelic language was seen to hold back progress, particularly in the schooling of girls. This was reflected in the example of the island of Lewis where women could read Gaelic, but few, especially compared to men, could read English or write in either language. Gaelic societies thus seemed more effective compared to those whose schools taught in English and tried to extirpate Gaelic, such as the SSPCK. Hence, in 1862 the percentage of signatures by mark in the marriage registers of the Hebrides was 64.8 for women but 47.6 for men, in contrast to the situation in Edinburgh where the percentage of those who could not sign their names was much lower, at only 4.33 for men and 8.75 for women.[34] Gaelic was not the only language barrier, however. For example, according to Lynn Abrams, in Shetland, where most of the schoolteachers came from outside the island, English was the language of the elite, whereas most Shetlanders spoke a strong local dialect which included a large vocabulary of words of Norse derivation.[35]

Schools providing for the poor in Britain both before but especially after the 1870 and 1872 Education Acts as well as the national schools in Ireland were often blamed for the loss of native languages which, since they were the language of the home, reinforced the sentimental notion of the wife/mother as the preserver of traditional culture. In practice, parents in Ireland, Wales and the Scottish Highlands identified their own languages with their traditional culture, morality and indeed emotions, whereas they saw English as the language of the economy and of the wider world. They expected, even demanded, that English be the medium of instruction in schools.[36] Native languages were often associated with poverty and English with opportunity in both employment and emigration, which in Ireland was reinforced by the Famine.[37] Not only, as noted above, had schoolmasters in hedge schools concentrated on teaching English as early as the start of the eighteenth century, but there is a lack of research into girls' education in these schools, while David Fitzpatrick has argued that the decline in agricultural employment in post-Famine Ireland, which hit women particularly hard, changed attitudes to female education. Of course, this was a regional development: in areas where there was alternative employment, such as northern Ulster where out-working was still widespread, there was low attendance at school, but where there was no paid work for girls, schooling was attractive to both them and their parents. It provided basic skills—literacy, numeracy and domestic—which equipped them to find jobs, particularly in domestic service, elsewhere. Indeed, in post-Famine Ireland, those areas of the country which experienced the highest rates of female emigration also demonstrated the higher levels of attendance and more years of schooling for girls than for boys; only in the more urbanized and industrialized province of Ulster did boys outnumber girls in attendance[38]

As the commissioners had reported of Wales 20 years earlier, the aim of education was literacy in English; however, whereas those commissioners had not spoken Welsh and had no sympathy for the language, Alexander Nicolson who reported to the Argyll Commission was a Gaelic speaker who held that 'any others but persons acquainted with the Gaelic language would in more parts of the district be entirely out of place in the position of teachers'.[39] As the 1847 Report had held for Wales, Nicolson saw the power of reading and writing in English as a force for developing what he identified as a backward society. At the same time, he focused on the empowering effect this would have on women, enabling them to communicate directly by letter with their men who were often absent for lengthy periods due to work. In addition to the advantages of literacy in English, Nicolson considered that skills in elementary arithmetic would make the women of the Highlands and Islands less vulnerable to being taken advantage of by merchants. No such hopes had been expressed in the Blue Books of 1847 for Welsh-speaking women in a similar situation.

The Welsh Blue Books did not result immediately in government action on education, but the Newcastle Commission's 1861 report on the schooling of the poor in England and Wales led to the Revised Code in 1862: government grants were to be allocated on the basis of the number of children in each school who passed an examination in reading, writing and arithmetic, as well as sewing for girls, overseen by the inspectors rather than the teachers. This was championed by Robert Lowe, who had been given responsibility for the Privy Council and its committee on education in 1859. Along with the committee's permanent secretary, Ralph Lingen, Lowe sought to raise both the standing of the committee and the standards of elementary education. At the same time, both men also looked for economies in government spending on education and sought to extend the system to the rest of the UK. The Revised Code was deeply unpopular in England and Wales, where it was seen by the clergy as an attempt to impose state control and by both teachers and inspectors as an additional burden. It was even less popular in Scotland where its application was postponed because Lowe's insistence on limiting government intervention in education to elementary schooling for the poor (the 'three Rs' plus sewing for girls) and on 'payment by results' seemed like a threat to the tradition of community schooling, notably the link between parish school and university and with it the status of the dominie, a crucial figure in the belief in Scottish distinctiveness as well as a reflection of the strength of Presbyterian patriarchy.

The dominie also represented a contrast to the English preference since parish schools in Scotland were traditionally mixed sex with male head-teachers; however, the Argyll Commission reflected what some saw as an aspect of Anglicization in the growing preference among the middle class for a more gender-specific curriculum. Still, whereas the 1870 Elementary Education Act was designed to fill the gap in the education of the poor in England and Wales, the 1872 Education Act for Scotland was to establish a state system for the whole country, to shore up Scotland's claim to a superior educational system. The two major churches (the Church of Scotland and the Free Church) handed over their schools to the new boards and the Scotch Education Department oversaw every aspect of school life to a degree unknown in England and Wales, or indeed Ireland. Nevertheless, while the 1872 Act aimed to preserve the Scottish national tradition, including mixed-sex schools, it also incorporated certain English practices, not least pertaining to gender.

THE GENDERED CURRICULUM BEFORE 1870

Whatever the denomination or the language, there was general agreement across the UK on gender roles and on how they should be reflected in the curriculum, though each denomination assumed that its women had (or should have) superior morals. In Wales, this became an expression of injured national pride in the face of Anglicization and the impact of the hated 'Blue Books'. The 1847 Report was regarded by the Welsh as a grossly unfair and inaccurate indictment by prejudiced Anglican, upper-middle-class English commissioners of three factors central to Welsh identity: the Welsh language and religion and, especially controversial, the morality of the Welsh people, in general, and of working-class women, in particular.

Yet the attitude towards the Catholic poor was similar, and like Welsh Nonconformists the Catholic Church in Britain insisted on separate schooling where possible. They saw church control of education as a means of preventing assimilation while achieving the integration of the impoverished Catholic immigrants into the wider community throughout Britain.[40] This was particularly the case in Scotland, where Catholics were a more significant minority than in England or Wales, making up around 12 per cent of

the population by the mid-Victorian period, with the 1851 census showing they constituted over 15 per cent of the population in the west-central
region.[41] The Catholic preference was, like the English generally, for single-
sex schooling, and where this was not possible (due to numbers or expense)
for mixed infant departments but segregation of the older children. However, in Wales where Irish Catholics constituted a much smaller minority
than in either England or Scotland, their poverty was so severe that they
often could not afford even to employ teachers or establish separate schools,
while families needed all members to contribute to the household economy
as soon as they were able.

Thus, apart from the parish schools in Scotland, gender segregation was
a notable feature of, or at least preference for, the education of the poor in
the UK, based on the shared belief that mixed-sex schooling was morally
dangerous. Catholics, especially in Ireland, went further in a preference
for single-sex schools run by religious orders, because they produced the
greatest number of religious vocations.[42] However, in isolated poor rural
communities in Ireland, it was not always possible to have separate schools,
or even separate departments within the same school, for boys and girls.
Indeed, it was more common for religious orders to establish schools in
urban than in rural areas. There were differences between male and female
orders. The former were willing to work with the national system from
the start. They also accepted the necessity of combining a literary with an
industrial training for poor girls who would have to find paid employment
as soon as they were able, often working with the local Poor Law Union
to teach pauper girls such skills as plain sewing, embroidery, lace-making,
crochet and netting, spinning and fancy knitting. Indeed, the founder of
the Presentation Convent at Castleisland in Kerry made a contract in 1854
with a firm in Belfast to supply material and employed a factory woman
from that city to teach the senior girls muslin embroidery.[43] More generally,
the Presentation Sisters recognised that many of the virtues which they
sought to impart to the children in their schools were also advocated by the
national board: regularity and order, cleanliness, neatness, truth and hon-
esty. Indeed, the schools established by the national board drew more girls
into education and in increasing numbers: whereas in the early nineteenth
century females made up less than half the number of pupils in schools for
the poor, by the 1840s that gap was narrowing rapidly.[44]

However, in contrast to most female religious teaching orders in Ireland,
the Christian Brothers worked with the National Board of Education for a
few years only, remaining outside the system from 1836. The Brothers took
an overtly political, nationalist stance and focused their educational efforts
on boys. Their schools played a major part in the revival of the Irish language and culture and also encouraged social mobility, teaching more than
the basics.[45] The female religious dedicated themselves to the health care
of the poor as well as to education, particularly of girls and infant boys.
Thus, for example, nearly all the convents of the Sisters of Mercy in West

Cork were involved in education, including of male infants.[46] Whereas the Christian Brothers focused on the inculcation in boys of Irish identity and national pride, the female religious concentrated on raising the standards of home life, with the aim of elevating the status and dignity of women.

Thus, nuns in Ireland played a very significant role in the growth of elementary education for both sexes, strengthening the Church's popular base, as well as inculcating an ideal of womanhood in keeping with the general Victorian understanding of separate spheres. Their wider remit was to improve the image of the Irish as a civilized people.[47] Since this entailed clearly defined gender roles within the family, the nuns paid particular attention to imparting both the ideology of domesticity and household skills to the girls. This was in keeping with the aims of the national board, reflected in the text books it published for use in schools, especially those which were aimed at girls, not only on the explicitly gendered topics of needlework and domestic science but also the implicit assumptions about feminine virtues. Indeed, domestic and family themes were to the forefront in the reading books for girls, while the books were used in schools throughout Britain and its Empire, reflecting both the absence of specifically Irish themes as well as the consensus on gender roles and separate spheres for the sexes.[48]

In general, the notion of a specialised curriculum for working-class girls reflected both the expectations of their gender in terms of employment as domestic servants and seamstresses prior to becoming wives and mothers and also the middle- and upper-class philanthropic interest in civilizing the working class. Lady Charlotte Guest's curriculum of basic literacy and numeracy and sewing and embroidery in her evening school for females in Wales, however narrowly conceived, may also be seen as 'enlightened'. Not only did she employ trained teachers and promote the education of adult women, but it was unusual for poor girls in the UK to be taught 'fancy' sewing. True, the latter was neither exceptional nor confined to Wales: for example, at Baggot Street charter school in Dublin the girls were employed at fine as well as plain needlework, with the fine work sold and the profits shared equally between the school and the master.[49] Still, before the 1870 Elementary Education Act for England and Wales, plain needlework was already a fundamental part of the curriculum for working-class girls, whatever the school. Indeed, by the middle of the nineteenth century, it had grown in importance, recognised by the middle classes as a sign not only of the domestic skills which working-class women needed for both home and service, but also of gender distinction, a symbol of the ideal of separate spheres for the sexes. Hence, following the Newcastle Commission's complaints about the poor quality of sewing instruction, its successful teaching became a condition of government grants to schools after 1862.

Sewing was central to the ethos and curriculum of charitable and private adventure schools for working-class girls, but there were widespread criticisms of these establishments by the early Victorian period. They were deemed to be inadequate in accommodation as well as teaching.[50] Indeed, it was reported to the Argyll Commission that benevolent ladies (in stark contrast to Lady Charlotte Guest in Wales) who established proprietary schools for poor girls did not consider that the teaching in these need be as good as in those for boys.[51] Similarly, dame schools, often considered no more than child-minding establishments, were the butt of criticism throughout Britain. Thus, the 1847 Report on Wales was harsh in its condemnation, except in those cases where the 'dame' could be re-classified as a 'governess' by virtue of the teacher coming from a higher social standing than her charges but having fallen on hard times. The Newcastle Commission agreed with the low opinion of dame schools, seeing them as 'mere nurseries' and expressing concern that 'a good many girls finish their education in them'.[52] Scholars have shown that there was a wide range of dame schools, which were as varied in quality as any other type of school and may be seen either as a precursor to infant schools or a barrier to their development. Dame schools have been portrayed as a popular social institution of the working class and infant schools as part of the middle-class effort to socialize the children of the poor.[53] Indeed, however harsh the contemporary criticisms of them, dame schools, especially for girls, continued to flourish in England into the 1880s and only began to die out as elementary education became compulsory.[54]

Moreover, despite girls spending so much time in domestic settings, with dame schools being conducted in the dame's home and with older girls expected to help with the dame's housework, as well as girls' frequent absences from school due to helping their mothers with their household tasks, there was concern that such a domestic training was deficient compared to what they should be getting through formal schooling. Working-class mothers, especially if they were in paid employment, had neither the time nor the ability to pass on domestic skills to their daughters; indeed, it was believed that the mothers often forgot what they themselves had been taught if their employment was full time. While the commissions into popular education throughout the UK all recorded complaints from parents about their daughters being expected not only to learn sewing but also to do chores in school, there were examples in which working-class wives said they had benefited from the sewing and knitting lessons which they felt had prepared them for a lifetime of 'making do and mend', notably among the wives of coal miners whose domestic responsibilities were particularly heavy.[55]

Generally, parents agreed that needlework was a necessary part of the girls' curriculum, but otherwise they displayed 'a strong dislike to other portions of female industry', considering such subjects 'below the dignity' of education and being of the opinion that they were best instructed at home.[56] While such views were voiced throughout Britain, they seem to have been held most strongly in Scotland where reports of parental resistance to daughters being taught even needlework in parish schools were widespread. For example, a report for the Church of Scotland schools in the north-east in the late 1850s noted that mothers insisted that their daughters could receive better instruction in housework at home or in domestic service than in school. [57] Indeed, it was only with the Education Act of 1861 that there was official recognition in Scotland of the domestic education of girls, in the sense that the Act accepted the need for more gender-specific schooling for the working class: 'Hitherto, boys and girls had been taught side by side in the parish schools and, as a rule, the curriculum for both was the same.' The 1861 Act allowed the appointment by parish schools of a woman 'to give instruction in such branches of female industry and household training, as well as elementary education, as they shall then or from time to time prescribe'.[58] This represented a small but significant breach in the male-dominated profession. However, although it had been stipulated that girls above the age of seven would not be counted towards the government grant unless they were taught sewing, the inclusion of domestic subjects was left to the discretion of the local authorities, and the Argyll Commission reported confusion among schoolmasters over whether sewing was compulsory or simply recommended by the Privy Council.

In fact, provision for sewing in parish schools in Scotland remained patchy before the 1872 Education Act: in the Hebrides, for example, the percentage of girls learning needlework in the 1860s was only 37.4, which was below the average for the rest of Scotland, at 42.6.[59] Categorized a vocational or 'industrial' subject, sewing was viewed as undermining the Scottish tradition of an academic curriculum in the parish school and in the process potentially compromising the position of the schoolmaster. The Newcastle Commission noted that sewing was often neglected in mixed-sex schools in England, but in Scotland it was often only on the curriculum in parish schools where female industrial departments were attached. Moreover, where these were established, there were warnings of possible deception if the cost of paying the sewing mistress fell on the treasured but poorly paid dominie. There was also concern that in a profession dominated by men, the sewing regulations might result in an oversupply of schoolmistresses, but that was to some extent mitigated by the preference to employ the wives or sisters of the schoolmasters as teachers of needlework, perhaps as a supplement to the dominie's inadequate salary.[60] At the same time, there was a fear that if insisted upon, adding a sewing department could bring hardship to poor districts. Thus, rather than having a sewing mistress in each parish school, one good sewing school was advocated for a wide district. And despite the fear of a potential oversupply, there were said to be too few sewing mistresses and too many practical difficulties in the way of introducing additional domestic subjects, such as laundry or plain cooking. This echoed complaints in the 1847 and 1861 commission reports for Wales and England, but whereas there was more of an expectation in England and Wales that a domestic curriculum for girls was intended to ensure a supply of efficient servants, the Scottish tradition valued the academic over the vocational. Nevertheless, in the 1850s inspectors of Scottish schools complained that female servants were ignorant of the science involved in such work as setting fires and generally the witnesses to the Argyll Commission supported the introduction of sewing.[61] Indeed, there was a suspicion that what was taught in schools for the poor throughout the British Isles failed to prepare girls for their domestic future.

Thus, across Britain there was concern over the state of education of the lower orders, but in contrast to Scotland there was an assumption that improvements should be based on social class: the poor were to be schooled apart from their social superiors and to accept and respect the social hierarchy. Hence the 1870 Education Act for England and Wales designated the schooling of working-class children as 'elementary', with the emphasis on the 'three Rs'. At the same time, government inspectors of schools and middle-class reformers insisted that something more was needed for girls: schooling in domesticity was seen as essential not just for the comfort of the individual home but also for the 'welfare of the nation'.[62] The belief was held so strongly that schools, especially if they were mixed sex, were criticized for spending too much time on book learning for girls and too little on domestic subjects.[63]

The emphasis on needlework in working-class girls' schooling reflected the general middle-class belief across the UK that poverty was a key indicator of bad household management. Thus the 1847 Report on Wales saw a causal connection between the lack of domestic education for girls and the 'social and moral depravity of the population', which was held to be particularly the case in mining districts. One witness from Wrexham lamented the lack of instruction in 'industrial' (that is, domestic) skills for girls:

> When they marry, they are unable to make and mend any article of clothing, even a pair of stockings for their husbands. The husband's wages must be spent on buying in the towns an article of clothing which costs twice the money, and does not last half the time. In consequence of this, though the wages are high, the people are often in a miserable condition. . . . The women have no knowledge of housewifery or economy; and their ignorance and inefficiency produce all kinds of domestic dissension and distress.[64]

That this opinion was held by a shopkeeper shows how strong the ideology of separate spheres was. It may also indicate that the poor were not yet considered worthwhile customers, either in terms of their purchasing power or social standing, at least by the more prosperous retailers.[65]

Hence, whatever the type of school, working-class girls were to be inculcated with certain domestic virtues as well as skills. The former included thrift, cleanliness, orderliness, punctuality and acceptance of their place both in the home and in society. These qualities, it was assumed, would make the working-class woman both a reliable servant and a sound homemaker. This was the case throughout the UK, though as we have seen it had particular resonance in Wales where the impact of the 'treachery of the Blue Books' became entangled with the issues of language and religion.[66] As a Celtic people, the Welsh, like the Scottish Highlanders and the Irish, were seen to be in dire need of the restraining influence of a domestically skilled and virtuous wife and mother. Indeed, there seems to have been a concern that however 'barbaric' their culture, it had an emasculating effect. This is reflected in Lingen's description of 'the Welshman' which gives the latter what were considered feminine characteristics: 'His feelings are impetuous; his imagination vivid; his ideas (on such topics as he entertains) succeed each other rapidly.' Such attributes, if unchecked, could lead to loss of virtue in a woman, while they made a man untrustworthy, 'naturally more voluble, often eloquent . . . [possessing] a mastery over his own language far beyond that which an Englishman of the same degree possesses over his'.[67] However articulate 'the Welshman' may be, the Welsh language was deemed 'a manifold barrier to the moral progress and commercial prosperity of the people'.[68]

Nevertheless, the commissioners who wrote the 1847 Report were insistent that the Welsh poor possessed both the capacity and the desire for an English education. Lingen acknowledged that 'so far as the Welsh peasantry interest themselves at all in the daily instruction of their children, they are everywhere anxious for them to be taught English'.[69] This was grudging praise: the criticism of the manners and morals of the poor in England and Scotland was not as harsh as it had been in Wales in 1847. Thus while illegitimacy was condemned in both England and Wales, one witness to the Newcastle Commission testified that despite high rates in the English manufacturing counties of Warwickshire and Staffordshire

> The behaviour and manner in other respects of girls and women is not in public less decent than that in places of better repute, and it is generally asserted that this early corruption of females does not hinder them from being very good neighbours, and excellent, hard-working, and affectionate wives and mothers.[70]

No such caveat was made for Welsh women. The commissioners of 1847 were convinced that however much the education of the English poor needed to be improved, the situation was worse in Wales, and the proof was that the 'disregard of cleanliness and decency is more observable in the purely Welsh than in the Anglicized districts'.[71] The key to raising the cultural and moral standards of the working class lay in the domestic education of their daughters in schools by trained teachers, since both the mothers and the untrained teachers were incapable of performing that role, let alone of understanding its crucial importance. The Welsh nation, but particularly its poor women, had been judged both uncivilized and inferior even to their English counterparts. Indeed, nearly a decade and a half later, the Newcastle Commission into popular education made many of the same criticisms as the commissioners of 1847. Moreover, the testimony of John Jenkins to the Newcastle Commission magnified the 1847 contrast between the north and the south of Wales: the people in the former area were 'sober, frugal, well-regulated and religious', whereas those in the south were immoral due to the extent of industrialization, urbanization and immigration.[72]

Some historians have suggested that while the Welsh were justified in 1847 in complaining about both the methods of inquiry and the lack of empathy on the part of the commissioners, nevertheless the subtext of the report went beyond the situation in Wales. It 'made a statement about education in England and Wales', embodying 'a philosophy of elementary education and a remedy to educational ills in England as well as in Wales'. The intention was to find 'irrefutable evidence for the necessity of a system of state education' for England as much as for Wales.[73] However, the 1847 Report provoked a markedly defensive reaction from middle-class Welsh commentators who were determined, on the one hand, to disprove the allegations of low female morality and, on the other, to raise the cultural level of the poor.[74] One result was an even stronger emphasis on the domestic role of women as mothers of the nation. Moreover, although the criticisms of school provision in Wales also applied to England, reaction in Wales against the charges of 1847 was so fierce, and the resistance from the churches, in both England and Wales, to a secular education so strong that it took nearly a quarter of a century before that was (almost) established by the Elementary Education Act.

Although in contrast the Scottish tradition had centred on a national system rather than one based on social class, in practice it was mainly the children of the poor who attended the parish schools. The assumption in Scotland had been that its education was superior to that pertaining elsewhere in the UK. Four years after the Newcastle Commission reported, however, the Argyll Commission was set up to examine the state of education in Scotland. While not limited to the schooling of the poor, it revealed weaknesses in the elementary education of the majority of children in the country districts of Scotland, which was precisely the area where the traditional parish system was assumed to be strong. One reason for this was thought to be the neglect of the basics by the schoolmaster in favour of teaching the minority of talented boys (the lads of parts) the higher branches to qualify them for university.[75] So committed were the dominies to the university subjects that if there were too few talented lads who could stay on into the higher standards, they taught the higher subjects to any girls whose parents could keep them at school, even though women had no hope of gaining a university education.[76] The Argyll Commission's reports on the education of the poor preferred the English practice of relying more on women to teach the basics as well as sewing. Yet there was unease among the assistant commissioners that an emphasis on elementary education, where the teacher was paid by the number of children who passed the elementary subjects and of girls examined in sewing, would hurt the higher branches so that 'the pride and glory of a schoolmaster's profession would be destroyed', reiterating the fear that Scottish education would be reduced to the uniformity of English elementary schools where the standard was deemed by the Argyll commissioners to be lower.[77]

If the sexes were separated after infancy, the best masters would remain with the boys, whereas the girls would have schoolmistresses whose own education and training had been limited, especially compared to the university-educated dominie.[78] Argyll's assistant commissioners underlined the national commitment to education for talented boys of any class by recording that whereas in Scotland there was at least one matriculated student for every 1,000 of the population, in England the proportion was one to 5,000.[79] At the same time, the Commission's endorsement of the growing emphasis on an education in domesticity for working-class girls within the UK reflected both the increasing influence of English practices and a response to tensions within the national community expressed in the fear that a country which had prided itself on its democratic tradition in education was now 'half-educated'.[80]

Indeed, the Argyll Commission recognised that the working of the parochial system was at best patchy: besides the weaknesses in the rural Lowlands where it had previously been considered to be fully operative, it was not only greatly restricted across the Highlands and Islands but had effectively collapsed in the large towns. As noted in the introduction, the educational tradition in Scotland had its origins in the Reformation and was bound up with the Established Church which, in contrast to the Church of England, had seen education as a means of uniting the nation in a common culture. The Disruption in the Church of Scotland in 1843, therefore, had an enormous impact on education. Evangelicals who left to establish the Free Church at once set up their own schools, replacing the ideal of the parish school serving the whole community with competition between churches over educational provision. One result was fear that the national system was considered to be collapsing so that the Argyll Commission accepted the state should assume responsibility for education, particularly in view of the demographic changes which had taken place under the impact of industrialism. The old ideal of one school in each parish simply could not meet the needs of the growing towns and cities and arguably never had met those of the huge, sparsely populated, scattered parishes in the Highlands.[81]

Nevertheless, whatever their problems, by the 1860s parish schools were taken as the standard by which to judge others in Scotland. Hence, adventure schools, the great majority of which were run by female teachers, were dismissed as harmful to the health as well as the education of their pupils, both girls and boys. Private charity schools, the majority of which were for poor girls and taught a very restricted curriculum, were also condemned as generally inferior to the parish and Free Church schools and were considered to be even worse for girls than for boys, with the former learning 'less than nothing'.[82] The commissioners noted that education of girls and boys began later in Scotland than in England (at six years of age, compared to four), yet although there was a larger proportion of pupils over 12 years of age in Scotland than in England, relatively few Scottish children remained in school after that age, mirroring the situation throughout the UK of early withdrawal from school.

Another concern was over co-education, a preference for which we have seen distinguished Scotland from the rest of the British Isles. However, the assistant commissioners who examined the country districts of Scotland in the 1860s recommended separating the sexes after infancy, preferring a schoolmistress to be in charge of the infants and the older girls. They echoed the view of the reports of 1847 on Wales and 1861 on England and Wales that mixed-sex schools resulted in ill-discipline. In contrast, 'in schools where girls alone were taught there was a much greater appearance of refinement'. They pointed out that single-sex education was the norm among the middle and upper classes, whereas among the poor, 'coarse and indelicate' behaviour by boys sparked unfeminine behaviour among the girls.[83] Nevertheless, it was more common that witnesses who reported to the Argyll Commission expressed regret that the English practice of single-sex education seemed to be spreading in Scotland. In this view, mixed-sex schooling encouraged the girls to compete academically with the boys.

Still, for the majority of parish school children in Scotland, as for work-ing-class children throughout the UK, the educational sights were low: by the age of 12 or 13, it was considered enough that they had attained 'a certain degree of intelligence, if not cultivation': they ought to be able 'to read a newspaper without effort and with intelligence; to write a well-spelled letter with ease; or to perform such arithmetical operations as occur in the ordinary business of life'.[84] And in that ordinary business of life, both girls and boys were expected to enter the work force at an early age; indeed, it was accepted that they would do so while still at school, even in Scotland where the half-time system of schooling was never as prevalent as in England and Wales.

ECONOMY, SCHOOL AND ATTENDANCE BEFORE 1870

Besides the two major influences of religion and language on working-class education of males and females in the UK in the nineteenth century, there was the economy. Indeed, throughout the British Isles, the local economy had a direct impact on the schooling of the poor. Thus, in Wales the process of industrialization which focused on the extractive industries had a crucial impact on female education in particular while there were similarities with Scotland where the economy grew dramatically in the second half of the nineteenth century and came to dominate key sectors in the world economy. Such phenomenal growth in Scotland was less concentrated than in Wales but was nevertheless narrowly based on the predominantly male sector of heavy industry (coal, iron and steel, shipbuilding and heavy engineering) and very dependent on the world market. Working-class women were concentrated overwhelmingly in domestic service, textiles and the clothing industries, though as in Wales farming in Scotland continued to depend more on female labour, both regular and seasonal, than in England into the twentieth century.[85] Wales, however, had an even more narrowly based industrial sector than Scotland which resulted in a decrease of employment opportunities for women outside of domestic service and agriculture.

Hence, to a much greater extent than elsewhere in the UK, the provision of schooling in Wales was also influenced by the concentrated nature of industry there. Certainly, the north of Wales was not completely agricultural, but the industries (slate quarries, copper and lead mining, woolen, cotton and linen manufacturers) were much more dispersed and provision of schools by employers was much less generous than in the south.[86] Still throughout Wales, the religious differences noted above meant hostility to schools established by employers since they were generally run along the lines of the voluntary Anglican National Society. Yet all churches perceived a decline in working-class morality which they associated with the growth of industry and towns throughout Britain from the late eighteenth century to the early years of Victoria's reign. This period also saw increased demand for child labour and a related increase in part-time schooling. Before 1833 in Great Britain and Ireland, factory legislation covering the textile industry, which depended heavily on female and child labour, required the owner to provide the child employees with an education, whereas the 1833 Factory Act required the child to attend external day schools.

In Wales, where coal mining and slate quarrying were central to the industrial economy in the south, the focus was on male labour. Education for child labourers in these industries was not covered by factory legislation until 1844, and the owners tended to establish work schools not attached to the workplace, which was especially the case in the coal industry. While factory legislation was intended to ensure that child labourers received some schooling, such works' schools were more generally for the education of the children of employees, girls as well as boys. In the south of Wales, there were girls' and infants' schools and occasionally mixed-sex schools; but the curriculum for girls was even more limited than that for boys: reading, writing, some arithmetic and a great deal of sewing. Even in the enlightened educational scheme at the ironworks of Sir (Josiah) John Guest, only the boys and men had an 'upper' level (at both day and evening schools) by the middle of the century. One reason was that as an employer, Sir John was interested in developing the skills and technical knowledge of the older boys, whereas the young women who attended his wife Lady Charlotte's evening classes were taught domestic subjects more as a way of preparing them for a domestic life than paid employment.

It was, in fact, common in Wales for industrialists to provide education, but it differed considerably between the regions of coal mining and heavy metallurgical industries and the textile manufacturing areas.[87] Moreover, that provision was concentrated in the south of Wales, where the process of industrialization saw a rapidly expanding population in the urban centres and industrial valleys, while there was a corresponding relative decline in rural areas which also lost population to England.[88] One aspect of this was a sexual imbalance in the population. The 1847 Education Inquiry noted that

> In Carmarthenshire the number of females exceeds that of males by one tenth, in Pembrokeshire by one-fifth, in Glamorganshire by one-nineteenth, in England by one-twentieth part (speaking in round numbers). The disproportion marks in what quarter the adult male labour in South Wales is drained off, *viz*, to the coal and iron districts, for, if we take the population under 15 years of age, the males are in each county in a majority.[89]

At the same time, Wales as well as England and Scotland attracted economic migrants, notably from Ireland since the late eighteenth century and including a significant minority of women. In contrast to Scotland and England, the Irish did not constitute a major immigrant group in Wales: that was the English. Nevertheless, the Catholic Irish throughout Britain were a despised minority, regarded particularly as less moral than Protestant women.[90] Hence, as noted above, what was so shocking about the 1847 Report was that the English and Anglican middle class had the same opinion of the Welsh Nonconformist working class, especially of the 'peasant girls' who were described as 'almost universally unchaste'.[91] Indeed, the same was said of women in the mining and manufacturing districts, where one Anglican vicar testified that 'nothing can be lower, I would say more degrading, than the character in which the women stand relative to the men. . . . Promiscuous intercourse is most common, is thought of as nothing, and the women do not lose cast by it'.[92]

The average age at which Welsh children, boys and girls, left school then was reported to be generally around ten, though in the mining districts of North Wales, that fell to eight.[93] It was recorded in 1847 that only 20.4 per cent of the children on the registers of schools in Monmouthshire were above ten years old; of those under ten, boys outnumbered girls by 26 per cent, whereas of those over ten, girls outnumbered boys by 20 per cent.[94] However, there was a higher rate of absenteeism among girls: although both sexes were often absent, with long intervals between attendance, the average rate of attendance of boys in 1846 was 62 per cent, compared to 54 per cent for girls.[95] Welsh girls, it seems, experienced an even briefer and more irregular period of schooling than boys, despite the fact that the form industrialization had taken favoured male employment. Indeed, it appears that even before industry took off in Wales, more boys received an education than girls.[96] That more boys than girls were kept on at school pointed to the parents' motivation: education would improve a boy's chances of finding a job in an economy where employment opportunities for girls were limited and contracting. The following extract from parish records for the 1840s shows that although there were regional variations, boys always out-numbered girls in day schools.

Percentage of Day Scholars to the Population of Each Sex

	Carmarthenshire	Glamorganshire	Pembrokeshire
MALES	8.6	9.5	11.6
FEMALES	4.9	8.8	6.4

Source: Parliamentary Paper, *Report of the Commission of Inquiry into the State of Education in Wales*, part 1, p.22.

The same was true of Sunday schools in these three counties: the number of male scholars under 15 years of age was 24,665 compared to 23,166 females; and above 15 there were 17,441 males to 13,445 females.[97] However, Jelinger C. Symons, commissioner for the counties of Brecknock, Cardigan, Radnor and Monmouth, believed that, while fewer in number, adult females had a better rate of attendance at the Sunday schools, which he felt went some way to reducing the inequality of schooling between the sexes in the day schools.[98]

Employers such as Sir John Guest who set up works schools expected their employees to contribute towards the upkeep. In contrast to the general type of works school, however, the Guest educational scheme was ambitious in terms of the numbers catered for, the organisation of the classrooms, equipment and curriculum, the employment of trained teachers, and the replacement of monitors with pupil teachers. In addition, there was the extension of the Guest philanthropy to the children of his Catholic workers who were taught in separate schools and administered by their clergy, all of which made it unique.[99]

As noted above, most Catholic communities in Wales were too poor to employ teachers and depended on the parish priest to take that role. When asked in 1824 whether Irish children who had gone to Scotland attended the parish schools, the Reverend James Carlile replied that they did not because there was employment for children there.[100] In Wales, one Catholic priest, who himself taught around 60 boys and girls, complained in 1842 that 'the children of both sexes are employed so early picking or piling minerals or coals [that] they are removed about seven years of age'.[101] There was a belief among Catholics that, in such a situation of desperate poverty within a hostile host community, the most basic ability to read was sufficient.[102] This, however, was judged to further differentiate the Irish migrants from the Welsh, among whom the tradition was more like the Scottish in the desire of the rural poor that their children, especially their sons, be educated as a means of social mobility.[103] Indeed, school attendance by poorer Catholic children remained irregular even at the end of the nineteenth century, though as throughout the rest of Britain, the Catholic Church sought both to increase school provision and decrease absenteeism.

In practice, before developments in factory and school legislation resulted in a system of half-time education, few working-class children of any denomination in the UK were kept on at school over the age of ten. While the boys went into the mines, quarries and ironworks of Wales, girls were expected to stay at home to look after younger siblings. Indeed, at the time of the commission the rate of illiteracy in Wales was much higher among women (70 per cent in the south, 66 in the north) than it was among men (45 per cent in the south, 41 in the north).[104]

The Newcastle Commission drew similar general conclusions regarding the education of the working class in England to that of the Welsh and Irish: its great concern was over the high rates of non-attendance and of irregular attendance, holding that 'to very poor children the school is a substitute for a home; they frequently have no other experience of domestic comfort and decency'.[105] There had been efforts to encourage attendance in England and Wales: the Committee of the Privy Council offered a capitation grant to schools with registered teachers for every pupil who went to school for a minimum of 176 days a year and who paid at least one penny a week in fees, from 1853 in rural parishes and from 1856 in towns. The grant differed, however, according to the sex of the child: schools could claim from four to six shillings for a boy but from three to five for a girl.[106]

Even as they complained that parents removed children as soon as they could find work, the commissioners accepted the need for child labour. The Newcastle Commission recorded that three children in a family over the age of eight could double the weekly income of the house.[107] Half-time education depended on the demands of the local economy. Hence Mr. J.S. Winder, who looked into the manufacturing districts of Rochdale and Bradford for the Commission, reported that it was much more prevalent in the former (a cotton-spinning town) than in the latter (a centre of the woolen industry) where children were more likely to work full time at an earlier age.[108] In both, however, most children had left school by the age of 13: in Rochdale, only 2.1 per cent of boys and 1.98 per cent of girls and in Bradford only 3.11 per cent of boys and 2.5 per cent of girls remained at school over the age of 13, most of whom were half-timers who could not get the certificate allowing them to work full time.[109] Indeed, 20 years later the Bradford School Board, under pressure from both employers and parents, reduced standards for exemption, arguing, on the one hand, that poor families needed their children's wages and, on the other, that half-time education was 'essential to the carrying on of the staple trade in the town'.[110]

Yet even in a city like Liverpool where there were fewer employment opportunities for children than in most of the industrial towns of the north of England, there was poor attendance.[111] This relative lack of jobs for boys in a port city contrasted with mining areas. In the latter it was felt that the exclusion of women from deep coal mining had resulted in the daughters of pitmen remaining at school 'a sufficient time to obtain as good and useful an education as the neighbouring schools [in south Staffordshire] are now able to supply', whereas boys as young as seven or eight could be found in the pits of Durham.[112] This seems a complacent judgment. The aim of girls' schooling in mining districts was to prepare them to be skilled wives and mothers: as Colin Griffin has elaborated, servicing the needs of miners, often including lodgers as well as sons and husbands, was a full-time job typically lasting from 5.30am until 11.00pm.[113] Little wonder, then, that daughters were frequently kept from school to help with such heavy and constant domestic work. Moreover, despite the lack of job opportunities for girls in mining areas which might indeed have kept them longer at school than their brothers, W.B. Stephens has pointed out that before the 1860s the daughters and wives of miners throughout Britain were less likely to be literate than their menfolk. [114]

Stephens has found a similar pattern among the daughters of skilled artisans, whereas, in contrast, the daughters of unskilled agricultural labourers tended to have better literacy rates than their brothers.[115] He emphasises the extent of variation depending on local factors, including among the latter the type of farming and the pattern of landholding. Meg Gomersall's study of rural Norfolk and Suffolk confirms this. Indeed, she found that there was a prejudice against educating boys for fear it would result in them abandoning agriculture.[116] At the same time, while boys were more able to find permanent employment in these rural counties from an early age, girls' attendance was erratic due to the demands of both seasonal labour and household duties.[117] The Newcastle Commission found that in the agricultural areas children of both sexes began to leave around nine years old, though the same witness calculated the average period of school life to be 6.3 years for boys and 6.88 for girls. Both boys and girls worked in the fields at planting and harvesting as well as clearing stones, but as in Scotland when it came to hunting game, boys were the preferred beaters, while girls worked in cottage industries, such as cutting cloth for factories.[118] The same Scottish witness voiced the general belief that working in the fields, whether in mixed-sex groups or single sex, lowered the moral standards of young people and in particular coarsened the girls.[119]

As noted above, in contrast to England and Wales, half-time education had never taken root in Scotland: indeed, by the 1860s only one per cent of factory workers were 'half-timers' compared to nine per cent in England.[120] Still, in textile areas, notably Dundee and Renfrewshire, half-time schooling was held to be the biggest obstacle to improving educational standards; and in such a female-dominated industry, it affected mostly girls. The same was true for the textile region of Lancashire where on the eve of the Victorian period the proportion of female day scholars was far lower than that of boys and far lower than the national average.[121]

Certainly, there was a general acceptance in the UK of the importance of female domesticity and of the notion of separate spheres for the sexes, but there were both national and local variations in the schooling of working-class girls which were related to the economy. For example, attitudes in Wales towards the teaching of domestic subjects were in contrast to those held in Scotland: in the parish schools of the latter, they were looked down on as non-academic subjects, whereas if forced to choose, Welsh parents preferred their daughters to be taught domestic economy to the Welsh language.[122] This may be related not only to the different educational traditions and the control which Presbyterianism retained over schooling in Scotland but also to the different employment opportunities on offer to girls. In Victorian Wales, there were lower rates of participation of women in the paid labour force than there were in Scotland, while the rate of female employment in England was ten per cent higher than in Wales. Moreover, women in Wales were concentrated in an even narrower range of jobs, with domestic service accounting for over 50 per cent of the total number of women in paid employment.[123] Thus, women in Wales did not share the same opportunities for industrial work that were available in England and Scotland.[124] In addition, there were fewer job opportunities in the industrial towns and valleys in the south than in rural west and north Wales. Indeed, whereas agriculture as a source of female employment was declining throughout Britain, it was crucial for women in north Wales, while, as noted above, it remained more important for women in Scotland than in England. In 1851, agriculture was the second biggest employer of women in Wales at 29.3 per cent, compared to 7.5 per cent of women in paid work in England.[125] One consequence was that young and single women tended to migrate to the south and south-east of England in order to contribute to the family income.[126]

Whereas demand for child labour throughout the UK depended on the regional economy, the general preference was for gender segregated work. The Newcastle Commission noted with disapproval that children employed in gangs to clear land of stones used 'shocking' language; furthermore, it was believed that such labour demeaned the girls more than the boys.[127] The investigation into Scottish education a few years later had a more nuanced opinion but shared the concern about the potentially baleful influence of unruly boys on girls. Boys who worked in the fields were generally considered to be much wilder than girls, with the result that the standard of boys' education in the Lowland country districts was below that of girls at the same age who were more likely to be kept at school until they were 12 or even 13, while boys as young as ten were sent out to herd.[128] Thus, one schoolmaster in East Lothian complained in the early 1860s that a walk in the countryside resulted in 'every feeling of decency [being] outraged': he had witnessed young female fieldworkers quarreling so violently that 'the language used exceeded anything I ever heard or indeed could have imagined'. In his view, boys and girls working together in the fields for much of the year resulted in the loss of 'any good impression made upon the young by teachers and clergymen'.[129]

In England as in Wales, but in contrast to Scotland, the Newcastle Commission found that in agricultural districts there was less opportunity for girls than boys to attend schools (and too few opportunities for either sex), whereas in mining areas it was the opposite, though even here there were differences. For example, there was a higher rate of literacy and less child labour among lead miners than among coal miners. Still, it was observed that in both there was a 'want of female delicacy and reserve'.[130] For children in England who did remain in school to 13, the preference was to separate the sexes and to have a woman teach the girls, as one inspector noted:

> the impudence of young girls in Weardale, Cumberland, etc . . . may be attributed in great degree to their mingling with boys at school until 13, 14 or 15 years of age, without the superintendence of a female. It is impossible to describe the coarseness of manners that prevails in these schools.[131]

Cumberland was a pastoral county with very little call on child labour, which may have encouraged children to remain in school until their teens. Additionally, the northern counties of England may have been influenced by the more positive attitudes to literacy in the neighbouring Scottish Lowlands.[132]

There was acceptance, though also unease, throughout the UK that mothers kept elder daughters at home to look after younger children when they had pressing chores, such as on wash-day, especially if the mother took in other people's laundry. In that case, daughters might be kept from school for two days a week, as at Clapham where clothes were collected for washing by the laundress on Mondays and returned to the customer on Fridays.[133] John Middleton Hare's report for the districts of Hull, Yarmouth and Ipswich in 1861 reveals the impact of the regional economy in addition to domestic responsibilities on girls' education:

> Girls, it has appeared from statistics, leave school earlier than boys; and the evidence derived from practical experience goes to show that, in general, their school attendance is both subject to more interruption and briefer in duration. Sometimes, like their brothers they are kept away for the sake of what they can earn by occasional employment (as stringing beads for 1s. 6d. a week in Ipswich); but more frequently they are required to help in domestic matters, in seasons of sickness, or when the mother is out at work, or is secluded by a new birth from the family. In Ipswich, there is little employment for women and girls but what can be done at their own homes. A stay factory, a shoe factory, a flax mill, and a silk-winding room are the only remarkable exceptions; but these are not to be compared in size with the cotton mills in Hull or the silk mills in Yarmouth. To the latter must be added various fish 'offices' of that town, which, however, create a demand for female labour only during the season and after each catch of herrings. These sources of employment excepted, my district calls for the labour of

the female hand only in those miscellaneous forms which are common to all parts of the kingdom alike. Upon the whole, therefore, it
may be concluded that the education of girls experiences no peculiar or
extraordinary impediment in the district committed to me. The poor
are more willing to spend money on the education of their sons than
their daughters.[134]

However, in Scotland there were believed to be particular problems in the
Highlands and Islands where, in common with other rural and remote areas
in the UK, attendance at school was very irregular. One factor was adverse
weather which was particularly severe in mountainous regions, preventing
both boys and girls from attending school. There was generally no distinction made between the sexes on the impact of such conditions, though
interestingly one inspector in London expressed an opinion to the Newcastle Commission that girls were less inclined to face inclement weather than
boys.[135] In most of rural Britain, and indeed in towns close to farming districts, both boys and girls were kept from school to do seasonal work in the
fields whatever the weather. Throughout the UK, however, it was mainly
older girls who missed school to allow their mothers to take seasonal jobs
by assuming the latter's domestic responsibilities. In the Highlands and
Islands, children were also expected to work on the family croft. In addition, in this region migration for work of adults of both sexes was essential
to the local economy. Thus, in areas where younger men and women left in
the summer for employment on the east coast and in east-central Scotland,
younger siblings would be taken out of school to help maintain the croft.
As in Wales, there was a lack of job opportunities for women apart from
domestic service and seasonal employment in the fields, and in both women
found more openings in the Lowlands. While men and older boys worked
in the fishing industry, often absent from home for long periods, as noted
in the introduction older girls were required to stay at home when their
mothers were engaged 'at the herring', which was similar to the situation in
Hull described above.[136]

SCHOOLING POOR GIRLS IN THE LATE VICTORIAN PERIOD

The Education Acts for England and Wales (1870) and Scotland (1872)
brought increased government intervention but also established local management through elected school boards in which, as discussed in Chapter
1, women could vote and stand on the same basis as men. The Acts reinforced the social class hierarchy since most pupils in board schools were
working class, but as the period progressed, increasing numbers of lower
middle-class children attended, especially girls who were attracted by both
the development of secondary level education through higher grade schools
and the opportunities offered by the pupil-teacher system (established in

1846) and the Queen's scholarships for entry to teaching, a respectable and relatively financially secure form of employment for women who were still faced with a very limited choice, constrained by notions of what was appropriate according to gender as well as to social status.

The local economy continued to influence the education of the poor after 1870. In mining areas, it was still boys who either left school as early as possible or became half-timers.[137] The textile industry, however, preferred girls: according to the 1871 census, between one and four girls aged between ten and 15 were employed in cotton manufacturing in Lancashire. The situation was worse in Dundee, a textile city with a marked reliance on jute manufacturing which made it more prone to fluctuations and unemployment. It also depended very heavily on female and child labour, making it a low-wage region.[138] There were more half-timers in Dundee than elsewhere in Scotland where the system had not been as strongly established as in England.[139] This was also the case in which cottage industries persisted: for example, in the lace and straw-plaiting trades in Bedfordshire and Buckinghamshire, school logs recorded complaints that poor attendance and the half-time system were holding back progress for the whole class. As Pamela Horn records, it was only with the sharp decline of the lace cottage industry in the later nineteenth century that this situation was alleviated. She found similarities in the straw-plaiting trade in which, although boys also participated, they did not do so to the same extent as girls. Moreover, these counties even in the 1870s contained many parishes without an ordinary day school. Horn concludes that while such cottage industries brought in much-needed contributions to the family income, the general education of the children was neglected 'while the women's constant preoccupation with their own plait or lace prevented them from looking after either home or family'.[140] That in turn led to older daughters being kept from school.

Religion continued to be a factor when church schools remained outside of the state system: the established churches in England and Ireland, Nonconformists in Wales, the Episcopal Church in Scotland and the Catholic Church throughout Britain. Whereas in Scotland after the 1872 Act, the main Presbyterian churches ceded their schools to the new boards which effectively constituted a national system of education, in England and Wales the Elementary Education Act was to fill the gaps in voluntary provision. As noted above, in Ireland there had been a 'national' system since the early 1830s, but it soon became effectively denominational, dominated by the Catholic Church. Whatever the denomination, however, all favoured a domestic education for working-class girls.

In this they agreed with the efforts of feminists and lady members of school boards to have domestic economy and especially cookery included in the girls' curriculum.[141] The issue of cost in establishing and maintaining the latter was particularly acute in small, rural, and Catholic schools. Other factors which made it more difficult to teach domestic economy, let alone cookery, in the schools for the Catholic poor than in board schools included the already heavy pressures on the mostly female teachers, the majority of whom were without teaching qualifications.[142] The church, however, was strenuous in its efforts to introduce domestic subjects which it saw as essential to raise the cultural and moral as well as health standards of its community and to have that despised minority accepted by the host nation.

The male educational establishment in Scotland, however, resisted middle-class ladies' efforts to have more domestic subjects than needlework in board schools, especially cookery which was expensive if it was taught in practice and not only in theory. The government, for its part, deemed practice especially beneficial for working-class girls and their families. Thus the Cross Commission into elementary education commended its teaching in 1886:

> We believe it is difficult to over-estimate the far-reaching effect upon the homes of our labouring classes of a knowledge on the part of the mother of the family of good and economical cookery. . . . it is said, among other things, that girls who attend cookery lessons acquire a taste for domestic employments, and are both useful at home and more intelligent in their general studies. The lessons are said to be a relief from over-pressure, and to tend to make the girls thrifty and careful housewives.[143]

Resistance to cookery in England and Wales was based above all on financial worries. Indeed, while the inspectorate in Wales (mainly Anglican) called for domestic deficiencies in female education, notably in terms of hygiene and budgeting, to be corrected by the teaching of domestic economy, poverty ensured that in most board schools it took the form of simple sewing.[144] Moreover, financial constraints also often meant that board schools were mixed rather than single sex, which was still considered to be injurious to morality, especially of girls, echoing both the damning indictment of Welsh women in the Blue Books of 1847 and the anguished Welsh response.[145] Additionally, while the emphasis on domestic subjects across the girls' curriculum intensified after 1870, there were continuing criticisms of the basic one of sewing. Thus, one male inspector for the south of Scotland complained in the mid-1880s that few girls left school with the ability to cut out the simplest garment.[146] There were exceptions, such as Maria Hull's experience of schooling in South Derbyshire. She recalled that she learned to make calico underwear when she was nine years old and also knitted vests and petticoats. In the early 1890s she progressed to 'scientific' needlework when she went to the Girls' Department of the local board school: 'we cut out paper patterns of undergarments—drawers, chemise and nightgowns—to our individual measurements.' Maria kept these patterns for a long time as she found them useful. She also recalled being taught to patch both calico and flannel, how to make buttonholes and a gusset and that she made a 'maroon-coloured flannel petticoat, feather-stitched in golden silk on the hem' while she knitted woolen gloves as well as stockings 'with either "Dutch" or "French" heels'.[147] Generally, however, many teachers in mixed-sex schools, notably in Scotland but also in England, regarded sewing, or at least so much of it, as a brake on girls' progress, keeping them behind boys in reading and arithmetic.

Only a minority of female school board members who were mainly responsible for the girls' industrial instruction tried to limit the time girls were required to spend on domestic subjects and, even more unusually, to propose that boys could also benefit from such subjects, though in some areas boys as well as girls were taught knitting, again depending on the local economy.[148] Jane Martin found that Ruth Homan and Emma Maitland got agreement on a pilot scheme in one school in Poplar for boys to attend the cookery centre for instruction in 'naval fare'. [149] Similarly Grace Paterson, who served on the Glasgow School board and championed domestic subjects for girls, acknowledged that some men at least had more than a passive interest in nutrition. As Honorary Secretary of the Glasgow School of Cookery, she reported to the Directors in February 1892 on 'the arrangements made with the Glasgow Shipowners' Committee for lessons in cookery of the articles of food usually provided for seamen'.[150]

Jane Martin also found that some female members of the London School board objected to the amount of time girls were expected to spend on domestic subjects at the expense of the other parts of the curriculum.[151] As discussed in Chapter 1, they were not unique. Flora Stevenson, who served on the Edinburgh School Board from 1873 until her death in 1905, expressed the opinion that board schools were 'not intended to do more for girls [than for boys] in preparing them for any special trade or profession' and that poor boys would benefit from being taught domestic subjects. Like the London ladies, she was concerned that the increasing emphasis on such subjects in the female curriculum was at the expense of girls' academic education. She pointed out that female pupils already spent up to five hours a week on sewing; if cookery was added, they would have little time left for academic work, let alone the basics of literacy and numeracy.[152] Mary Burton, also of the Edinburgh Board, went further, arguing for 'the desirability of having boys taught to work a sewing machine, and the girls to hammer nails'.[153] Nor was such a view limited to the larger boards.[154]

Still, such views were not held by the majority of school board women, most of whom fretted that working-class girls did not receive an adequate domestic education at home. They held that the aim of a domestic curriculum in school was primarily to preparing future wives of working men. This reflected a belief that gender roles as well as housewifery skills were not 'natural' or instinctive and had to be learned, but that the working-class mother was either not skilled enough or had lost the skills because of the need for her to contribute to the family income. In Scotland, with the exception of knitting and sewing in areas where socks and sacks were produced by children (boys as well as girls in the case of the latter), domestic economy was not intended to prepare girls for paid employment.[155] However, some local studies in England have found that it helped prepare them for particular labour markets. For example, girls in Norwich schools spent a lot of time on sewing and found jobs available in clothes and shoe making as well as in food and drink factories, though typically they were employed in the latter not in producing but in packing.[156] In Ireland where, as noted above, employment opportunities for women were shrinking in the second half of the nineteenth century, and in Wales where the structure of the economy meant a very restricted range of jobs open to women, elementary education nevertheless opened up opportunities for girls in the same areas as were expanding for female labour throughout the UK: teaching, the service sector and white collar occupations. The female religious orders continued to include a range of industrial subjects in their curriculum, with considerable success in some cases: in 1890, the Lady Inspector with the national board commended the industrial department of the Presentation Sisters' school at Tralee:

> The Sister who acts as industrial teacher is highly gifted as a designer, especially for the Limerick 'run' lace, of which she also thoroughly understands the working. She has received no fewer than nine medals from the South Kensington Schools for excellence in lace design.

One result of such teaching was the revival of this traditional skill, but generally the trades taught in industrial departments of national schools and in industrial schools reveal how restricted the labour market was for working-class women in Ireland.[157]

There was always domestic service, of course. Despite the lack of industry outside of the north of Ireland, there had been a process of urbanization so that there was a constant demand for servants. In 1891, 255,000 females in Ireland earned their living as domestic servants.[158] Yet proportionately even domestic service was in decline in Ireland by the end of the Victorian period. Hence, since females greatly outnumbered males in the workhouse, the Commissioners of National Education suggested that an organised system of assisted emigration to the colonies as domestic servants would relieve the Poor Law Guardians and ratepayers of a considerable financial burden. The scheme was open to both boys and girls, but the latter consistently outnumbered the former.[159] Girls who attended the national schools saw education as a means to make them attractive emigrant workers as well as to enable them to maintain communication with family left behind: thus, girls' attendance rates at national schools were higher than boys even before it became compulsory in 1892, while girls also attained better results. David Fitzpatrick has recorded that by the beginning of the Edwardian period, female migrants (mostly single and in their early 20s) outnumbered males by a sixth.[160]

Throughout the British Isles in the later Victorian period, there were eugenicist arguments about the need to improve the health and fitness of the imperial nation, the key to which was the mother. In Ireland, this was reinforced by a concern over the high rate of emigration among the youngest and fittest of the population compared to the rest of the UK. Indeed, this was believed to be a major factor in the persistent economic stagnation and widespread impoverishment among the labouring class. Generally, eugenicist concerns as well as campaigns for improved sanitation and public health put increasing demands on the poor housewife: her children, especially her daughters, were staying on longer at school and family size was declining but not so noticeably among the working class. Further, the Irish or Welsh wife's chances of employment inside or outside the home were very restricted. She was, therefore, more confined to the domestic sphere at a time when she was most harshly criticized for her perceived lack of domestic skills. Hence, in Ireland and Wales especially the emphasis on domestic skills in school was to make up for the mother's perceived inadequacy and to ensure that the next generation would raise the living standards of their families. In both countries, an elementary education in English was the key to opportunities in employment and emigration for daughters as well as sons.[161]

Due to Scotland's different educational tradition, the Board of Education (1873–1878) recorded concerns that the 'university' subjects, notably Latin and Greek, were in decline both in terms of the teachers who could offer them and the pupils who were taking them, which led to a fear that 'under the Educational Code the ancient high character of the public schools in Scotland cannot possibly be maintained'.[162] This tradition, of course, was male centred, while the Board was pleased that 'the important and valuable subject of "Domestic Economy" has now for the first time taken root in the public schools of Scotland'.[163] Besides being taught only to girls, as noted in Chapter 1, it was the sole higher or 'specific' subject which was made compulsory for every girl who wanted to be presented in any other specific subject. Still, by the 1880s, specific subjects were valued as a means of providing some level of secondary education which, it was lamented, was not yet available 'for every boy and girl of promise throughout Scotland'.[164]

Whereas secondary education developed informally through the elementary schools by means of higher-grade departments and schools and pupil-teacher centres in the larger towns of England and Scotland, Wales was the first part of Britain to secure legislation which allowed it to be formally established through the Intermediate Education Act of 1889.[165] It was in Ireland, however, that state support for secondary education was first introduced by the Intermediate Education Act of 1878. Initially, girls had not been included, but Isabella Tod (1836–1896), founder of the Ladies' Institute in Belfast, and Margaret Byers (1832–1912), principal of Victoria College in the same city, campaigned successfully that girls be offered the same opportunities as boys to sit the public examinations. As will be shown in the next chapter, this affected mainly middle-class girls, which was similar to the intermediate schools established in Wales after 1889. According to Gareth Elwyn Jones, these schools were 'an amalgam of the grammar and higher grade models, deemed especially suitable for a predominantly working class society, but with a growing middle class element'.[166] Deborah James, however, has found that the school in Pontypridd attracted and indeed encouraged working-class girls to apply for scholarships supplied by a local charity.[167] Gordon Roderick also charts an increase in working-class girls and boys entering intermediate schools in the early twentieth century, but again he points to the limited expectations girls had of paid employment in Wales: the majority still went into teaching and shop work, whereas boys who sought to avoid mining took up the increasing opportunities in clerical work which in other parts of Britain were attracting women.[168]

What was particularly important about the Welsh intermediate schools was that they would not be under the Church of England, and whatever the limited labour market for girls, they provided them with educational opportunities. Indeed, by 1900 there were 3,513 girls and 3,877 boys in the Intermediate Schools of Wales.[169] While the intermediate schools seem to have represented progress for girls in particular since their curriculum, like that in the boys' schools, privileged academic over technical subjects, domestic subjects in the girls' curriculum were not thereby rendered peripheral. Indeed, in South Pembrokeshire, domestic economy, cookery, needlework and laundry work were prominent among the subjects offered to girls. Moreover, the Pembroke Dock Intermediate School which opened in January 1895 offered four scholarships to girls but six to boys from the borough and the same for children from rural districts, which helps explain that its first enrolment was 35 girls and 50 boys.[170]

This Act is generally seen as improving and extending educational provision in Wales: it established a statutory system of (fee-paying) secondary education which in turn established links with both elementary schools and university colleges, an aspect the Scots were keen to emulate, establishing secondary education committees to receive and distribute grants to the counties and boroughs in 1892.[171] Yet the Welsh Act is also recognised as having an Anglicizing effect. One aim of intermediate schools was to enable their pupils to compete on English terms: notions of Welsh identity were not included in the curriculum but were left to the home, the chapel and the Sunday school, though as in board schools, the fact that teaching was in English did not preclude the teachers themselves, who tended to come from within the community, being proficient in the Welsh language.[172] It was also to inculcate middle-class values and for the girls a culture of femininity. Intermediate schools certainly opened up more opportunities for women as teachers but this also reflected the paucity in the choice of professional work open to women in Wales in the late nineteenth century.[173]

At the end of the Victorian period as at the beginning, there was still a fear in England that the poor were in danger of being over-educated. Hence there was resistance to the establishment of secondary education paid for by the state. The children of the poor were expected to follow their parents into similar employment, which mostly did not require much training in the way of skills except on the job. Advocates of technical and scientific education thus had to emphasise the values over the skills this would impart, particularly in the education of children to think methodically.[174] Yet secondary education had developed. Thus a commission was set up in 1894 to consider establishing a secondary system, and since its chairman James Bryce was a supporter of female education, it was included in its remit. The Bryce Commission noted that the bigger boards throughout Britain had established 'ex-standard' classes and 'higher' departments in elementary schools as well as 'higher grade' elementary schools going beyond the limits which had been fixed by the parliamentary grant. The Elementary Education Act of 1870 had not envisaged either secondary schooling for the poor or a system of education which would allow progression from primary to secondary and university. Scotland's educational tradition had rested on a link between the parish school and the university for the clever but poor boy, but its board schools were also subject to the grant system which was not intended to support secondary level education. The commission accepted that there was apparently less demand among working-class girls for secondary education: more of their brothers attended and completed higher grade schools, reflecting the facts that there were still fewer well-paid jobs open to girls with a secondary education than boys and that older girls were still needed at home to help with domestic chores. Bryce reported that of the grants made to secondary schools by local authorities under the Technical Instruction Act (1889) by far the largest share went to boys. Indeed in some cases, girls were excluded, and when there was open competition, between two-thirds and three quarters were awarded to boys.[175] Whereas he noted with approval developments such as the Intermediate Education (Wales) Act of 1889, the proprietary schools established by the Girls' Public Day Schools Company (1872) and the University Extension Movement, he recognised that these affected the middle class and accepted that 'girls of the industrial classes will need to be trained for domestic duties'.[176]

Bryce also recorded that there was now less opposition to mixed-sex schooling which he considered was 'better than either feeble separate departments or a neglect of girls', especially in rural districts where it was difficult to provide separate secondary schools for boys and girls.[177] There was, however, lingering concern in England that mixed-sex schooling would upset the gendered curriculum, to the detriment of girls' domestic education. Thus, Mrs Kitchener, a former school board member, reported to the Bryce Commission on Manchester, Liverpool and Rochdale that the disadvantages of mixed-sex schooling in the higher standards of elementary schooling were

> attributable to the undue preponderance of scientific subjects forced on them, through their depending for their very existence on large grants from the Science and Art Department. . . . Chemistry, applied mathematics, mechanical and geometrical drawing have their definite value

in a good many trades . . . for boys; but for girls, they lead to nothing but a blind alley.[178]

Moreover, there was still resistance among middle-class parents to sending their daughters to elementary schools. As Mrs Ella Armitage reported to the Bryce Commission in the mid-1890s, those who considered themselves 'upper-class' baulked at the mix of social classes: 'girls should be kept from any contamination with people who drop their Hs or earn their salt.'[179]

CONCLUSION

As this discussion has shown, however elementary the curriculum was for both sexes in the Victorian period, gender is fundamental in any consideration of the schooling of the working class throughout the UK. Richard Aldrich pointed out that the Newcastle Commission had revealed that across England and Wales girls attended public weekday schools in substantial numbers, while returns from the Catholic, Sunday and ragged schools indicated a preponderance of girls. He concluded that the sons and daughters of the poor attended school in broadly similar numbers and received a broadly similar education, while at the lowest end of the school spectrum, girls outnumbered boys.[180] Yet as Aldrich has also acknowledged and as previous studies have shown, it is difficult to generalize because local variations were so great.[181] Indeed, there was significant variety of educational experience not just between rural and urban regions but within both of these. This overview confirms the importance of local factors, both between and within the constituent parts of the UK. These were most notable in the economy and in the relationship of each constituent part to the state, reflected in the resistance to the efforts of Westminster to impose secular education and the resentment of Anglicization. Religion was a factor in all parts of the Union, but one which needs to be situated within the context of established versus 'minority' churches, notably when the former was not numerically dominant, as in Wales and Ireland. Divisions within the established church, especially in Scotland, and tensions within Nonconformity, notably in Wales, also had a bearing on concerns over control of education. The economy was localized throughout the UK, making different demands on, and offering different opportunities for, child labour, and even though girls and boys worked at the same jobs, as in agriculture, it was more common to have a gendered division in the employment of children. As the century progressed that was an increasing trend, which, in turn, was reflected in the curriculum as well as attendance.

The various commissions into the schooling of the poor often contained explicit statements that the aim was social control, but there was also recognition of the significance to the economy of child labour, especially that of boys. Girls, who had fewer options for employment and who were generally paid less than boys, were destined to be wives and mothers and so were crucial to ensuring social stability: hence the attention paid to their education in domesticity, both in terms of the ideology and the skills. Yet all the reports reveal not only concern about the quality of teaching domestic subjects but also alarm that in too many schools they were not taught at all. There were also, as noted above, similar criticisms of the standard of teaching in charitable sewing schools. Sewing, it was held, could be both easily and cheaply provided and might also bring in funds to the school, but in practice most attention was paid to it and other domestic subjects in the schools for paupers and delinquent children where, as noted in Chapter 1, an even narrower curriculum was followed.[182] Yet even in workhouse schools where girls were taught with a specific view to their entry into the domestic sector, there were problems. As Mary Carpenter complained of the education of pauper girls in 1862, if the institution was large:

> the managers usually endeavor to economize labour by the introduction of washing machines, wringing machines, drying closets and other contrivances, which are most valuable if the object is to save labour, but most injurious if the object is to train the girl. She must leave such a laundry not only utterly incapable of going through the necessary processes in an ordinary house, but what is worse, with her mind quite unprepared to use its faculties in actual life. The dormitory work does not teach girls how to perform the housemaid's ordinary duties, and the cooking is necessarily on so large a scale, and so managed, that few comparatively out of only one hundred girls can learn it at all, and even these may be quite unacquainted with the way to boil a potato, or make a common family pudding.[183]

A similar concern was expressed that larger industrial schools in Ireland in the later Victorian period did not provide a satisfactory training in domestic service which would fit the girls for work in a family home.[184] In smaller workhouse schools, as in ordinary day and dame schools, an education in domestic skills was on a more appropriate scale, but the reports all expressed concern that it was of poor quality. It was felt particularly in England, Wales and Ireland that a domestic education for girls was essential but that it could not be adequately imparted in either the home or independent working-class establishments; and whereas the Scottish educational tradition favoured the academic over the vocational in the curriculum of the parish school, there was the influence of government policy which tied grants to sewing from 1862, as well as of the English ideas on the centrality of domesticity to a poor girl's schooling.

When it was realized that philanthropic efforts alone, whether by church, society or individuals, could not ensure the moral order through offering a sound domestic training for girls, the state had intervened. Notwithstanding the variations and taking into account the different emphases, the reports into popular education in the Victorian period reveal that what was common to the schooling of working-class girls throughout the UK was both concern that the daughters of the poor were peculiarly vulnerable to the lure of immorality presented by the new economic conditions, as well as hope that they were also potentially the moral linchpin of their families.

3   The Education of Young Ladies

Even before the Victorian period, British society assumed that boys and girls would be brought up differently, and parents accepted they had a key role to play in ensuring their children were trained for adulthood, or rather for manhood and womanhood.[1] Upper-class boys were prepared for their adult life of work (for the state or for the church) and public life in 'public' schools and universities.[2] To become a man, they had to shake off feminine influences, including that of their mother and sisters, usually by being sent to boarding school from an early age. Boys were not to be 'soft' but to learn the virtues of endurance, perseverance, self-reliance and emotional continence, encapsulated in the phrase 'the stiff upper lip'. These boys were taught manliness, for example, through sports and by hunting.[3] In particular, boys were to learn to keep their emotions in check and generally exercise restraint, leaving the finer feelings and sensibilities—or rather, the display of such—to their sisters.[4]

Whereas formal education was to prepare boys for an adulthood of family breadwinner, their female counterparts were not considered in need of such an education as their future was in the home. They should receive an education which would instil in them the domestic ideal and train them in the social graces to make them attractive marital prospects and companionable wives.[5] However, since the late eighteenth century such an education had been criticized by both radicals and conservatives as frivolous, incapable of preparing them either for marriage and motherhood or for the one respectable post open to them, that of governess. Maria Edgeworth (1768–1849) and her father Richard Lovell Edgeworth (1744–1817) asked what was the point of such an education, outlining the common assumptions that it was for the young lady to win admiration and entry to fashionable society, to increase her chance of a 'prize' in the matrimonial lottery, to fend off ennui through innocent and amusing occupation. Apart from the dangers of turning the recipients of such an education into vain and flighty creatures, they wondered if, once married, a lady had the leisure to continue with her accomplishments.[6] Middle-class parents, however, continued to have their daughters schooled in the social graces. Echoing the Edgeworth critique in 1865, Dorothea Beale declared

I think that the education of girls has too often been made showy, rather than real and useful—that accomplishments have been made the main thing, because these would, it was thought, enable a girl to shine and attract, while those branches of study especially calculated to form the judgement, to cultivate the understanding, and to discipline the character (which would fit her to perform the *duties* of life), have been neglected; and thus, while temporary pleasure and profit have been sought, the great moral ends of education have too often been lost sight of.[7]

This did not mean there was no place for the accomplishments in a young lady's education. At Cheltenham Ladies College, founded in 1854, where girls were taught English language and literature, modern languages (French and German), natural science, astronomy and physical geography, there were options of music, singing and dancing. Reforming headmistresses like Beale valued the intellectual and moral lessons which could be imparted from teaching accomplishments such as music.[8] They ensured, however, that accomplishments were taught in a more professional way.[9] Indeed, from the middle of the century, women could attend publicly funded music and art schools and earn a respectable living as performers and teachers, though generally on lower salaries than those offered to their male counterparts.[10] Boys at the public schools could also take music and drawing as 'extras', but the term 'accomplishments' had a rather derogatory connotation, implying superficiality.[11] Thus Samuel Whyte, a Dublin schoolmaster whose 'English' Academy was co-educational, wrote scathingly in 1772:

The present style of educating daughters is altogether *mechanical*, and either from misconduct, or utter neglect in early days, rendered ten times more imperfect, troublesome and expensive than it might be. Without idea, without sentiment, just at the moment they are introduced into the circle of dissipation all at once, the *French* master, the music master, the drawing master, the dancing master, the writing master, etc. etc. are poured in upon them. The accumulated expense appears a serious object; the first rudiments of everything are unpleasant; their amusements possess their minds; they are hurried from master to master, comprehend little, retain less, and are disgusted with all, so contract whimsical, desultory habits, and can settle to nothing as they ought.[12]

Whereas Christine de Bellaigue has pointed out that even before the educational reforms of the mid-nineteenth century, the accomplishments might be taught both systematically and seriously, nevertheless critics of middle-class girls' schooling focused on what they judged to be the lack of depth and rigour in subjects intended to add polish and refinement to a lady's education.[13] That they remained in the curriculum of reformed schools was a sign that even if parents sent their daughter to such an institution, they still expected her to learn the social graces. Reformers like Beale often charged parents with neglect of their daughters' education, but as Marjorie Theobald has argued, a key issue which they faced was how to reconcile female learning with propriety.[14]

THE PROPER EDUCATION FOR A LADY

If the emphasis in a young lady's education was to be shifted from the accomplishments, it was not clear what it should consist of, except that the purpose of her education would remain different from that of her brother whose own schooling was under scrutiny by the early nineteenth century. Thus, calls for reform of middle-class girls' education were echoed by the declining reputation of England's public schools for boys, and in 1861 a Royal Commission (Clarendon) was set up to investigate the nine leading public schools in England.[15] Rugby had already had its reputation restored by Thomas Arnold (1795–1842) who became headmaster in 1828. He reinvigorated it by setting high standards for behaviour from the boys and of teaching from the masters, raising the status and salaries of house masters and assistant masters, developing the position of prefect, with older boys responsible for the behaviour of the younger ones, introducing regular examinations and pupil reports for parents.[16] In terms of what was taught, however, Arnold did not implement curriculum reform: the classics remained central as he believed that Greek and Latin formed the youthful male mind. He also insisted on the relevance of the study of history for understanding contemporary affairs. But whereas he established modern languages and mathematics on a surer footing, Arnold did not pay the same attention to science, which although taught in public schools was not seen as essential to a gentleman's upbringing. The aim of the public school was to build a boy's character and make him a gentleman, not prepare him for work.

While Ruth Watts has shown that there was a place for science in middle-class girls' education, she accepts that the Victorian royal commissions into education of the middle classes exhibited little commitment to promoting science and that discussion around the place of science in secondary schools and universities focused on male education. She also pointed to the gendered reasoning given for including science in the female curriculum: thus the phrenologist George Combe emphasised the need for a scientific education for girls and women precisely because of their domestic and familial role.[17] Combe considered that health was of crucial importance to the mother and so girls should be taught about the workings of the body and the mind: hence he recommended they be taught anatomy, physiology, phrenology and mental philosophy and that they should take physical exercise in the fresh air.[18] Watts has found that by the mid-nineteenth century some private schools for girls, notably those run by Unitarians and Quakers, taught science well.[19] However, growing elitism and professionalism were tending to exclude women from science, while the continuing preference in boys' public schools for an education in the classics also affected them: in arguing for equality in the education of middle-class girls reformers emulated the curriculum of boys' schools.

Arnold, moreover, aimed to have Rugby produce Christian gentlemen. Loyalty, devotion and sacrifice were key elements of the public school ethos; these virtues could also be expected of gentlewomen, though they may have been expressed in terms of forbearance, fidelity, purity and self-denial.[20] Arnold wanted thoughtful and dutiful boys; his focus was on character rather than intellect. That was reflected in the popular novel, *Tom Brown's Schooldays* (1857), written by a former pupil, Thomas Hughes (1822–1896). This novel promoted the idea that competitive games were essential to the public school spirit, suggesting that team sport was important for inculcating the notion of the common good, not just of team or school, but of nation and empire.[21] Arnold became known as the founder of the modern public-school system with sports at the heart of it, though he had in practice not advocated this while Hughes himself later criticized what he thought had become a 'cult' of sport or games' mania, focusing on 'muscular Christianity' rather than the 'Christian manliness' which Arnold had hoped to develop in his pupils and which Hughes wrote about in *The Manliness of Christ* (1879).[22]

The public schools were mainly for the upper classes and those wealthy businessmen who wanted their sons to rise in the social scale. Most middle-class boys were educated in grammar or private schools. The former had often been established to teach poor boys but in the Victorian period had raised their status and usually required fees, putting them out of their reach.[23] A minority of grammar schools came to rival the public schools, emulating their focus on the classics. Lower middle-class parents preferred a curriculum which would prepare their sons for jobs in the professions and commerce, clerical work and bookkeeping. Most grammar school boys remained at school for only a few years, leaving around 16 years of age; few went to university, though some benefited from university extension classes from the early 1870s.[24] As Christina Bremner observed in 1897 of the University Extension Movement, 'there is a tendency for the women to be sisters of university men, and for the men to belong to a non-university class'.[25] The introduction of examinations for entry to the civil service in the mid-1860s opened up the opportunity of a relatively secure and respectable job for the clever lower middle-class boy.

A number of these themes can be detected in the developments championed by those who campaigned for reform of middle-class girls' education in England. Key figures included Frances Buss (1827–1894), Emily Davies (1830–1921) and Dorothea Beale (1831–1906).[26] Buss had had to earn a living as a teacher from the age of 14 which convinced her of the need for a serious education to prepare middle-class women like herself for employment. She had been among the first to attend the evening classes at Queen's College (1848–1849) which had been established to raise the educational standards of girls expected to become governesses. In 1850 she set up the North London Collegiate School for Ladies. Her aim was to prepare girls for Queen's College and for jobs as governesses. She also advocated that girls sit external competitive examinations, just as boys did, and was successful in 1863 in persuading the Cambridge local examination syndicate to open its exams to girls. Two years later, the universities of Durham and Edinburgh followed suit, while London, an examining and accrediting rather than a teaching body, opened its degrees to women in 1868.

Though Dorothea Beale came from a wealthier background and had a good private education, she too was one of the first to attend Queen's College; within a year she was teaching mathematics there, while continuing her own studies of Latin and Greek. In 1858 Beale became principal of Cheltenham Ladies' College, but in contrast to Buss, she was wary of girls sitting the same examinations as boys. For her part, Emily Davies set her sights from the start on gaining entry for women to the universities. Whatever their differences, these reformers opposed domestic training in the education of middle-class girls: that was for servants. What they wanted was parity of education with boys of similar social standing. All three were acutely aware that middle-class women needed an education which would equip them for respectable employment. Not only had census returns revealed that women outnumbered men in the population, but the later Victorian period saw an increasing trend for middle-class men to delay marriage while building their careers.[27]

ROYAL COMMISSIONS AND CRITICISMS OF MIDDLE-CLASS GIRLS' EDUCATION

In the same decade as the Clarendon Commission, the education of young ladies came under parliamentary scrutiny. In 1864 the Taunton Commission was established to enquire into the condition of middle-class, or 'secondary' schools. Although originally the focus was boys, feminists and educational reformers lobbied successfully to have girls' schools included. The report noted the limitations of what it could state on female education:

> Girls are more often educated at home, or in schools too small to be entitled to the name, and both the number and value of the endowments which are at present appropriated to their education bear an extremely small proportion to those appropriated to boys. Moreover, the privacy of girls' schools occasions greater difficulty in obtaining satisfactory information than is found in the case of boys.[28]

Hence, the importance of the ladies who gave evidence and expressed opinions on, and impressions of, the state of middle-class girls' education. All agreed that it was a 'grave' subject, since an educated mother was of even more importance to the family than an educated father. The commission also recognised that there were many unmarried middle-class women who had to support themselves.[29] Its reports are a key source for studies of middle-class girls' education in England and Wales at a time when campaigns to improve it had made some headway, at least in the south of England, and where some individuals were already arguing for both parity with boys and access to university. The general points made here have been made before; what is less often noted are the reports on and the comparisons drawn between the education of young ladies in other parts of Britain, notably Scotland.

The commission acknowledged the prejudice that girls were less capable and had less need of a serious education than their brothers, noting that girls' schools were often spoken of as intended to be a substitute home with the mistress concentrating on moral rather than intellectual training.

> One of the advantages of a large boarding school for boys is supposed to be the formation of a strong hardy character, and both a large school and a boarding school may be thought unfavourable to the formation of the gentle and feminine character which it is desired to form in girls.[30]

Indeed, some lady teachers in private schools feared that 'too much' serious study would render their pupils 'masculine' and unattractive as wives.[31] Of course, in many cases the mistresses themselves lacked a serious education, while they responded to what parents, especially of the lower middle class, demanded: a sufficient education in the accomplishments as would make their daughters appear to advantage in 'society'.[32] Often, girls had been taught at home until about 14 years of age, then sent to a private boarding school to be 'finished'. Upper- and middle-class girls from both Wales and Scotland were sent to such schools in England in order to lose their provincial accents and 'habits'.[33] This was also the case in Northumberland where, as in Scotland, significant numbers of middle-class girls were taught by masters in mixed-sex schools. Hence, the upper middle class tended to send their daughters out of the county; even at the end of the century, the professional classes in Bury sent their daughters out of the county 'in order that they may both "make nice friends", and get rid of their provincial accent'.[34] In Ireland, too, particularly if based outside Ulster and therefore in a minority within the local population, wealthy Protestant parents sent their children to English boarding schools to be educated as they were unwilling to have them schooled with the mass of Catholic peasant children.[35] Some sought a more liberal curriculum for their daughters: for example, one girl had been sent to the Quaker school in York in 1835 which taught both classics and science.[36]

For their part the growing Catholic middle-class in Ireland looked to the boarding schools run by mainly French religious orders. Anne O'Connor sees the French influence as different from the English reformers, but religious orders had similar ideas to the general education of ladies across Britain, offering similar subjects to boarding schools in England, including the accomplishments, but not teaching Latin or mathematics. They too believed that the secondary education of girls should be distinct from that of boys because of their different prospects in adulthood. Perhaps the main distinction was in the very religious atmosphere and the even stricter separation of the girls both from the lower classes who attended the day schools and from their own families.[37]

There were similarities with the Catholic girls' schools established in England. Although the biggest Catholic effort was expended on elementary schools, there were private day and boarding schools which remained outside the government grant system and so are difficult to quantify. Barbara Walsh has found that most religious congregations responded to the growth of a Catholic middle class and in the latter half of the nineteenth century established day, boarding schools and high schools which educated girls for the university examinations. Some of these targeted the young ladies of the upper middle class, emphasising their 'broad curricula and modern facilities': Walsh quotes from one prospectus which called attention to a 'Demonstration Kitchen and completely fitted chemical Laboratory' as well as a large gymnasium and well-heated swimming bath. Such schools were set in extensive grounds and offered the same types of sports and games as the non-denominational high schools for girls did, including lawn tennis, croquet, hockey, horse riding, and Swedish drill.[38]

This prospectus and related advertisements were from the early twentieth century (1909 and 1920) which suggests that curricular developments in such exclusive Catholic high schools may have lagged behind the non-denominational ones, though Susan O'Brien gives an example of the St Leonards-on-Sea boarding school which dated from the 1850s and was considered by an HMI to offer an outstanding education.[39] They may also have been competing for non-Catholic girls: O'Brien has drawn attention to the increasing number of middle-class Anglican families who sent their daughters to convent schools and suggested that by the late nineteenth century the trend may have been growing.[40] Anglican clergymen had run schools for middle-class girls, usually daughters of the less well-off professionals, including the clergy themselves, since at least the previous century but notably from the 1820s; and Anglican sisterhoods established schools for young ladies from the 1850s.[41]

Catholic provision for middle-class girls in England tended to be situated in the wealthier south-east, especially around London. In contrast the numbers of convents grew very slowly in Wales, yet while these also concentrated on the Irish immigrant poor, schools for middle-class girls were being established from the early 1870s.[42] This was similar to the situation in west and central Scotland where poor Irish Catholics were concentrated; in the east, the French order Ursulines of Jesus catered for the daughters of the elite.[43] As elsewhere in the UK, religious orders founded boarding schools both to cater for the growing Catholic middle class and to subsidize the work they did for the poor.

Wherever young ladies were educated, the Taunton Commission registered a generally unfavourable view of their schooling: it was said to lack thoroughness and be unsystematic; too little attention was paid to the basics, too much to the accomplishments and all were poorly taught.[44] While there were similar complaints about the organisation and standard of teaching in boys' schools, the judgment was that the girls' schools were inferior. As the report on the extra-metropolitan parts of Surrey and Sussex complained, 'young ladies are made to devote themselves to what are at most the graces of life, and merely nibble at the bone and sinew of sound instruction in the moments which can be spared from the piano and the easel'; or as another witness testified, 'the education given at girls' schools is partly answerable for the vapid characters and frivolous pursuits of idle women, who have nothing particular to do'.[45]

Yet there was little difference in the cost of girls' compared to boys' education. Although girls attended school for considerably briefer periods (often only up to two years), there were additional costs incurred by the range of accomplishments, some of which might be taught by more expensive visiting masters. Whereas two-thirds of the cost of a middle-class girl's education could be spent on these 'extras', there was general agreement that not one teacher was well, or even adequately, paid.[46] Emily Davies also argued that the very smallness of so many girls' schools made them relatively more expensive, even as she acknowledged that the schoolmistresses were on very low salaries. A study of Birkdale, a suburb of Southport, confirms this. Most of the private schools for both sexes, but especially for girls, were small, with the emphasis in the curriculum of the female schools on the social graces. Indeed, 'their livelihoods depended on their demonstration of linguistic and artistic accomplishments', while their economic prospects were 'gloomy': 'even successful principals of small schools could not expect to make a profit of more than, say, £300.' They were at the mercy of parents who could withdraw their daughters at any time and who made demands of the school not only in terms of the curriculum but also of whom the headmistress accepted as pupils.[47]

In many cases, both the pupils and their mistresses in private schools were deemed ignorant. The preference of the lady witnesses was for single-sex education and female teachers in girls' schools, but campaigners, including Davies and Buss, were in favour of girls being offered the same academic education as boys so that they could sit the same public examinations. Davies called for a 'fixed standard which has a recognised value' and in her view girls 'would rather be tried by that than by a new standard invented especially to accommodate some supposed peculiarities of their own'.[48] Not all the ladies agreed. Mary Porter, who had set up and run a private school for training governesses near Tiverton, considered that 'the generality of girls could not go so far in mathematics and classics as boys' because, while girls were 'quick' at learning, they were not 'capable of applying themselves for such spaces of time'.[49]

The commission acknowledged that parents generally preferred a liberal, humanist schooling for their sons to a vocational one, and those who advocated reforms in female education sought to emulate that. There was to be no schooling in domestic subjects. Indeed, there was criticism of the poor teaching of 'ornamental sewing' which it was considered could be learned more effectively and appropriately at home. Again there was some difference of emphasis, perhaps due to which section of the middle class was being educated. Whereas Frances Buss thought it desirable that every girl should know how to sew, Emily Davies declared that the importance of instruction in needlework for a young lady was decreasing, due to the use of sewing machines and the preference for ready-made clothes.[50] Moreover, Miss E.E. Smith of Bedford College's managing council observed that while young ladies should 'be at all times helpful and handy, I should deprecate making needlework and housekeeping the subjects of special instruction during the brief school years'.[51] Like other domestic skills, sewing was seen as the work of servants and seamstresses. Indeed, it was believed that if, for example, cooking was taught, it would bring the pupils into too close contact with the servants.[52]

Taunton compared the state of secondary schooling in England with other European countries (France, Germany, Switzerland and Italy). Within Britain, the most detailed comparison was with Scotland. There was some disagreement, particularly over co-education. The commission noted that in the 'Scotch system', burgh schools or academies offered secondary education to the middle classes of both sexes, though in practice fewer girls attended than boys. This was confirmed by the Argyll Commission into the state of education in Scotland which was appointed in 1864. Its remit was more comprehensive than the various English commissions (Newcastle into elementary schools, 1858–1861, Clarendon into the public schools, 1861–1864, and Taunton) since it covered all types and stages of education up to teacher training, except for the universities and private, or adventure, schools for girls.[53] In smaller towns the sexes tended to be taught together in academies, though often with considerably fewer girls. Thus, at Elgin Academy there were 40 scholars on the roll in the classical department, only four of whom were female; 80 boys but 16 girls taking mathematics; 100 boys but 21 girls taking English; and 12 boys but four girls taking modern languages. At the other end of the country in Kirkcudbright, there were 31 boys and 11 girls learning Latin and eight boys and one girl taking Greek. Only in a minority of small town academies, as in Stirling and Inverness, were the sexes separated.[54] The highest praise went to Inverness Academy:

This system seemed to us to meet what was wanted in a burgh school much more completely than any system arrived at in any other school. The total separation of the sexes is most desirable, and it is not effected by teaching the boys one hour and the girls another hour in the same classroom. At Inverness they never meet. The girls have their own class-rooms, under the supervision of a lady superintendent; but they have the advantage of being taught by qualified masters and in the same system as the boys. This feature is well worthy of notice. The tone both in the boys' and girls' school struck us as being decidedly higher than what it is in many, indeed in most, of the schools we visited.[55]

This implied that it was advisable for questions of morals and refinement that the sexes be kept apart at least over the age of 12 but that they should both have access to the best masters and a similar curriculum. Inverness Academy again was unusual in that the girls were not offered Latin but were taught needlework.

Assistant Commissioners Harvie and Sellar were keen to underscore the higher standing of education in Scotland compared to England, claiming that the Scots were more disposed than the English to take up whatever educational opportunities were on offer, as well as to preserve what they termed 'our scheme of national education' with its links between the parish and burgh schools and the universities.[56] The Taunton Commission like-wise felt that the burgh schools contributed to 'that general diffusion of intelligence for which Scotland is remarkable'.[57] Assistant Commissioner Fearon visited Scottish burgh schools for Taunton, noting that rather than follow a standard curriculum students paid by subject. He accepted that there was a more 'popular' basis to burgh schools than to middle-class schools in England but put that down to Scotland's poverty; he also agreed that the universities likewise had an 'intensely national and popular char-acter', supplying the schools with a higher standard of teacher than was the case in England. But precisely because of this 'democratic' aspect, Fearon considered that both burgh schools and Scotland's universities were less suitable to the 'wants' of a wealthy and refined class which preferred the more socially exclusive nature of education in England.[58] This notion of exclusivity was influential in Scotland: Harvie and Sellar emphasised the 'democratic' or 'national' nature of schooling for younger children, but they noted that 'if society be divided into three classes' by wealth and social position, 'the minds and the tastes of those classes should be distinguished equally'. Whereas the education of the working class would normally be finished by 12 or 13 years of age and the children of the middle class should be expected to have reached the same level of intelligence by that stage, the latter should have three or four years further schooling to equip them with the degree of 'cultivation' appropriate to their status.[59]

Taunton noted that many burgh schools admitted girls, only a few taught them separately from the boys, but others (such as Hamilton Academy) were co-educational only until a certain age, usually around 12. That some high schools in the most important cities (Glasgow, Edinburgh and Aberdeen) excluded girls was more like the situation in England; other similarities were that the two countries' universities were closed to women. The impression Fearon had, however, was that co-education did not cause any 'harm': rather he felt that 'the presence of girls both civilizes and stimulates the boys, and that the opportunity of working with the boys strengthens the judgement and braces the mental faculties of the girls'. Still, he noted that it was mainly the daughters of the lower middle class who attended burgh schools and that the majority of middle-class daughters were sent to Ladies' Academies or Colleges.[60]

Another contrast with England was that Scotland did not favour boarding schools for girls nor believe that there was an urgent need for reform in middle-class girls' schooling. Yet there were growing reservations among the middle classes about the desirability of continuing the tradition of mixed-sex schooling, at least for their own children. Harvie and Sellar considered that in terms of 'mental training', mixed schools had much to recommend them, whereas from a social point of view, they had little to commend them, at least after childhood. It was, they reflected, a 'delicate' matter, difficult to provide evidence to support one system over the other. Their impressions, however, led them to support separating boys and girls of the higher orders: 'it seemed to us, that in almost every school in which boys and girls of 15 and 16 years of age were brought together, strangers could not help noticing the existence of irregularities that were unnoticed by teachers.' Whereas the testimony of some teachers that the presence of girls had a civilizing effect on masters as well as boys concurred with Fearon's impression, Harvie and Sellar considered that such an influence was imperceptible and were concerned that the behaviour of the boys prevailed, coarsening the manners of the girls, the reverse of 'civilizing'. They felt this to be the case not only when the sexes were taught together but also when they were in separate departments and met in common spaces, such as stairs and corridors. Yet while they favoured single-sex education from the age of 12, they acknowledged that there could be disadvantages, having observed that when boys and girls were pitted against each other, the latter did at least as well as the former:

> At Kirkcudbright Academy where for a small school the classical attainments are high, the second best scholar, both in Latin and Greek, was a girl of 16 years of age, who was reading Homer and Virgil. At Dumfries Academy, where mathematics was taught and learned at least as well as in any school in Scotland, the best geometrician in the class that was examined was a girl of 14 years of age; and in the highest Latin class at Arbroath High School there was a girl of 17 who had been five years in Latin and was reading the First Book of Livy quite as successfully as the boys in the class with her.

The lesson they took from these examples was not that co-education was superior academically but that girls were as capable of studying the more difficult subjects as boys. They noted that girls generally performed better than boys at modern languages and did as well as boys in English, while history was unpopular with both. They also admitted that when the sexes were taught in the same school, the girls appeared to be more industrious and conscientious than the boys and that in examinations 'girls always do their best for themselves and their teachers, while boys not infrequently are satisfied with getting the work done, and are indifferent however inadequately it may represent the pains that the master has taken with them'.[61]

Emily Davies reported that she had been told by schoolmistresses in England that 'the Scotch girls are much better taught than the English girls', but she preferred single-sex education for educational as well as social reasons, while Frances Martin, a superintendent at Bedford College, disparaged the 'Edinburgh' system of girls going from class to class and master to master.[62] Lindy Moore has found that there was a blurring of the separation between home and institutional schooling of young ladies in Scotland, notably from the end of the Napoleonic Wars when refugees from Europe took up teaching there. This they did in the girls' homes, holding classes in their own homes, and being employed in private schools as specialist masters. Girls, mainly from the age of 12 but sometimes younger, might attend a number of different masters and schools, depending on what their parents could pay for and approved of their daughters studying.[63] Except for the very small private schools run by women, then, middle-class girls' education in Scotland was dominated by men. Parents looked for a university-educated master, while women filled the role of governess who ensured that the girls practiced what the master had taught or of lady superintendent who oversaw both the girls and the governesses and performed an administrative role, freeing masters to concentrate on their subjects.[64] Indeed, where possible, smaller private schools boasted of employing the best masters, which was also the case in London.[65] Thus, while the practice of girls attending several different schools or masters at a time, going for the teacher and his subjects, was seen as distinctively Scottish, there were instances of girls who attended private schools in England doing the same.[66]

FEMINISM AND EDUCATIONAL REFORM

Lindy Moore has pointed out that reforming initiatives began earlier in Scotland than in England, influenced particularly by the movement to improve scientific instruction of the middle class.[67] The reforming pioneers were men, though there was already a move to single-sex education by the 1850s among those who could afford it. This trend continued: as seen in the next chapter, after 1872 some school boards in Scotland actively tried to attract middle-class girls, with a few schools becoming single-sex by the end of the century. The Scottish middle-class generally was not as well off as the English and fewer could afford to send their daughters to private schools which resembled the situation in Wales and Ireland.

Men were involved in the efforts to improve middle-class girls' education across the UK. Two who were associated with the establishment in 1848 of Queen's College, London, the Reverend Frederick D Maurice (1805–1872) and the Dean of Westminster, Dr Richard Chenevix Trench (1807–1886), also influenced the establishment by Anne Jellicoe (1823–1880) of Alexandra College in Dublin in 1866. Trench, who had been appointed archbishop of Dublin in 1864, persuaded Jellicoe to follow the London model, including close links with academics at Trinity College Dublin who lectured and examined the girls and prepared them for public examinations.[68] Jellicoe was also influenced by Maria Grey (1816–1906) and her high schools for girls established under the aegis of the Girls' Public Day School Company (GPDSC): set up in 1872, it grew out of the National Union for the Education of Girls of All Classes above the Elementary, known as the Women's Educational Union (1871). Like both Queen's College and Bedford College in London, Alexandra College focused on an academic education, with a view to sitting university examinations; and also as in the London colleges, a school was set up (1873) to prepare people for the college.

Another Jellicoe enterprise, the Queen's Institute (1861), paralleled the efforts of the Langham Circle in London with which Jellicoe was familiar, in providing a reasonably priced academic, technical and commercial education for young ladies, especially those with limited incomes, to train them for respectable paid employment. In post-Famine Ireland there was not only a high rate of emigration but also a growing number of single women often in straitened circumstances who needed appropriate careers.[69] Jellicoe had considerable success, as within a decade the civil service in Ireland began to employ women as telegraph clerks, but the Institute closed after two decades.[70]

There were similar developments in Belfast, notably Margaret Byers' Ladies' Collegiate School established in 1859, later known as Victoria College with separate secondary and university departments. Byers had the support of the Presbyterian Church and Jellicoe of the Church of Ireland, but with such a prominent individual as Archbishop Trench involved, Jellicoe did not have the same decision-making power as Byers and indeed served as Lady Superintendent of Alexandra College from 1866 to 1880.[71] In 1867 six women founded the Belfast Ladies' Institute with the aim of providing 'advanced classes for ladies of a higher class than hitherto attempted in the neighbourhood' though its examinations gained only limited public recognition. The ladies of the Institute petitioned Queen's College Belfast (one of three constituent colleges of the Queen's University of Ireland) to set examinations for women, which it agreed in 1869.[72] Margaret Byers, like Frances Buss, aimed to present girls in public examinations, Isabella Tod, like Emily Davies, quickly sought to gain entry for women into the universities.[73]

Feminists, then, were more closely and earlier involved with the campaign to improve girls' education in England and Ireland than in Scotland or Wales. The reforms in England, however, had a knock-on effect in Wales, though it was not until 1886 that the Association for Promoting the Education of Girls in Wales was established. The religious question, noted in the previous chapter, also had a bearing on middle-class girls' education. The association's members believed that not only was too little attention paid to female education but also that the Church of England had too much power over Welsh education. Hence the struggle for improved female education was part of the Nonconformist struggle for equality with Anglicanism.

Religion was also a significant factor in Ireland where the Catholic Church's suspicions of Protestant proselytising and of government intervention held back the development of secondary education for middle-class Catholic girls. The church welcomed the French female religious orders who established boarding schools in Ireland. They reinforced church control over education: that the majority of secondary schools in Ireland were run by religious orders ensured lay people were largely kept out of the secondary teaching profession, confining them to insecure and subordinate positions, while such schools helped the church resist government interference, notably in discussions over the Intermediate Education Act for Ireland in the 1870s.[74] The church had previously blocked suggestions for mixed-sex intermediate schools from the commissioners of endowed schools in the late 1850s, believing that this system would spread English utilitarian ideas about female education.

The original Intermediate Education Bill had been for boys only, but feminists involved in the campaign to improve Protestant girls' schooling in Ireland—including Byers, Jellicoe, Tod, Anna Haslam (1829–1922) and Alice Oldham (1850–1907)—lobbied vigorously and successfully to have them included. Indeed, the activities of these women paralleled those of feminists in England around the Langham Place circle: for example, Anna Haslam was a founder of the Irish Society for the Training and Employment of Educated Women in Dublin in 1861.[75]

When the Intermediate Education (Ireland) Act was passed in 1878, there were around 30 secondary schools for girls run by female religious orders, and their decision to associate with the Intermediate Board's examinations meant a more rigorous and academic curriculum. Grainne O'Flynn has noted that while the numbers of girls sitting the examinations gradually grew, advertisements for male and female schools differed: the former boasted of their successes in Intermediate, Royal University and Trinity College examinations, whereas the latter continued to emphasise the accomplishments as well as 'home comforts'.[76] In contrast, even private schools in England boasted of preparing girls for Cambridge local examinations, though this was not the most prominent feature in the advertisements.[77] Students at both Alexandra and Victoria colleges performed significantly better in the Intermediate Examinations in the late Victorian period than those in convent schools. Increasingly the Catholic Church had to listen to the demands of the Catholic middle class who wanted their daughters to receive as good an education as their Protestant counterparts and were prepared to send them to the new colleges for want of a Catholic alternative.[78] Hence, the bishops agreed to convent boarding and day schools offering such an academic curriculum and entering girls into the public examinations. At least the Intermediate Commissioners recognised denominational schools and examined but did not (until the end of the century) inspect them so that the state was still kept at a distance.

In Wales, efforts to establish secondary schools for girls might also be seen as an attempt to assert a specifically Welsh identity, since wealthy middle-class parents tended to send their daughters to be educated in English boarding schools. Welsh 'exiles' in London who were associated with the Honourable Society of Cymmrodorian and the National Eisteddfod provided an influential platform for those who wanted improvements in female education. [79] The Aberdare Committee which looked into intermediate and higher education in Wales in 1880 tended to equate nationality with Nonconformity, but it recognised the centrality of the Welsh language, even if the majority of people now spoke English. In practice, despite administration (including inspecting, examining and rewarding certificates) of intermediate schools through the Central Welsh Board which was set up in 1886, the Welsh language was neglected, partly perhaps because head teachers, both male and female, tended to have been educated at universities in England.

The Association for Promoting the Education of Girls in Wales (1886–1901) had close connections with the campaigns to improve middle-class female education in England, and the English GPDSC quickly extended its operations to Wales. Welsh feminists sought to improve a situation which they believed lagged behind other parts of Britain: thus Miss Elizabeth P. Hughes declared in 1884 that whereas in England 'the chief work has been to enable women to share the educational advantages of men', in Wales 'we have to create a higher education system for both sexes'.[80] The association was not setting itself apart from the English reformers, and indeed there were links between them: for example, Dilys Glynne Jones of the Welsh Association had taught at the North London Collegiate School in 1887, while other key Welsh reformers had themselves been educated in England, such as Elizabeth Phillips Hughes at Cheltenham Ladies' College, where she also taught for four years before studying at Newnham College Cambridge in 1883.[81]

The Taunton Commission found that middle-class boys' education in Wales had serious deficiencies, but that the situation for their sisters was worse: there were only 24 endowed schools for boys and two for girls. Moreover, little had changed by the time the Aberdare Committee reported in 1881; if anything the situation for girls had, compared to boys, deteriorated. Aberdare found 27 endowed grammar schools for boys but only three for girls.[82] Still, Malcolm Seaborne has claimed that in one respect Wales led the way in secondary education for girls by providing two pur-pose-built schools, the Howell's schools at Llandaff and Denbigh, opened in 1860.[83] The Aberdare Report recorded the dissatisfaction of Noncon-formists with Anglican influences on grammar schools and recommended non-sectarian intermediate schools with governing bodies representative of the local population.[84]

However, Welsh endowed schools were not innovative in the curricu-lum they offered, which like their counterparts in England included English grammar, French, geography, history, music and drawing. Whatever the desire for a distinctively Welsh middle-class schooling, reformers of girls' education sought to emulate the boys; and although there may have been more support for co-education in Wales, the key issue was cost rather than a preference for the Scottish system. Indeed, as in England, and increasingly in Scotland and Ireland, the emphasis in Welsh secondary schooling was social differentiation. Thus, in middle-class Penarth, there were to be sepa-rate schools for girls and boys with relatively high fees, but in the industrial and more remote rural areas, where most pupils were lower middle and upper working-class and fees were lower, mixed-sex schools were more common.[85] The most exclusively middle-class of these schools were urban, notably Cardiff, Swansea and Newport. In Cardiff when the local borough authority established separate intermediate schools for girls and boys, the principals of those schools had both been educated in private schools in England and were determined to adopt the practices and ethos of English public and grammar schools, including house systems, compulsory games and the spirit of competition, clubs and societies and high fees.[86] Although there was a relatively small middle class in Wales, the establishment of such schools indicated that it was growing and that while parents wanted their children, particularly boys, to be able to compete with their English coun-terparts, they did not always want to send them to England.

The focus of the Aberdare Report was very much on class; grammar schools were to be for the wealthier middle class, intermediate schools for the children of the less well-off. But there were echoes of the Scottish prac-tice of enabling talented working-class boys to enter university: Aberdare recommended that they be helped by a limited number of scholarships and exhibitions.[87] Moreover, as will be discussed below, while the campaign to establish a university of Wales from the 1860s focused on men, 20 years later women were admitted to the newly established university colleges in Wales on equal terms with men.

Such developments in middle-class education came later in Wales and clearly benefited from government intervention as well as the efforts of individual reformers, both male and female. While the Taunton Commis-sion provided more of a stimulus to reforming girls' schooling in England, the Aberdare Committee, which reiterated many of Taunton's criticisms, was very important for developments in Wales, most notably the 1889

Intermediate and Technical Education Act. As Gordon Roderick has shown, secondary education in Wales did not simply replicate the English provision, though there were distinct similarities: what emerged from the 1889 Act was 'not a uniform, cohesive pattern of secondary education, but rather a multi-layered, uncoordinated patchwork of different types of school, each type with its specific objectives and curriculum and related to the perceived needs of a particular sector of society'.[88] Among the examples he provides is the decision by the joint education committee in Swansea that there should be two single-sex schools catering for pupils up to the age of 18: a grammar school for boys and the High School for Girls established in 1882 by the GPDSC, both of which were taken over by the committee at the beginning of 1895.[89]

The Aberdare Committee accepted the need for improvement in the provision of education for middle-class girls and recommended that their schools be assisted by public funds and that women be appointed as governors.[90] The subsequent Act of 1889 urged equal provision for the sexes, and Roderick has recorded that by the end of the Victorian era this had almost been attained: in 1900 there were 93 intermediate schools, of which 43 were co-educational, seven were mixed sex, 22 were for boys only and 21 for girls; these accounted for a total of 3,877 boys and 3,513 girls.[91] While, as Roderick notes, parity in numbers had been attained by 1905, in the 1890s there were still instances which favoured boys: one intermediate school in South Pembrokeshire which opened in 1895 with 50 boys and 35 girls on the roll offered more scholarships and bursaries to boys than girls—six scholarships for boys and four for girls from the borough, four for boys and two for girls from rural districts and 12 bursaries to boys but eight to girls for those most in need of aid.[92]

As noted in the previous chapter, compared to England girls' employment opportunities were fewer and in a narrower range in Wales. This is confirmed by Deborah James' study of intermediate schools and career opportunities for girls in the East Glamorgan valleys. She notes the tendency to celebrate the 1889 Act as not only an important stimulus to improving both the provision and quality of secondary education for girls in Wales but also as opening up higher education and new careers to them. Her detailed examination of three schools (Aberdare, Pontypridd and Rhondda County schools) in this area reveals that in practice the secondary education they received did not offer the same opportunities in the white-collar sector or nursing and midwifery as were increasingly available in other parts of Britain. Girls were channelled into teaching because of the absence of alternative careers which would have been accepted as appropriate to women in the region.[93] This confirms Roderick's study of secondary education in Glamorgan: of a sample of 69 girls who went to secondary school at Gowerton, 44 per cent became teachers, 26 per cent remained 'at home' and 17 per cent became shop assistants or took up millinery and dressmaking; at Ystalyfera the choices were even narrower: half went into teaching and a few became shop assistants. The vast majority in the area either became teachers or entered no vocation.[94] Thus, geographical location and economic and cultural influences as well as gender have to be taken into consideration to grasp the impact of the 1889 Act.

For England, Sheila Fletcher has identified a slowing down in the movement to improve middle-class girls' schooling in the 1880s. There was no English equivalent to the intermediate education acts of Ireland and Wales. She notes that the new high schools affected a minority of middle-class girls: 'The pioneers' success is so well known, and they put such a stamp on girls' education that it is only too easy to forget the void that lay between these rising stars and anything approaching a girls' school system.' Whereas Geoffrey Walford saw the North London Collegiate School which Frances Buss established in Camden as a model for the growing number of day schools, including those of Maria Grey's GPDSC, for Fletcher the Camden school was more 'a prototype' than the foundation of a system.[95] She also pointed out that the Endowed Schools Act of 1869 did not insist that girls should share in every endowment, while the wealthy continued to favour an education in the accomplishments for their daughters over subscribing to a secondary school which offered girls a serious academic education. Hence, Grey's GPDSC would only found a school once a certain number of shares and of pupils were pledged: by 1900, around 30 schools had been established.[96] The Taunton Commission had identified 820 endowed schools of which only around a score were for girls; the Endowed Schools Commission set up 178 grammar schools of which 47 were for girls and one was mixed sex; that was replaced in 1874 with the Charity Commission, which established 335 grammar schools, of which only 47 were for girls and six were mixed.[97]

Despite relatively modest results, however, Rosemary Thynne argues that the significance of the high schools far outweighed their numbers because they set the standards for middle-class girls' schooling, though she acknowledges that when it came to the serious study of science it was the non-GPDSC schools outside of London which led the way.[98] Nevertheless, pupils at the GPDSC high schools performed disproportionately well in examinations compared to those at either the endowed or Church Society schools into the twentieth century.[99] Moreover, for Lindy Moore those women who pioneered educational improvements for middle-class girls in England had no equivalents in Scotland so that whereas the headmistresses of these secondary schools for girls constituted 'an early and visible part of the women's movement', the masculine educational tradition both held back the development of such a movement in Scotland and limited the opportunities of female teachers.[100] This suggests complacency in the Scottish attitude that there was no need for radical improvements in middle-class girls' education, to which Gillian Avery adds reluctance to appear to be imitating an English initiative. As in Wales, it was the late Victorian period before secondary schools for girls were promoted in Scotland. Avery argues that setting up a high school for girls along English lines was seen as a criticism of the traditional Scottish system, pointing out that it was only in 1888 that St George's High School for Girls was opened in Edinburgh which like the boarding school St Leonards (near St Andrews), stood apart from other schools in Scotland.[101] Yet while there was little in the way of overtly feminist thinking behind developments in Scotland, English feminists used similar arguments to Scottish reformers: an intellectual education was not only compatible with a woman's domestic future but also essential for her to fulfil that role. Indeed, one factor in the development of a serious education for middle-class girls lay in the increasing claims for the importance of motherhood in the later Victorian period.

Ironically, Carol Dyhouse detected an attitude of complacency among the feminists who pioneered educational reform in girls' schooling in England by the late nineteenth century. She points to the stark criticisms of girls' middle-class schooling made by Christina Bremner in 1897.[102] Whereas Josephine Kamm claimed that the GPDSC's fees were 'moderate' and Mary Cathcart Borer described them as 'reasonable', in Bremner's view they were relatively expensive and for the better-off only. She agreed that the schools had set high educational standards but pointed out that parents did not always want this for their daughters. She also recorded that the endowed and proprietary schools for girls received a 'less than equal' share of the funds from the Charity Commission and an 'unequal share of technical instruction—in some cases even being excluded', while there was a growing need of scholarships and exhibitions to enable girls to go on to university.[103] Still, by the end of the century, some upper middle-class parents were concerned about the pretensions of their social inferiors in sending their daughters to private schools, and this anxiety to maintain the distinction of rank led them to seek a serious education for their daughters. They had come to consider the new high schools and colleges for young ladies as superior to the genteel schooling of lower middle-class girls.[104]

GENDER, CLASS AND CURRICULUM

As Joyce Goodman has pointed out, 30 years after women were invited to give evidence to the Taunton Commission, women were not only witnesses to the Bryce Commission into secondary education but also sat as commissioners (Sophie Bryant, 1850–1922, Lucy Cavendish, 1841–1925, and Eleanor Sidgwick, 1845–1936) and were appointed as assistant-commissioners tasked with reporting on girls' education.[105] The lady assistant commissioners were given separate instructions from the men: the former were to consider the main differences that might exist in the education required for girls as compared to that of boys.[106] The underlying assumption was that there were differences. As one lady reported to the commission, the curriculum best suited for girls was 'not quite the same' as for boys, and while this was particularly the case for the working class, 'girls, no matter what may be their social status, have always to prepare themselves to some extent for home life'.[107]

In addition, they were to examine whether there was the same demand for secondary schools among the working class as among the middle class. Bryce showed that while provision for secondary education for girls was particularly uneven in England, there was demand for it, stimulated by such developments in female education as the establishment of university colleges for women—Hitchen/Girton (1869/1873) and Newnham (1871) at Cambridge, Somerville and Lady Margaret Hall (1879), St Hugh's (1888) and St Hilda's (1893) at Oxford and Royal Holloway (1886) at Egham—as well as the opening of local examinations to girls and the University Extension Movement (1873).[108] Bryce (who was associated with the GPDSC) considered that since the Taunton Commission had reported, there had probably been more change in the secondary education of girls than in any other department. He pointed to the different types of schools, endowed and proprietary, and among the latter, particularly those of the GPDSC and the Church Schools Company.[109] These tended to be single sex, but Bryce noted that across the sector there was a considerable amount of mixed-sex schooling, notably in rural districts, in higher grade schools and pupil-teacher centres. Bryce also noted that mixed schools were the norm in the USA, parts of Canada and Scotland, and in these boys and girls were successfully taught together.[110]

The lady assistant commissioners were required to consider what the differences in provision were for girls, how to meet those in mixed-sex schools, and whether the sexes should be taught separately after a certain age.[111] As noted in the previous chapter, one of these, Ella Armitage, observed of Devon that among those who considered themselves socially superior there was still resistance to sending their daughters to be taught with the daughters of the poor. This social prejudice, she believed, held back the development of secondary education for girls in that county, especially when combined with parental indifference to their daughters' education. Middle-class parents worried that girls' health could be harmed by education, still prevented their daughters from taking public examinations and were concerned only that they learned ladylike accomplishments. Another assistant commissioner, Mrs Kitchener, recorded examples of maternal concern that too much education would make daughters ineligible for marriage: the headmistress of 'a good and fashionable school' related that one of her more intelligent pupils, a 17 year old, was to be withdrawn because 'she was too much interested in her classes' and showed signs of 'getting blue'. This fear of 'blueness' led the parents of another pupil to prevent her from going to Newnham College, while the mother of a girl who displayed considerable ability in mathematics complained of her being a 'tiresome child' who showed no interest in music or French 'or something that's some use'.[112]

In rural areas, governesses employed in the family home and in small private schools were still more common than what she considered the superior education offered by the new high schools. Where these existed, as in the endowed school in Exeter, they 'extinguished' employment opportunities for the governess.[113] Mrs Armitage was of the view that the higher the school fee, the more likely a girl was to be prepared for marriage rather than paid employment, and she regretted that no attempt was made to train them for the former 'but more stress is laid on the piano, guitar, mandolin, watercolour painting, and French'.[114] Since such subjects drove up the cost of girls' education, less well-off parents sought lower fees; if they could not find them, they kept their daughters at home, preferring as one assistant commissioner put it, refinement over education.[115] It was at least acknowledged that while lower middle-class parents in England were less willing to pay for the education of their daughters than their sons, this should not simply be equated with indifference; rather, it was now related to the few opportunities for girls to obtain a socially respectable job at a reasonable salary.

Yet even in industrial areas where there had been considerable progress in girls' secondary education, it was uneven. Thus, whereas in Birmingham the provision of secondary education for girls was 'exceptionally good', it was very deficient in the rest of the county, both in terms of numbers of schools and quality of teaching.[116] Despite reporting that 'bad schools still exist, but they are driven into holes and corners' by the new high schools and that boarding schools had also improved, Mrs Kitchener observed that the education within the reach of the lower middle-class girl was 'comparatively worse' than it was 30 years ago. Even at the 'excellent' Liverpool Institute, about half the pupils left at 15, the majority employed 'mainly in shops, dressmakers' or milliners' establishments, or the post office'.[117] This was also the case in suburban districts of Norfolk where lower middle-class girls went into shops, did clerical work and typing, were taken on by the post office or began teaching; girls from the high schools often took up governessing as soon as they left or found posts in the cheaper private schools.[118]

As noted above, the reformers wanted a similar education to the boys. This search for equality meant that the new secondary schools for girls were not notably innovative in the curriculum: not only did it privilege classics but also the teaching of what were considered 'girls' subjects' such as modern languages emulated, as Ruth Watts has recorded, the teaching in boys' schools by changing to grammatical over oral methods. At the same time, girls and boys tended to study different sciences, with chemistry and physics for the latter, biology, physiology and botany for the former.[119] Christina Bremner noted in 1897 that women focused on those three sciences plus hygiene, but they constituted a small minority among female students: in 1894–1895 there were only ten women to 202 men at the Royal College of Science.[120] Geoffrey Walford reiterates the different reasons given for teaching science to boys (for future occupations) than girls (their domestic future). He accepts that at a time of strong opposition to reforms in middle-class girls' education and resistance from the professions, notably of medicine, to the entry of women, such a cautious strategy regarding curriculum was understandable.[121]

There were exceptions, though mainly for adult lower middle-class women. Julie Stevenson's study of women students at University College London and the Polytechnic at Regent Street shows that they studied scientific and technical subjects and that they were not as marginal as has been assumed; but their choice was restricted by the employment barriers they faced. Most women avoided courses in which there were few if any openings for them, tending to study subjects such as hygiene and physiology which strengthened their career prospects.[122] In another study based on London, Joyce Goodman looked at the committees established by county councils after the Technical Instruction Act of 1889. Though women were not eligible to stand for election, they could be co-opted: only 14 councils had done so by 1896. While it was the general belief that technical education for girls should focus on domestic economy, Goodman records that a range of non-domestic, vocational subjects was introduced, including bookbinding, glass painting, secretarial and commercial and gardening.[123]

There were indeed a number of specialist colleges for female technical education, with examples given by Christina Bremner, including the Women's Department of Swanley Horticultural College (1891) as well as the various cookery schools in major urban centres, beginning with London in 1873, but she also noted that in technical education women were both in a minority and usually limited to domestic economy; girls and women of the wealthier middle class were unlikely to attend; the education received in the Mechanics' Institutes was for lower middle-class and upper working-class women; and the Home Arts and Industries Association (1884) had the aim of spreading artistic handiwork among the working classes.[124] As Joyce Goodman concludes, training initiatives did not challenge the separation of the sexes in the trades: skilled women were not to compete with their male counterparts.[125]

Generally, the Bryce Commission found that 'technical education' for girls was largely based on domestic economy and more likely to be found in the intermediate schools than in the high schools. Gender difference was also a social class issue, and there was considerable disagreement over the question of whether there was a place for domestic economy in middle-class girls' schooling. Under the influence of social Darwinism, there was pressure to introduce domestic education into the curriculum in girls' secondary schools and even of the universities. The pioneers of female secondary and higher education, however, insisted on the same academic standards as in male education and most resisted the inclusion of domestic economy in the girls' curriculum because of its association with working-class women. Headmistresses of high schools regarded needlework and other domestic subjects as unsuitable for their girls, though some regretted that academic subjects crowded out such practical work, believing that it 'would serve as a relief to certain of the delicate and backward girls'.[126] There were exceptions: cookery was taught at the Belfast Ladies' Institute, though like chemistry, it was difficult to accommodate, and Sara Burstall introduced cookery, laundry and needlework to Manchester High School in 1898: though she aimed these at the less academic pupils, she considered that 'the normal work of a woman is to be the maker of a home, to be a wife, and above all a mother'.[127]

There were differences between middle-class parental expectations of their daughters in the north compared to the south of England. Many Yorkshire towns had a small professional class whose women were expected to know how to discharge the domestic tasks and not simply to rely on servants: thus, girls attending secondary schools in the West Riding were proficient in cooking from the practical experience of their own homes.[128] As for the rare labourer's daughter who won a scholarship to a high school, it was maintained that she would gain little benefit; indeed, her life chances could be harmed since girls of her class required 'a more efficient training for domestic life than can be given in their homes' so that she would be better off at a school which taught domestic economy.[129] In any case, few of the very few working-class children who won scholarships could stay on at school for more than a year or two, while it was noted that by the late nineteenth century, lower middle-class parents in bigger cities were sending daughters as well as sons to elementary schools to benefit from the opportunities of scholarships to the grammar schools: those for girls in Birmingham were said to be 'exceptionally good'.[130]

The Aberdare Committee and the Bryce Commission tended to equate technical education for girls with domestic economy. The lady assistant commissioners to the latter were asked to consider how technical education for girls could be organised in urban and rural districts with 'regards being had to the varying wants of the different social strata'.[131] While the 1889 Welsh Act for intermediate schools was also concerned with technical education, the desire of reformers to see middle-class girls' education on a par with boys meant that technical education, including domestic, was neglected: the curriculum of secondary schools was predominantly academic. The secondary schools which developed in Wales (grammar, high schools, intermediate schools and higher grade schools) followed the English model, though provision in Wales was much broader, covering the country by the end of the century.[132]

Indeed, the Bryce Commission revealed that not only were there no secondary schools for girls in large parts of England but also that such schools as existed offered girls very little technical education. Generally, local government grants favoured boys, though in Bolton where all scholarships and exhibitions were funded by private philanthropy, girls had more opportunity of 'ascending the educational ladder than in any other town in Lancashire'.[133] That seems to have been an exceptional case: of the grants made to secondary schools by local authorities under the Technical

Instruction Acts, boys' schools received 'by far the largest share'; where there was competition between girls' and boys' schools, between two-thirds and three-quarters of the grants went to the latter, while in some places girls were excluded.[134]

The Aberdare Report insisted that for girls it 'should be distinctly higher than elementary, but should be of a practical character, including some kind of industrial or economic training'.[135] The charity commissioners who examined the curricula of the intermediate schools following the 1889 Act recorded that 'girls' subjects' such as needlework, dressmaking and cookery, were included in the curriculum at the expense of science. Whereas in mixed-sex schools, girls had access to laboratories for practical work in science, there was little or no provision for this in girls' schools: time spent on domestic economy was at the expense of girls' scientific education.[136] A study of secondary education in the Rhondda valleys noted similar differences in the curricula for girls and boys which increased in the higher standards: in the girls' departments music, drawing, domestic economy and needlework were taught from the fourth standard, with French added in the sixth, whereas boys were taught algebra, Euclid and mensuration and offered Latin and chemistry.[137]

There were similarities in the curriculum of secondary schools in England. One headmistress reported to favour separate 'technical schools' for girls meant in practice a school for domestic training, though in her view domestic subjects should not be added to the curriculum of the secondary school partly because they were not 'purely educational' and also due to the cost of the necessary apparatus. Thus, the Yorkshire Ladies Council of Education had established a well-equipped school for training in cookery, laundry and other related household subjects in Leeds, with branches at Wakefield and Sheffield.[138]

EDUCATION, FITNESS AND FEMININITY

As noted above, George Combe had insisted that health was crucial for women, especially mothers.[139] They not only had to study it, they should ensure that they themselves were fit and healthy. Dorothea Beale was of the opinion that serious study was good for a girl's health: the want of wholesome occupation, she insisted, 'lies at the root of much of the languid debility of which we hear so much after girls leave school'.[140] For each girl from the higher middle class who was said to suffer from overwork and strain due to her studies, Beale held that there were 'hundreds whose health suffers from the irritability produced by idleness'.[141] James Bryce agreed: ill health was more frequently caused by the frivolity and languor of boarding-school life than by being overly studious.[142]

The belief in the relationship between a healthy mind and a healthy body had been recognised by writers on female education from the late eighteenth century.[143] However, the emphasis was on the differences between the sexes, on a femininity which deemed women to be not only physically weaker than men but frail creatures whose very delicacy constituted the marks of their social distinction. Critics of the education of young ladies argued that such weakness fed on itself. The third issue of *The English Woman's Journal* began with an editorial on 'Physical Training' which was very critical of boarding schools, accusing them of forcing girls to study from early morning to late in the evening, learning by rote and cramming for examinations, with no attention paid to their health and fitness. Moreover, once a young lady leaves school for home, she continues to lead a sedentary life except when she is dancing until the early hours, all of which takes a grave toll on her health and ensures that she really is a delicate being. The editorial was also scathing about the lack of fitness of her brother, but at least he had physical recreations such as boating, skating and cricket. It was declared that

> the *first* [emphasis in the original] duty of a good schoolmistress, a duty higher than that of any mental (we had almost said of any moral) superintendence, is to see that all the young girls join, *more than once a day*, either in outdoor exercise, or in dancing, blind-man's buff, or some similar active exercise in the house. No house is fit for a boarding school which has not a room sufficiently large for such a purpose.[144]

In practice, such schools often developed out of a family's school room, were short lived and had no administrative oversight.[145] Yet it was precisely because they tended to be small domestic establishments based in the teacher's home that was reassuring to parents.

The same issue of *The English Woman's Journal* called for gymnasia to be established in cities for girls and young women who attended colleges, lectures and museums; 40 years later a similar recommendation was made to the Bryce Commission.[146] The journal had included a short extract from Dr Elizabeth Blackwell (1821–1910) on the physical education of girls, which both argued for its importance and lamented that it had so little place in their schooling. Neglect of exercise during youth, she argued, led to 'weakness of the whole muscular system' leaving women 'unfit for duty'.[147] The Taunton Commission agreed, noting that except for 'callisthenics' which was taught in the better schools, bodily exercise was neglected which it felt was an obstacle to successful study and was responsible for girls' poor health.[148] Frances Buss testified that a course of four half-hourly lessons in callisthenics was compulsory among the older girls at the North London Collegiate School precisely because they got so little bodily exercise. The younger girls, she explained, were more willing to play in the playground. Dorothea Beale reported that at Cheltenham an experienced teacher was employed to teach callisthenics twice a week in a room specially fitted for the purpose. However, in unreformed schools exercise was reduced to deportment.[149]

As noted above, sport was generally seen as a masculine pursuit. However, increasing wealth and a surfeit of free time for the middle-class lady, as well as the determination among educational reformers to emulate the curriculum in the public schools for boys, gradually led to a growth in female interest in sport and games. The arguments against women participating in sporting activities were very similar to those which considered that higher education was dangerous for them: both would harm the delicate female body and mind, wreck her reproductive organs and destroy her femininity.[150] Victorian feminists and educational reformers believed in the relationship between a healthy mind and a healthy body, seeing a need to cultivate both.[151] Most, however, thought that physical exercise should be 'moderate' and ladylike. Moreover, as Kathleen McCrone observes the majority of women who took up sport did so because

> sport was enjoyable, fashionable or companionable, not because they rejected patriarchal notions of female frailty and inferiority or because they viewed sports participation as a means of emancipating themselves and their sex from restricting social norms.[152]

There was increased interest in eugenics in the latter part of the century as well as concern for the health of the imperial nation. The poor health and physique of working-class men were put down to lack of domestic skills on the part of their women with, as noted in Chapter 2, the consequent campaigns to increase the time girls of that class spent acquiring these in elementary school. When it came to fitness, however, working-class children, and especially boys, were at most given military drill exercises, though in some cities, such as London and Glasgow, boys and girls in board schools also received swimming lessons by the later Victorian period. It was only with the shock of the evidence of the Boer War when thousands of working-class men who sought to enlist in the armed forces had to be rejected on medical grounds that more consideration was given to physical exercise in elementary schools, though the emphasis remained on military drill for boys and domestic education for girls.[153]

Most studies of female schooling and physical education in the Victorian period are not much concerned with the working class who did not possess the necessary educational culture or facilities, leisure time or money.[154] Elementary schools also did not have playing fields, another mark of class distinction, while it was generally only in the early twentieth century that the training of elementary school teachers included physical exercise and games, mainly as part of the wider question of personal hygiene. Outside of school, working-class girls had very little time and few opportunities to participate in sport, although from the 1880s middle-class philanthropists taught games and gymnastics in the various clubs and societies set up to 'save' and to civilize their social inferiors, such as the Girls' Friendly Society and the Mothers' Union.[155]

In contrast, the emphasis in the schooling of middle-class girls was the relationship between mind and body. The report of the Taunton Commission in 1868 was very critical of the lack physical education in girls' private schools and the failure of the teachers to understand the importance of bodily exercise, though the inspectors themselves had little to say about games for girls.[156] Even the medical profession, which was hostile to women's entry into higher education, at first saw physical exercise as a balance to academic study. However, when some women participated in competitive sports, medical practitioners echoed the eugenicist argument that 'strenuous exercise, especially during puberty and menstrual periods, drained energy from vital organs, thus damaging women's bodies irreparably and threatening the survival of the race'.[157] Fear among parents, often shared by teachers, that too vigorous exercising would de-sex daughters, led to campaigners prioritising academic reform. Their aim was to improve the intellectual education of young ladies without attracting controversy about the end product being not only un-marriageable but manly.

Witnesses to the Taunton Commission agreed that there was still a need for the accomplishments in a young lady's education in order to avoid her gaining a 'hardness of manners'.[158] Hence proponents of physical exercise for girls developed the argument around health and well-being to show the benefits to a girl's moral character through the inculcation of self-discipline which proper exercise could bring. Far from de-sexing girls, it would enhance womanliness. Even those who sought entry into higher education emphasised that the goal was to make better wives and mothers, not to turn girls into boys.[159] At Cheltenham College, Dorothea Beale, who was adamantly opposed to competition in any form, at first banned hockey. Yet as noted above, she was convinced that physical exercise, including swimming, was beneficial and gradually relaxed restrictions on games, eventually renting land for a playing field in 1891.[160] Her watchword was 'moderation' or as Sara Burstall expressed it, 'not too much'.[161] The transition from gentle callisthenics to physical education was, according to Kathleen McCrone, gradual and did not occur to any extent before at least the 1880s; indeed, competitive games really entered girls' schools with the first generation of Oxbridge-educated mistresses who had learned to appreciate them at university.[162]

One of the biggest differences between the secondary schools for girls and boys examined by the Bryce Commission was that the latter enjoyed considerably more provision of playing fields and more regular and systematic organisation of outdoor games. Though more was being done for girls, doubts were expressed that this was likely to bear much fruit in the near future. Still, there were schools in which games were compulsory as in one in Dewsbury which owned a large playground and four tennis courts. Girls also played hockey and cricket, with the older girls challenging the younger boys in both. Swimming was also compulsory for the Dewsbury girls.[163] But it was unusual to have such provision for sport and games in day secondary schools for girls even in the late nineteenth century, whereas bigger boarding schools were recorded as providing a variety of both (for example, golf as well as tennis, hockey and boating) and also gymnasia. As one lady commissioner observed

> It was pleasant to see the zest with which some of the younger mistresses entered into the play; on inquiry, I usually found that they had been at Oxford, Cambridge or Holloway. Several headmistresses spoke of the value of this phase of university training for teachers in secondary schools.[164]

Women who attended colleges and universities had to maintain their femininity and so justified their sporting activities on very different grounds to their male counterparts. A healthy physique and a competitive spirit were clearly useful to middle-class men in their public lives in a variety of ways, whereas women argued it was a means of preventing over-strain in their studies. There were very similar arguments about the moral and spiritual benefits girls as well as boys could derive from sport: honour, loyalty, determination and discipline.[165] However, there was still a gender division between male and female sports which was based on the continuing belief in women's inferiority to men. Even proponents of physical education for girls accepted the notion of separate spheres for the sexes and insisted on the co-relation between girls' sports and moral rectitude.[166]

Getting exercise in whatever form onto the curriculum of schools for young ladies opened up another way into the teaching profession for middle-class women. When girls' private schools, especially elite ones such as Roedean and St Leonards, began to offer gymnastics and games, there was the possibility for a few women to become physical education teachers.[167] Like cookery, as will be seen in the next chapter, training in physical education was separate from teacher training. The specialised training of the games mistress developed before that of the master.[168] The guiding force was Madame Bergman-Österberg (1849–1915), a Swedish woman who had been employed by the London School Board in 1881 to train teachers in Swedish (Ling) gymnastics. She gave classes to women teachers from 1882, and by the time she left in 1887 over 700 mistresses in London's board schools had received the certificate of proficiency with perhaps as many again who had received some training but not the certificate.[169] She founded a training college for women in Hampstead in 1886, resigning from the London School board a year later.

Bergman-Österberg's focus shifted to middle-class girls attending the new high schools. She now believed that she could not lay the foundations for a healthy race among the working class without improvements in its conditions of life.[170] By the turn of the century, there were five physical education training colleges in England, of which three were residential, catering for the daughters of the professional middle classes. The two-year courses were intensive, combining theory, practice and teaching practice, Swedish gymnastics and English games. The idea of the latter was more controversial than the former which could be construed as therapeutic. As noted above, even in boys' schools, sport, or rather the emphasis put on it, had its critics. Again, the emphasis in arguments for the importance of physical exercise was to make a healthy mother and child, linking fitness to hygiene and a scientific understanding of the body. Indeed, it appealed to eugenicists and those worried about the degeneracy of the upper classes: training women in this way would lead to improvements in the 'racial quality of the elite'.[171] Thus the *English Woman's Journal* concluded its editorial on physical exercise in 1858:

> . . . we may indeed inaugurate great sanitary reforms, destroy the virulence of epidemics and lengthen the lives of the masses in very appreciable degree,—but we shall continue to see our foremost battalion perish in the pride of its progress, our most ardent workers in the field of the intellect fall in the flower of youth.[172]

HIGHER EDUCATION

The Taunton Commission acted as a spur to reform in the direction of greater educational equality between middle-class girls and boys, especially but not only in England. Yet as Michèle Cohen has observed, it also contributed to new constraints and inequalities in female education: examining the language deployed by the commissioners, she concluded that it was 'already gendered because it had been elaborated precisely to construct or consolidate gender difference'.[173]

Once secondary school improvements were under way, the reformers, notably Emily Davies and Elizabeth Garrett (1836–1917) in England, turned to higher education. This does not mean that women had not attended university before then. Long before the University Extension Movement of the 1870s, indeed from the early eighteenth century, academics delivered public lectures to women as well as men, both inside and outside the university, while pioneers of adult education, who focused mainly on working-class men, accepted women, usually of a higher social standing, to their classes.[174] Some women achieved an impressive level of education, notably in science.[175] Nevertheless, they were generally not accepted within the professions and the Victorian period saw the tightening of regulations which deliberately sought to exclude women.

Certainly, the professional sector was a tiny part of the economy even by the middle of the century, and women were not totally excluded; but they were limited to what was related to their domestic role.[176] This process of professionalization was constructed on a masculine ideal of the 'learned professions' and it became increasingly difficult for women to achieve professional recognition. While women were being excluded from the 'learned professions' from the late eighteenth century, they developed their own form of professionalism, especially teachers as will be seen in the next chapter.[177] Thus, whereas some campaigned to gain entry to the male professions, others sought to develop specifically female professions, including certain areas of teaching (notably kindergarten, infants, domestic science and in single sex girls' schools).

While there were key figures in the campaigns to secure women's entry into higher education and the male professions, Christina Bremner pointed to the importance of local initiatives.[178] Thus, the Association for the Higher Education of Women, founded in 1878, had its origins in various urban bodies, such as the Ladies' Educational Associations in the main towns and cities across the UK, and regional associations, notably the North of England Council for Promoting the Higher Education of Women (1867), which had developed from the 1860s.[179] The Central Association of Irish Schoolmistresses (1882) worked closely with the Ulster Schoolmistresses' Association (set up by Isabella Tod and Margaret Byers), campaigning to persuade Trinity College to admit women.

That this was a mainly Protestant campaign did not mean Catholic women lacked interest. Religious orders still dominated Catholic teaching in Ireland, and they were forbidden to join such bodies, but three orders in particular, Dominican, Loreto and Ursuline, were interested in preparing girls for higher education. Thus in 1893 the Dominican St Mary's College and High School for Girls and in 1894 the Loreto College were opened: indeed, headmistresses of all Loreto schools were ordered to send their 'university girls' to the College.[180] While Protestant women could campaign openly, Catholic religious had to work within a male-dominated church which was for the most part opposed both to higher education for women and mixed-sex education. Indeed, Judith Harford suggests that the movement for higher education for Irish women was fuelled by denominational rivalry, showing how female religious manipulated this in their efforts to get higher education for Catholic women.[181]

The various campaigning bodies across the UK arranged for visiting university tutors to give lectures and provide accompanying materials (such as reading lists), while Cambridge University was persuaded to set a special 'women's examination'. This led to cooperation with working-class men who sought to improve their education and resulted in the university establishing a syndicate for local lectures with the examinations being renamed the Higher Locals. Ellen Jordan has observed that these developments perturbed Emily Davies who feared they had potential of keeping university education for middle-class women separate and inferior to that of their brothers.[182] Her focus was the upper middle-class woman, whereas the University Extension Movement was open to both men and women further down the social scale who took advantage of correspondence classes which prepared them for examinations.[183]

Davies concentrated on getting girls to sit university examinations on the same basis as boys. She did not agree that the sexes were so different that they required a different type of education; nor would she accept that the main use of a university education was as a kind of intellectual finishing school for the clever young lady. At the same time, however, the emphasis on high academic standards in middle-class female education was accompanied by insistence on ladylike behaviour.[184] For Davies this was largely to reassure parents about the propriety of sending their daughters to university. Dorothea Beale, however, felt it was necessary to show that a serious education would not 'unsex' a woman.

> I do not think the plan for admitting girls to the same examination with boys in the University local examinations a wise one: the subjects seem to me in many respects unsuited for girls, and such an examination as the one proposed is likely to farther a spirit of rivalry most undesirable. I should much regret that the desire for distinction should be made in any degree a prime motive, for we should ever remember that moral training is the end, education the means; the habits of obedience to duty, of self-restraint, which the process of acquiring knowledge induces, the humility which a thoughtful and comprehensive study of the great works in literature and science tends to produce, these we should specially cultivate in a woman, that she may be the true woman's ornament of a meek and quiet spirit. As for the pretentiousness and conceit which are associated with the name of 'blue-stocking', and which some people fancy to be the result of education, they are only an evidence of shallowness and vulgarity; we meet with the same thing in the dogmatic conceit of the so-called 'self-educated man' who has picked up learning, but has not had the benefit of a systematic training and a liberal education.[185]

This reflects the social and cultural obstacles in the way of women's entry into higher education. Resistance came from those who considered women would be a disruptive influence at the university; from parents who were afraid higher education would 'change' their daughters and perhaps make them un-marriageable; from clerics and the medical profession which believed that higher education would harm women morally as well as physically.[186] Yet while the Church of England is often seen to be among the more resistant of denominations to the higher education of women, paradoxically by the end of the century, it was an important provider of not only secondary education for girls, for example, through its Church Schools Society, but also of higher education through particular foundations (such as King's College Ladies' Department) and key individuals (including Frances Buss, Dorothea Beale and Emily Davies). It was noted of Beale in particular that she looked on her role as principal of Cheltenham Ladies' College as a religious vocation.[187]

Whatever the obstacles, higher education for women increased. In 1878, London University began to award women degrees on the same basis as men which set a precedent for the inclusion of women in the Irish University Act of 1879: both of these were examining bodies, and it was only from the early 1890s that women were legally allowed into the universities.[188] In the face of resistance from universities to allowing women on to their campuses, Emily Davies established Hitchen College in 1869, moving in 1873 to Girton College at Cambridge. As already noted, she insisted on parity of entry and examination with male students. Others, such as Anne Jemima Clough (1820–1892) and Elizabeth Wolstenholme (later Elmy, 1833–1918) were willing to compromise through utilising the university-based extension system, consisting of a lecture programme for women with special university-based examinations, which would allow women to become teachers.[189] Clough developed it for women by establishing Newnham College at Cambridge. Davies, however, believed that university extension classes did not amount to serious, systematic studies and considered that they undermined her attempts to get equality with men. She may also have associated these classes with the extramural public 'afternoon' lectures offered in cities across Britain from the middle of the century.[190]

Carol Dyhouse's study of women in British universities has shown that the pioneering feminists and educational reformers were also divided over such issues as segregation of and separate spaces for the sexes, as well as the notion of women being in need of protection.[191] Yet all used the language of femininity and domesticity both to defend their initiatives and to reassure parents. Thus, Emily Davies refuted the notion that higher education would 'spoil' a woman for a domestic future. The hall of residence would be a substitute home which would oversee the morals as well as the health of the residents, protect them from the temptations of 'society' and better prepare them for their future whether 'as mistresses of households, mothers, teachers, or as labourers in art, science, literature, and notably in the field of philanthropy'—it would not, she stated, be specifically directed towards changing the occupations of women but rather 'towards securing that whatever they do shall be done well'.[192] Such rhetoric not only accommodated contemporary concepts of femininity but also may have served to reinforce them.[193]

Indeed, throughout the late Victorian period, there were restrictions on the activities and behaviour of female students, often imposed by those who championed their right to higher education. It was not simply a question of propriety and 'tone' (the continuing threat of female students turning into masculine bluestockings) but also, by the turn of the century, of curriculum as well, with universities under pressure to introduce 'home science' for women.[194] As noted above, technical education for girls, which had tended to be equated with domestic economy, had not been considered academic and was associated with the employment needs of the daughters of the poor. Hence there was resistance to the inclusion of domestic subjects in secondary schools and universities. This had resulted in a curriculum which favoured the humanities which in turn limited the subjects taken by the small minority of women who went to university. Still, by the end of the century, there was increasing pressure from social Darwinists and eugenicists for domestic subjects to be introduced to middle-class girls' education.[195] Thus, at Royal Holloway College—opened in 1886 and admitted as one of the schools in the Faculties of Arts and Science of the University of London in 1900—cookery and needlework were among the subjects offered: the impressive kitchen facilities were not only for the preparation of the students' meals but also for teaching them cookery.[196] Nor was this was simply a case of such subjects being forced on female students by educational authorities, since there were efforts among some feminists to improve the status of home economics and to carve an exclusive place for the women who taught it. Indeed, the Glasgow Association for the Higher Education of Women (1877) recognised the Glasgow School of Cookery (1875) as an important development for the higher education of women in the city.[197]

While other occupations (for example, white-blouse and service sector) opened up for women, even at the end of the Victorian period, teaching was their main profession. As will be discussed in the next chapter, elementary schools were still considered socially beneath the middle class and even the establishment of higher grade schools by the larger boards in the late nineteenth century were unattractive to the majority of university-educated women who sought posts in the new high schools for girls. Only gradually did such women take posts in the training colleges and pupil-teacher centres. Thus, it was those ladies who had gone to cookery schools, the first of which was established in Kensington in 1873 with other large cities quickly following, who ventured into the schools for the poor, though they found the working-class and lower middle-class schoolmistresses reluctant to accept the peripatetic cookery teacher as their professional equal.[198]

As for university, Carol Dyhouse has observed that 'neat chronological lists of dates of entry are not easy to draw up and can be misleading' as women were often admitted to classes 'before or in some cases after' being allowed to sit degree examinations. Dyhouse also records that there were sometimes special qualifications for women, notably the distance qualification higher certificate of the LA, later LLA, from St Andrews University.[199] As Robert Bell and Malcolm Tight have noted, such certificates were a means of meeting the demand for higher education without having to admit women to degrees.[200] Whereas University College London opened to women on the same terms as men, there were also separate colleges for women, such as King's College for Women in London, Queen Margaret College which opened in Glasgow in 1883 (known as the 'Scottish Girton') and the colleges at Oxford and Cambridge where women were admitted to examinations but were not eligible to be awarded degrees. Some offered restricted access: for example, University College Liverpool (1881) admitted women from its foundation to study for the degrees of London University and Victoria University, but they were not accepted to the medical faculty until 1903. Even where women attended the same lectures as men, the sexes were separated, and the women were chaperoned to and from the classes.[201] Queen Margaret College effectively became the women's department after incorporation into Glasgow University in 1892, but Sheila Hamilton has observed that in the long term, separation limited the provision and facilities for female students.[202]

Although Wales did not have a university until 1893 when a federal examining university was set up, what became the University Colleges of Cardiff (1890), Aberystwyth (1892) and Bangor (1894) all took women on the same terms as men from the start. Robert Anderson has recorded that by 1900 women made up 15 per cent of students at universities in England, 14 per cent in Scotland but 38 per cent in Wales.[203] The movement for the admission of women to university in Ireland closely followed that of England. In both, fewer women at universities came from the lower classes than in Wales or Scotland, which may have been related to differences in social structure in the smaller and less well-off parts of the UK as well as to the high rates of female emigration from Ireland and the continuing reservations among the Catholic hierarchy over admitting women to higher education.

There were local as well as national differences. In her study of Aberdeen University, Lindy Moore found that the women who matriculated between 1894 and 1920 were overwhelmingly local, a quarter coming from professional (especially daughters of rural ministers and teachers) and a fifth from farming families. Working-class students (daughters of tradesmen and skilled manual workers) were under-represented. Moore suggests that, in contrast to other universities in Britain, there was at Aberdeen a belief that girls who were not ladies should still have an opportunity to study at university. The relative poverty and lower social class composition of female students at Aberdeen was due, Moore explains, to the relatively low cost of attendance and greater availability of financial assistance and to free or cheap secondary education. The practice at Aberdeen was for students to stay in lodgings, possibly the cheapest in Britain. Aberdeen lacked the funds to follow the moves towards residential accommodation for women students which elsewhere in Scotland, and notably in England, was considered essential for the protection of female morality; the lack of it meant that almost no upper-class girls attended Aberdeen, and few upper middle-class girls did so unless they lived with families or relatives.[204] Some in Scotland saw residential accommodation as Anglicizing: even by 1919 only 14 per cent of female students at Scottish universities lived in residential accommodation, compared with around 33 per cent of students at the English provincial universities and over 66 per cent of women at the Welsh university colleges.[205]

The university colleges in Wales were associated with the strength of Nonconformity while the Queen's Colleges in Ireland were associated with the Presbyterians. However, when Queen's University was replaced by the

Royal University of Ireland in 1870, which, like London, was an examining institution whose degrees were open to other institutions and individuals, it allowed women to sit the examinations and encouraged secondary schools and ladies' colleges to prepare their pupils for them. Alexandra College in Dublin and Victoria College in Belfast were quick to take advantage of the opportunity.[206] Indeed, it soon replaced Trinity College Dublin which catered for the Anglican-landed and professional classes and had established examinations for women in 1870.[207]

Of course, passing examinations did not necessarily provide women with recognised qualifications, but inroads were made. Whereas Oxford and Cambridge would not confer degrees on women, those who passed the examinations found posts in prestigious girls' schools. Ellen Jordan has recounted the successful struggle for professional recognition of three women who in the early 1870s had passed the examinations that entitled them to be listed as pharmaceutical chemists.[208] It proved much more difficult for women to enter medicine.[209] Whereas Elizabeth Garret Anderson claimed in 1895 that 'it is almost as easy at this moment for a woman to get a complete medical education in England, Scotland or Ireland, as it is for a man', once women graduated, they found their career opportunities were limited, while there was no similarly concerted campaign to gain entry to other elite professions.[210]

CONCLUSION

Middle-class girls' education was influenced by a variety of factors, including parental and cultural expectations, social class, religion and the economy as well as gender; and as in the previous chapter, how these interacted was linked to the local and regional context. Even at the end of the Victorian period, young ladies were educated mostly at home or in a homelike environment, and the expectation was still that they would not enter paid employment. Like their brothers, they were to be educated, not trained with a specific occupation in mind. Both married and single middle-class women were, of course, expected to perform socially useful unpaid roles related to or motivated by their religion.

There were significant advances in the formal education of Victorian young ladies, though a focus on key figures and their achievements may lead to an exaggeration of the extent of their influence. Whereas feminists and other reformers pointed to the increasing need for single ladies to find suitable ways of supporting themselves which necessitated a serious education and the opening up of the professions to women, as well as the establishment of female professions, there was still the question of the purpose of educating young ladies. It seemed clear what that was for their social inferiors: to prepare them for a life of domestic service, whether in their own home or an employer's. Certainly, a 'domestic' future was also envisaged for the young lady, but there was no agreement on how to prepare her for running her own home, though it was generally agreed that whether or not she was taught domestic skills, it was unlikely that she would perform them: even the less well-off among the middle classes employed a servant. The main argument for keeping domestic subjects out of the curriculum for young ladies was as a mark of her social superiority; the call for parity with middle-class boys' education was also a sign of social class.

That, however, was a challenge to gender divisions and male superiority within the middle class which had to be made palatable by reassurance of continuing distinctions between the sexes: hence, the emphasis on ladylike behaviour and feminine traits. The stern critics of a schooling in the social graces were stereotyping the characters of its recipients as vain, shallow and selfish, yet they did not advocate removing the accomplishments from their education for these were another mark of social standing, of superior cultivation. The educated lady would continue to value marriage and motherhood as her ideal future, but even if she had to work for a living, as increasing numbers did, she would approach whatever she did in a 'womanly' way: caring and nurturing, paying attention to detail, striving to do her best to meet the expectations of her teachers, always for the good of others and not out of personal ambition or desire for fame. The education of young ladies was not to challenge, at least not explicitly, the ideals of domesticity and femininity, but to enhance them and extend their influence.

4   The Making of a Female Teacher

This chapter looks at the development of teacher training in a broad sense, both formal and informal. There was a wide variety of teaching roles, not all of which are covered here. Rather than an attempt to be all encompassing, the focus is on social class and in particular on middle-class notions of 'training' as appropriate to the teaching of working-class children through its associations with a very limited curriculum and a relatively brief course that concentrated on practice rather than theory. This alludes to a perception of elementary school teaching as a 'craft' rather than a 'profession', though there were differences in the status of teaching the poor across the British Isles. Yet the division between the two was not as sharp as this suggests. The governess, for example, often gained classroom experience through teaching the poor (both children and adults) in charity schools, visiting and observing teachers in schools for the poor and in a minority of cases through becoming pupil teachers. The increasing demand for elementary school teachers, especially after 1870, attracted lower middle-class women, and in turn their entry into pupil teaching and training colleges led to developments in the curriculum, including a move away from the focus on the basics in the education of both. As seen in Chapter 2, however, the curriculum was always gendered; indeed, by the late Victorian period domestic subjects took up much of a working-class girl's schooling and her mistress's training. Yet while that restricted the education, in breadth as well as in depth, of both the girls and their teachers, from the early 1870s it opened up a specialism for middle-class women who studied in cookery schools.

   This chapter begins with the governess who was among a minority of the women in paid employment throughout the century but whose 'plight' so worried the middle classes that it led to significant reforms in their daughters' education, as discussed in the previous chapter. The focus then shifts to the working class and the pupil-teacher system established in 1846, among whom girls outnumbered boys from the start, a reflection both of the limited job opportunities open to girls compared to boys and of the fact that teaching was considered the most respectable way for girls of all social classes to earn a living. It was through this system that a significant number of lower-middle as well as upper-working class women entered teaching;

indeed, they came to dominate the work force numerically by the end of the century, though the pace of this 'feminization' process differed across Britain. The next three sections explore developments in the training of adult teachers, mainly but not exclusively, for the elementary sector and the colleges themselves. The emphasis remains on social class, but regional, national and, not least, religious factors also influenced the making of a female teacher and her efforts to achieve professional recognition.

THE GOVERNESS AND HER PLIGHT

Writers on female education since the eighteenth century favoured education in the home for the middle classes and in a school run by the ladies of the latter for the daughters of the poor, though boarding schools did become fashionable among the lower and middling sections of the middle classes. Teacher 'training' in the sense of improving the teacher's own education and professionalism was a subject of concern for the middle classes which persisted into the Victorian period, though typically it was not institutionalized and relied on the female teacher's own efforts to improve her skills. While her efforts have generally been admired, that has been tempered with some disdain for the assumed lack of systematic study and what Mary Wollstonecraft (1759–1797) termed a 'disorderly kind of education'.[1] Nevertheless, teaching was one of the very few respectable occupations open to such ladies, either running small schools or working as a governess in someone else's home. Indeed, Wollstonecraft herself spent an unhappy period as governess.[2]

Published in the year after Wollstonecraft's death, *Practical Education* by Maria Edgeworth and her father Richard Lovell Edgeworth advised parents not to choose a governess for her fashionable accomplishments but rather to look for a discriminating and enlarged understanding, a steady temper and an open mind, integrity and good manners. Further, *Practical Education* asserted women's right to dignity and respect through an education which would develop their rational faculties. Maria's works in particular were based on optimism about female potential and capacity for moral judgment, affirming the power of education and women's claim to it. She advocated that the job of governess should be recognised as

> an honourable profession, which a gentlewoman might follow without losing any degree of the estimation in which she is held by what is called *the world* [emphasis in the original]. There is no employment, at present, by which a gentlewoman can maintain herself without losing something of that respect, something of that rank in society, which neither female fortitude nor male philosophy willingly forgoes. The liberal professions are open to men of small fortunes; by presenting one similar resource to women, we should give a very strong motive for their moral and intellectual improvement.[3]

To the question of what young ladies were being educated for, Hannah More insisted that it was not to produce female scholars; rather, 'the great uses of study to a woman are to enable her to regulate her own mind, and to be instrumental to the good of others'.[4] More generally, writers on female education from the late eighteenth century criticized the showy and ornamental level of female accomplishments which many parents, especially in the aspiring lower middle class saw as a necessary gloss for their daughters in a competitive marriage market. But those writers did not simply dismiss the accomplishments; rather they valued them as a means of forming a girl's character, making her more rational as well as more moral.[5] Thus the Anglican clergyman and religious writer Thomas Gisborne (1758–1846) remarked at the end of the eighteenth century that although they may have been ranked too high in parental priorities, the accomplishments were necessary in a young lady's education which should 'call forth the reasoning powers of girls into action and enrich the mind with useful and interesting knowledge suitable to their sex'.[6] At the same time, a young lady was not expected to call attention to her education. Erasmus Darwin (1734–1802) advised, 'The female character should possess the mild and retiring virtues rather than the bold and dazzling ones [as] great eminence in almost anything is sometimes injurious to a young lady.'[7] Men, warned Dr John Gregory (1724–1773), 'generally look with a jealous and malignant eye on a woman of great parts, and a cultivated understanding'.[8]

This emphasis on the suitability of content in terms of gender was common to the bulk of writings on female education from the later eighteenth century. Still, the list of subjects deemed appropriate for a young lady's education was broad: music and dancing (though never so much as to forget the delicacy of the female sex); reading and reading aloud; writing, grammar, languages (specifically French and Italian, while the classics, and especially Greek, were considered less necessary, and even 'masculine'); arithmetic, geography, history, natural history, an outline of the sciences (including botany and chemistry); mythology (though care had to be taken since much of it was seen to consist of 'vices'); polite literature including plays (though the theatre was regarded as too often a shock to female delicacy), poetry and romances (though the senses and the imagination should not be over-stimulated); drawing and embroidery; and the rudiments of 'taste'.[9]

Whereas Mary Wollstonecraft advised day schools rather than boarding and Erasmus Darwin preferred a school education to home schooling, most writers on female education advocated the latter, with the mother as first educator and the employment of a governess. Generally, however, they deplored the poor rewards and low esteem in which the governess was held, insisting on the importance of her responsibility for the education of her charges. All these writers realized that governesses themselves needed a sound education and suggested that they should continue to improve their own education when their charges were young. It was the view of the

Edgeworths that between 12 and 14 years was necessary for the education of a young lady: hence, the importance of the governess.[10]

Similarly, Sarah Trimmer (1741–1810) had very definite views on governesses whose role she saw as the mother's representative but whose actual position, she felt, was too often difficult and even humiliating:

> Numbers of unhappy governesses, and amongst them persons who once moved in a higher sphere than their employers, daily experience mortifications, the recital of which would shock the feeling mind. For it is among the inconsistencies of the present age, that while *musical* and *theatrical* talents, will often gain a low bred woman admittance into the first circles, she who possesses a talent of superior value, that of being able to form the mind to goodness and virtue, and give a proper direction to all different branches of education, is thrown into the *background* [emphasis in the original], as a person of no consequence at all.[11]

Complaints both about the treatment of governesses and their own low level of education continued over the next half century. In the 1840s, for example, one writer complained about the tide of frivolity in the education of young ladies, observing ironically that whereas women 'had been the first to help themselves to the tree of knowledge', it seems as if now 'the flaming sword of public opinion [was] employed to drive them away from all approach to its vicinity'.[12]

Sarah Trimmer was active from the 1780s in establishing and running Sunday schools and schools of industry in her hometown of Brentford, Middlesex, and working with the Society for Promoting Christian Knowledge. Mother of 12, Trimmer built on her experience of two decades in the home classroom to offer practical advice for teachers (both amateur and professional). She did not write works of theory, producing instead a series of teaching aids and school books, though there were resemblances between her ideas on education and those of, for example, Locke, Rousseau, Fénelon and Madame de Genlis. [13] Indeed, from the late eighteenth century, there were many similar books directed at the governess. These included detailed instructions on how and what to teach, sometimes written in epistolary form and also memoirs of governesses.[14] In a publication of 1826, the anonymous but self-professed 'experienced teacher' who had been a governess for 20 years, had chapters on English grammar, history, arithmetic, geometry, natural philosophy, chemistry, astronomy, geography, botany, zoology and the 'accomplishments'. In the introduction, the author complained that attention was paid to 'the fingers, the ears, the tongue, and the feet' which are 'schooled in all those little arts and elegances that are calculated for momentary and external effect' but that

> the mind of the young lady, upon whom the most fashionable and expensive education has been bestowed, is left in nearly the same state

of ignorance as that of her whose external education is limited to the business of housewifery and the drudgery of domestic life. A learned man is, mentally speaking, altogether a different being from a peasant; but a lady, except in the elegance of her accomplishments, does not in many instances, at least in as far as depends on her school education, differ materially from the menial who is deputed to attend upon her.[15]

Interestingly the chapter on the accomplishments is the briefest, although the author protests both that they still have a place in female education and that the aim of educating a lady is not to make her 'learned' but a 'rational and prudent wife and mother'. This writer, like her eighteenth-century predecessors, argued that too great an emphasis on the accomplishments in both the governess and the education she imparts results in the pupils never reaching maturity, gaining only an education in 'mere externals'. At the same time, a lady should not be expected to be an expert in all the subjects covered in the book, but she should know the 'general principles of all these matters and their relation to each other', in order to prepare her to be the mother of 'well-informed and virtuous offspring' and to give her moral influence over men.[16] Whereas the previous chapters in her 'manual' for governesses were on subjects which all required knowledge and understanding, the accomplishments needed 'doing': thus, dancing and music and 'indeed all the arts by which the voice, the carriage, and the hand can be improved, must be tried and tried again, before they can be acquired'. The exception, the author held, was drawing, which, like the previous subjects, depended on 'general principles of perspective and the practice of drawing'.[17]

Nor should parents expect the governess to possess all the accomplishments; if necessary, specialists (such as musicians) might be employed in addition to the governess, and they might be male. Again, this was not new to the nineteenth century. Thus, the first announcement of the school for young ladies which Hannah More and her sisters were to open in Bristol in April 1758 had advertised that a dancing master would 'properly attend'. [18] Indeed, in Scotland even if a middle-class family could afford to employ a governess, there was a continuing preference for hiring university-educated men to teach their daughters specialist subjects, either in day schools or in the family home, into the 1860s and 1870s.[19] There was, however, always a tension, at least in England, over the employment of male teachers in girls' homes or schools. Thus, Priscilla Wakefield (1750–1832), Quaker author and philanthropist, asked whether it was 'compatible with propriety or decency' for a young lady to be 'exposed to the wanton eye of a dancing-master' or indeed a musician. In her view, only women should be allowed to instruct their own sex 'in these seductive arts'.[20]

The education of ladies in the Victorian period was still to prepare them for marriage (to be not only the husband's pleasant companion but also by implication his moral 'governess') and motherhood (as the first educators of their children). Hannah More herself never married and nor had the author of *The Complete Governess*, reflecting the relatively high rates of spinsterhood.[21] The Victorian period saw concern grow over the fate of the spinster lady who had to support herself. How could the education of the middle-class girl fit her for a career other than marriage without giving the impression that she was destined for paid employment and so undermine her social position? Critics of the standard of education among governesses argued that a woman in that position required a thorough mastery of the branches she was to teach even though she could not be expected to know everything.[22]

How, then, was how the employed lady to preserve her social standing? Governesses who became authors of works on teaching tended to insist that it was a calling, a vocation.[23] Like the writers of the late eighteenth century who either addressed governesses directly, or focused on the plight of the governess, Victorian reformers sought to convince their readers that the role was an honourable one which society ought to recognise. This was particularly the case for clergymen's daughters who were expected to make a living. Thus, Jane Hay Brown (later Hamilton, 1827–1898), the eldest daughter of a United Secession Church minister in a small town in Ayrshire, worked for much of her adult life both as a governess and in private girls' schools.[24] After the death of her father in 1847 and the family's removal from the manse, Jane followed her widowed mother Margaret to Glasgow where the latter took in lodgers, and Jane worked as a day governess to two families. A member of a secessionist church, she had no formal training as colleges were run by the Church of Scotland and, after 1843, the Free Church of Scotland, but it was generally acknowledged that 'A large proportion of ministers' daughters must depend upon their own exertions in teaching or some other mode of employment. And society, as a whole, is interested in whatever tends to elevate their intellectual status and practical uses.'[25]

Agnes Porter (c.1752–1814), born in Edinburgh and daughter of a Church of England clergyman, may also have expected to work for a living, but to protect her social position, she too did not receive formal training.[26] In this she was like the majority of governesses. Although Clara Reeve (1729–1807) had suggested a Ladies Seminary to educate destitute young gentlewomen and prepare them to be self-supporting members of society in the early 1790s, this was a minority view even in the early nineteenth century when there was increasing competition for governess positions.[27] Some did exist, such as the Cork Preparatory Seminary for Young Governesses (1828), but it was the middle of the nineteenth century before there was a serious attempt to educate and professionalize the post of governess. Indeed, even then there were reservations: Kathryn Hughes records as unusual the school in Tiverton run in the 1860s by Mary Porter (noted in the previous chapter for giving evidence to the Taunton Commission) which offered the general education of middle-class girls with the addition of 'the art of teaching'. Mary Porter's aim was to help the impoverished daughters of professional men become proficient governesses. As Hughes point out, however, even feminists and educational reformers such as Emily Davies saw vocational training as an issue of status; indeed, it was a mark of separation between social classes, with training for the lower middle-class woman who would become a teacher in a school for the poor, whereas a middle- and upper middle-class lady, however financially distressed, would lose status by entering a training college.[28] As summarized in the report of the Taunton Commission (1868), the evidence of Davies and other female reformers 'especially disclaimed' special training for teaching:

> Miss Kyberd would have good inspected schools, and girls trained to teach as part of their education; and Miss Davies thinks special Training Institutions very undesirable, while she would add, for such as desired it, six months' special training to the course of instruction [in their own school].[29]

This was at least recognition that their own education as well as their experience of, for example, teaching younger sisters and doing philanthropic work in Sunday and charity schools would not necessarily 'fit' ladies for the role of governess; but the 'special training' advocated was to be part of their liberal education, an 'add-on' but not separate. Indeed, there was a firm determination to keep the two occupations of governess and elementary schoolmistress apart: hence, resistance to training for the former was both to ensure its social and moral standing as a calling and to prevent the narrowly educated and trained teacher from climbing the social ladder by becoming a governess.[30]

PRESERVING STATUS, IMPROVING EDUCATION

Training, then, was appropriate only for those who would teach the poor. Yet complaining about the deficient education and inefficient teaching of governesses was an enduring middle-class trope from the later eighteenth century. Moreover, governesses themselves sought both to improve their skills as a teacher and their attractiveness to a potential employer. Memoirs show governesses intent on furthering their own education, as well as their interest in the theory and practice of teaching. They could read up on both: in 1860 one seasoned governess advised ladies embarking on such a career to 'buy Isaac Taylor's *Home Education* and Abbotts' *Teacher* . . . [and] have them always at hand'; to talk to successful teachers but also to gain access to 'all the schoolrooms you can, good or bad' to observe and learn from the experience of others.[31] Writing in the late 1840s, Margaret Thornley had likewise advised would-be governesses to observe schools and practicing teachers closely; moreover, some young ladies' institutions in Scotland offered additional classes in teaching methods for intending governesses.[32] Of course, this did not amount to formal training and depended on the conscientiousness and indeed the energy of the individual governess, but the writers did advise ladies to be methodical in their efforts to improve both their own education and their teaching skills.

While the continuing preference was for home education, Susan Skedd has noted that the growing practice of employing a governess among the middle classes in the early nineteenth century did not result in a reduction of the numbers of girls' schools.[33] Sometimes sisters joined forces in establishing a school for young ladies in their own homes or in a building which they could present as a substitute home for boarders, though it was also a business venture. As noted above, the More sisters did this in the south of England in the mid-eighteenth century—the highest concentration of governesses in Britain was in London and the Home Counties.[34] The experience of the Keddie sisters revealed that the same limited opportunities for respectable employment for middle-class women applied in Scotland as elsewhere in the UK. Henrietta Keddie (1827–1914), who later became a successful novelist writing as Sarah Tytler, was the seventh of eight children of a Fifeshire lawyer whose modest and diminishing income, as well as severe losses in coal mining investment, meant he could not support them in adulthood. Her elder sisters worked for several years as governesses before four of them combined forces in 1848 to open a girls' school in the small town of Cupar, where Henrietta taught for over 20 years. As she remarked in her memoirs: 'When learning dressmaking and such posts as housekeeper and waiting-maid had fallen quite out of court for girls of the middle class, there was absolutely nothing for them by which they could earn a living except as teachers.'[35]

Most if not all governesses took up a paid position out of necessity rather than by choice. In practice, it was an insecure way of earning a living, with many unable to save for retirement. Whereas the Edgeworths in the late eighteenth century had advocated that wealthy parents pay a salary of £300 a year, most governesses were paid considerably less than that. Only those who were employed by the wealthier families could command a relatively high salary, such as Ann Porter who was in the employ of Lord Ilchester in the last two decades of the eighteenth century. Even she did not meet the Edgeworths' ideal: Porter is estimated to have earned around £105 a year while she had an annuity of £30 on her retirement in 1806.[36] Indeed, Porter's annuity was more in keeping with the annual earnings of the governess: in 1809, for example, Miss Weeton's annual earnings were 30 guineas.[37] Nor did the Victorian period see much improvement: by the middle of the nineteenth century the average salary was between £20 and £45.[38] Given the fierce competition which kept payment so low, governesses had to pay attention to strengthening their bargaining power. Thus, Ellen Weeton (later Stock, 1776–1849) regretted that she had never learned French 'for, if I had only understood that in addition to my other attainments, I could have had a situation where I should have received a salary of a hundred a year, in a family of distinction'.[39]

Yet French was the most commonly learned foreign language among a young lady's accomplishments. Hence at the age of 30, Jane Brown left her day governess positions in Glasgow and went to Germany: since she could already offer French, perfecting German, it was hoped, would increase her opportunities in the educational marketplace. She is also an example of how women in her position helped each other: she was tapping into the network of her former German teacher from whom as a girl she had taken lessons in Glasgow in the 1840s and to whose East of Scotland Institution for Young Ladies Jane would send her own daughter in the 1870s.[40] In 1857 Elise Schultzen arranged a position for Jane in Hildesheim, Lower Saxony, as a 'parlour' mistress in an establishment for young ladies.

She did not, however, earn enough to pay her employer for lessons in German and drawing and to support herself without occasional remittances from her mother and brother. When their mother lost money in 1858 with the collapse of a Glasgow bank in which she had invested, Jane was concerned that her studies meant she was a continuing burden on her family. Her brother, James, was a United Secession minister like his father, though as yet without a settled parish; but on this occasion he was able to reassure his sister that he had earned enough that year to support their mother. He urged Jane not to return to Scotland but to take a governess post offered in Hanover. He even encouraged her un-chaperoned travel as he felt it would deepen her knowledge of German culture and add to her accomplishments, strengthening her chances of employment.[41]

When Jane returned to Scotland in 1859. she arranged for her friend Agnes Nichol, daughter of the professor of astronomy at Glasgow University John Pringle Nichol (1776–1859), and his first wife Jane Tullis (1809–1850), to take her place in Saxony. Twenty-five years later Miss Schultzen who was still teaching in Scotland helped Miss Yorsten, a governess who had been employed by Jane from the late 1870s until her small seminary for young ladies ceased to be a profitable venture: Miss Yorsten also went to improve her German and so her employment prospects. Thus, from the early to the late Victorian period, this small network of governesses took their studies seriously, approached them systematically and saw self-improvement as a means of adding to their curricula vitae as well as developing their skills as teachers, but their prospects remained precarious.

Hence, from the start of Victoria's reign there was much middle-class concern over 'the plight of the governess'. One result was the establishment of the Governesses' Benevolent Institution (GBI) in London in 1843, and five years later Queen's College for Women and Bedford College were founded. The two London colleges were more concerned with improving middle-class female liberal education than with imparting vocational skills, however. The Victorian middle classes had a stereotype of the elementary school teacher as uncultured and unrefined, not just because of the narrowness of their education and of the basic curriculum which they were expected to teach the children of the poor, but precisely because they were trained either (as will be discussed below) in colleges from the early nine-teenth century or as pupil teachers from the mid-1840s. This was not only a view held by ladies, since among schoolmasters only those who taught in schools for the poor were expected to have been trained: for those who taught the sons of the middle and upper classes, a university education was the usual requirement. It was not, then, until the late 1840s that a formal qualification was issued, while the certificate of academic compe-tence from Queen's College for the GBI was effectively restricted to London and to those who could afford annual fees of around £25. This amounted to the basic annual income that most governesses were able to ask for, as reflected in advertisements placed by those seeking a position.[42] It would take improvements in middle-class girls' education after the 1860s before a more systematic training was offered to ladies.

Christine de Bellaigue, however, has argued that not all governesses were either reluctant or inadequate teachers. Her study of the correspon-dence, memoirs and biographies of 83 schoolmistresses born between 1780 and 1860 has found not only that many were educated to be governesses but also that for significant numbers becoming a governess was a positive choice and not always a necessity. Moreover, she found that in this period governesses became increasingly interested in educational theory and spe-cialised training through self-study, attendance at public lectures, teaching abroad (notably in France where schoolmistresses had been examined and certificated since 1810), working in Sunday schools and in some cases even as pupil teachers.[43] Whereas de Bellaigue focuses on England, the Scottish case study of Jane Brown supports many of her arguments. It also reveals how family duties could upset even the best laid plans.

Whereas Jane had sought to improve her prospects as a governess through intensive study of the German language and culture in the late 1850s, she was not able to fulfil that plan due to the serious illness of a younger sis-ter who had emigrated to the Australian colony of Victoria earlier in that decade. She died soon after Jane's arrival in 1859, and Jane remained to look after her young nephew and niece. She married a widower, Andrew Hamilton, a year later, but when he became gravely ill in 1867, she opened a small private school for young ladies to support the family. Although the two schools she ran successively over the next couple of years were short-lived and modest ventures, they have nevertheless been recognised as con-tributing positively to the development of female education in Victoria.[44]

On being widowed in 1869, Jane returned to Scotland. She now had to support her own two children as well as her mother who was very ill. Jane took as boarders the children of overseas missionaries sent to Scotland for their education. She continued to teach but not as a day governess. Instead, she found a better-paid post as Lady Superintendent at Dowanhill Institute for Young Ladies in Glasgow, which took both boarders and day pupils. The Institute was run by a man, which was not unusual in Scotland.[45] Jane's position seems to have departed from the norm due to her family circumstances. The Lady Superintendent usually lived on the premises, but Jane did not, perhaps because her employer's wife did and also because of her own children and child boarders, as well as her sick mother. Moreover, whereas the expectation was for the Lady Superintendent to have had teaching experience, she was generally not expected to teach, but Jane did.

When her mother died in 1871, Jane was no longer tied to the city. Although the Dowanhill Institute had a good reputation for teaching older girls and indeed had 136 on the roll in 1873, Jane felt her prospects in Glasgow were uncertain, reflecting the competition between such private schools. As she had done in Australia, she decided to set up her own small school, assured of an excellent reference from her employer testifying both to her moral character and her teaching abilities. Since there was less competition back in Ayrshire than in Scotland's largest city, she decided on the coastal resort town of Largs where there was a market for a private girls' school and where costs were cheaper than in Glasgow. She established a Ladies' Seminary in the home she rented in 1873. It was a day school, but she offered to board young ladies who lived at a distance, usually from farming families. To supplement her income and in recognition of the generally limited size and often short-lived nature of such ventures, she continued to board children of missionaries, girls as well as boys under eight years of age; the latter she taught separately. Jane also advertised to take in the children of holidaying summer visitors.

Jane's employment history confirms that however well-educated and whatever the extent of her teaching experience, the life of a governess in the Victorian period remained financially precarious and socially insecure This was especially the case for an untrained teacher who would not, or could not, teach in elementary schools. In 1877 Jane's school had 26 on the roll and earned praise from the local school board despite the fact that it was private: the board believed that an 'institution of this kind was much required, and now that it has been provided we are glad that advantage is being taken of it'.[46] Yet even though demand grew high enough for Jane to employ two female assistants, by the early 1880s her seminary was becoming less profitable, and Jane increasingly relied on boarders. By then, such small private schools were being overtaken by larger establishments boasting qualified teachers. Feeling by 1885 that she could no longer make a living from the school, she moved to Edinburgh to be near her student son. She continued to take in missionaries' children as boarders, but rents in Edinburgh were high, while boarding was neither well paid nor reliable. Jane's brother supplemented a small annuity left by their mother with £30 a year, but by 1890 he was dead. Although her daughter was now living with her and contributing to the family income by teaching music, both privately and in girls' schools, this was another insecure way of earning a modest living. In 1895 Jane had to apply to charities for help. Her situation only improved the following year when her son opened his own preparatory school for boys in the town of Melrose in the Scottish borders, and she went to live with him and his family.

As this case study confirms, even at the end of the Victorian period most governesses did not have, or seek, formal qualifications, though Jane herself regretted that she had not possessed a certificate. Even those middle-class schoolmistresses who accepted the need for a more systematic education still tended to identify training with elementary teaching, which was not deemed respectable for the middle-class lady. The Victorian period, however, saw two important developments which by the late nineteenth century had resulted in both the feminization of teaching and the entry of women from the lower middle class into the elementary classroom: pupil teaching and teacher training.

PUPIL TEACHING AND SOCIAL CLASS

As noted above, some governesses had had experience as pupil teachers.[47] The system of pupil teaching introduced in 1846 by James Kay-Shuttleworth and the Committee of Council on Education is seen as opening up educational and employment opportunities for working-class and, increasingly in the later nineteenth century, lower middle-class girls; but it is also considered to have delayed the professionalization of elementary teaching, notably in England and Wales.[48] Moreover, the imposition of the pupil-teacher system on Scotland was seen as a threat to the profession as well as to the educational ladder which could lift the poor but talented boy to the university.

James Kay-Shuttleworth considered elementary teaching to be unsuitable for middle-class children who were unlikely in any case to attend the same schools as the poor. His own family employed governesses.[49] Hence he conceived pupil teaching as a means of raising the standards and efficiency of elementary schools by training within the classroom. It was a form of apprenticeship which required children to stay on at school between the ages of 13 and 18, to teach in the school during the day, then to be given instruction in school subjects for 90 minutes from the master or mistress and to be examined annually by HM Inspectors. The pupil teachers were paid £20 per annum, rising to £25 over the five-year apprenticeship, very similar to the salary of a typical governess though with responsibility for significantly higher numbers of pupils. Interestingly, as pupil teachers, boys and girls at first received the same wages, but the 1862 Revised Code decreed that girls should receive less than boys. This was part of the effort to reduce expenditure, but it was also recognition that more girls than boys were attracted to pupil teaching because the latter had more opportunities for better-paid work outside of school.

The code, however, was not simply to reassert a gendered hierarchy among pupil teachers. As Richard Aldrich has pointed out, there was alarm among politicians and administrators concerned with education that those teaching the poor who had gained qualifications were now displaying aspirations above their station and the 'necessary drudgery of teaching the basic subjects'. Hence, the code decreed that in future all grants would be made to managers who in turn would decide on the salaries of both teachers and pupil teachers.[50]

What children were taught in schools for the poor was indeed significantly narrower in scope than the education of their social superiors. Yet even such an elementary curriculum was gendered along the lines of what male and female pupil teachers were expected to teach. Girls were not examined in the 'masculine' subjects, such as algebra and the geography of the British Empire. They were expected instead to focus on domestic subjects. Indeed Kay-Shuttleworth saw this as essential for social stability. Writing in 1846 he reflected that

> The domestic arrangements of the poor are often extremely defective, from want of knowledge of the commonest arts and maxims of household economy. A girl who works in a factory or a mine, or who is employed from an early hour in the morning until the evening in field labour, has little or no opportunity to acquire the habits and skill of a housewife.[51]

While this reflected both the reality of poor children's and women's paid employment and endorsed the generally accepted division of labour between the sexes, one complaint was the extra burden on both pupil teachers and teachers; another was that the latter neglected the instruction of the former, even as (or precisely because) they relied so heavily on the pupil teachers. As one witness to the Royal Commission into the Working of the Elementary Education Acts, the Cross Commission, remarked in 1886, there was 'a great tendency to accentuate the "teacher" part of the contract and to neglect the "pupil" part'.[52] To compensate for this, larger school boards set up pupil-teacher centres. Wendy Robinson's research has shown that the evening and sometimes weekend classes which the pupil teachers had to attend gradually gave way to a half-day system, with pupil teachers spending half in school and half in the centre. Thus, the responsibility for training pupil teachers was taken from the school teacher, while the staff in the centres had higher certificates or university degrees by the end of the century.[53]

At the same time, the restriction in the hours spent by pupil teachers working in schools led boards, especially in England, to make savings on salaries by increasingly employing un-certificated and untrained adult women[54] James Kay-Shuttleworth had envisaged that by the end of their apprenticeship pupil teachers would be efficient classroom managers and the successful ones could compete for Queen's scholarships to go on to teacher-training colleges, but in practice the majority of pupil teachers in England did not do so because that required a further two years of study in which the colleges spent more time on academic (effectively secondary) and moral education than on practical skills. Instead, most former pupil teachers in England remained un-certificated teachers, paid at lower rates than those who qualified.[55]

This was also the case in Ireland, where the majority of national school teachers were untrained, but it was particularly the case in Catholic schools throughout Britain and notably in Scotland where Irish Catholics constituted a more significant minority than in England. The earlier arrival in Glasgow of female religious orders, the Franciscan Sisters of the Immaculate Conception (1847) and the Sisters of Mercy (1849), meant that, contrary to the situation in the parochial school system, Catholic girls had a better (relatively speaking) education than Catholic boys.[56] Within a decade this seemed to change with the arrival of the Marist Brothers (1858) and of the Jesuits (1859), although the latter concentrated on schooling middle-class boys.[57] However, the pupil-teacher system may have compensated for the girls' apparent loss of that early advantage as it gave opportunities for those Catholic girls whose parents could afford to do without either their wages or their help at home. There were efforts to attract boys to pupil teaching: special grants were given to male pupil teachers and to male students and their teachers at training colleges which were not offered to females. This not only failed to bring more males into pupil teaching, but only a minority of Catholic girls became pupil teachers and even fewer went on to training college. Whereas the church considered teaching a respectable occupation for a woman, for parents the needs of the family came first so that daughters took factory work as soon as possible.[58]

Nevertheless, Catholic schools in Britain relied very heavily on pupil teachers, mainly because they were unable to afford the wages paid to certificated teachers. As a result the pupil teachers could turn to their own lessons only after an exhausting day's teaching.[59] Thus, the Catholic School Committee recorded a Scottish Inspector's assessment in 1889:

> Our Catholic candidates are kept hard at work all day in school (in some cases till six in the evening), having, as a rule, no more than one hour of instruction five times a week, from a teacher worn out with her hard day's work. The Board candidates, on the other hand, are allowed to leave their schools to attend afternoon classes taught by first-rate masters—men who have taken university degrees, and who devote themselves to special subjects—and by mistresses engaged for tuition at the 'Centres', who come fresh to their work, and have no school duties to absorb their time and strength. The same tutors and governesses succeed each other throughout the day on Saturdays; while every facility that money can procure in the shape of books and apparatus is at the command of their fortunate pupils. Until something of the kind is done for Catholics they can never meet their competitors on equal grounds.[60]

Although the inspector spoke of 'candidates' without specifying gender, girls outnumbered boys as pupil teachers from the start. He did identify the teacher as female: by 1880 there were already three to four times as many women as men at all levels of the teaching profession in the Glasgow Archdiocese.[61]

This reliance on pupil teachers reflected the poverty of the Catholic minority, not only in Scotland but throughout Britain. Indeed, it was typically also the case in rural areas where they lacked the benefits brought by pupil-teacher centres. More generally, the pupil-teaching system was intended to reinforce both social and gender hierarchies and to segregate the social classes. Yet studies have shown how lower middle-class parents came to see elementary school teaching as an acceptable occupation for their daughters, especially with the development of higher grade schools in the later nineteenth century. Frances Widdowson has claimed that lower middle-class girls were becoming pupil teachers as early as the 1860s and in increasing numbers once school boards were established in England and Wales with the Elementary Education Act of 1870. Moreover, once universities became associated with day training colleges from the 1890s, academically better educated middle-class students who did not have the experience of pupil-teaching apprenticeships began to attend, though Widdowson also points out that elementary school teaching was still generally considered an unsuitable occupation for such ladies up until 1914.[62]

Indeed, the pupil-teacher system was both to improve the schooling of the poor and limit their education to the basics. It offered a restricted social mobility to the pupil teachers, while it aimed to socialize the working class generally and raise their moral standards.[63] It was the socially exclusive nature of the English system of elementary education, its reliance on pupil and un-certificated teachers which upset educationalists in Scotland, with its tradition of a national system of parish schools and university-educated schoolmasters.[64] More generally, the pupil-teaching system contained formal distinctions in the curriculum according to gender which, as discussed in Chapter 2, were seen as undermining the academic content of Scotland's parish schools.

Yet the development of the pupil-teacher system revealed similarities between England, Wales and Scotland. Throughout Britain, the system was quickly dominated by girls. Whereas in 1876 there were just under 19,500 female pupil teachers, there were just over 11,102 males; within 20 years there were 26,757 females to only 7,245 males.[65] At the same time, in regions where there were better-paid job opportunities girls who might have been expected to stay on at school and train as pupil teachers—mainly daughters of skilled workers and small-scale tradesmen—left to add to the family income. The list of occupations of girls attending evening classes of the Edinburgh School Board in 1893–1894 showed how much competition there now was: of 830 young women who attended only one was recorded as a pupil teacher. At the same time, that nearly half of those in attendance were listed as 'at home and unemployed' suggests that not only were daughters often needed to help with housework and childcare but also that such a long period of apprenticeship followed by two years of training was a costly burden for working-class parents.[66] Nevertheless, as early as 1851 an inspector noted that in many places in Scotland girls were being kept on at school longer than boys.[67] The same was the case in England and Wales: as Chapter 2 has shown, by the later Victorian period, girls were more likely to remain at school in rural or mining areas where there were more employment opportunities for boys, whereas the situation was reversed in textile areas.

Generally, then, where parents could afford to keep daughters at school and where there were few job opportunities for girls, pupil teaching was attractive, both in terms of future pay and social status. The latter point was important: elementary schoolgirls had a rather limited range of poorly remunerated jobs open to them, while pupil teaching provided a way into the profession, even if not on an equal basis with men. In Scotland and Wales, then, it offered a rise, albeit modest, in social status since teaching was more highly regarded than in England. On the other hand, there was concern in Scotland that as schoolmistresses came to outnumber masters, the educational tradition, based on the university-educated dominie, was under threat of being reduced to the elementary level of England.[68]

However, as school boards throughout Britain introduced higher grade schools in the later nineteenth century, the education of pupil teachers broadened to enable them to teach above the lower standards.[69] Both Wendy Robinson and Meriel Vlaeminke found evidence of academic progress for girls in English higher grade schools, many of which were co-educational.[70] That was more like the preference for mixed-sex schooling in Scotland where higher grade schools were designed with university requirements in mind as a means of reviving the national tradition. However, they went against the 'democratic' aspect of the parish schools since they tended to be designed to attract middle-class pupils. Indeed, Garnethill Public School in Glasgow followed the trend in England by becoming a High School for Girls in 1898 to attract middle-class girls who would not have gone to a mixed-sex public school. Both as a board school with a mixed-sex higher grade department and then a single-sex high school, girls were taught the university subjects of Latin and Greek.[71]

While this was in contrast to the more limited curriculum offered in England, Garnethill was unusual in Scotland in following the English preference for single-sex schools. As noted in previous chapters, traditionally Scots saw the element of competition between the sexes as stimulating the girls' academic performance. Mixed-sex schooling continued to predominate in Scotland, and for reasons of economy spread in England and Wales. Pupil-teacher centres, moreover, were usually mixed sex, though girls predominated numerically. As in board schools, the curriculum in the centres was gendered, with domestic subjects compulsory for girls who were assumed to be less 'intellectual' than the boys, even where, as Wendy Robinson has pointed out, the latter did not perform as well as girls in the examinations.[72]

There was growing concern about the education of pupil teachers by the later nineteenth century. This may partly have been a result of improvements in elementary education under the larger school boards which persuaded some lower middle-class parents to see elementary school teaching as an acceptable career for their daughters.[73] By then, it was increasingly thought that pupil teachers needed the experience of secondary education. Indeed, there were complaints in the 1880s about the low level of education of both pupil teachers and trainee teachers and the low numbers of certificated teachers. One witness to the Cross Commission, Rev. Warburton, complained that the ratio of trained to untrained schoolmistresses was decreasing every year 'by bounds and strides'. He advocated more training colleges for women, particularly non-denominational ones.[74] In response the larger boards had established higher grade schools. However, the Bryce Commission into secondary education in 1895 accepted that these schools carried the education of children 'beyond the limits which the parliamentary grant had fixed': i.e., they were secondary, rather than elementary. [75] The Bryce Commission also highlighted what it saw as a significant change in attitude: ' . . . the idea that a girl, like a boy, may be fitted by education to earn a livelihood, or, at any rate, to be a more useful member of society has become more widely diffused.'[76]

As noted in Chapter 2, however, there was continuing resistance among middle-class parents to sending their daughters to elementary schools.[77] One factor was the growth of mixed-sex schooling in England, especially in rural areas, which reflected lingering concern that mixed-sex schooling would upset the gendered curriculum, to the detriment of girls' domestic education.[78] This, it was held, and not such 'male' subjects as mathematics and the sciences, prepared a girl for her future: working-class boys and girls would have different adult roles and their schooling should take account of that.[79] The specific subjects and the higher grade schools, then, were seen to provide an education which was useful, even necessary, for working-class boys but unsuitable for their sisters who could not gain entry into the relevant trades.

Indeed this gendered division of labour was reflected in the pupil-teacher centres where girls far outnumbered boys. For example, at Manchester's Central Pupil-Teachers' School, there were 240 girls in 1895 but only ten boys.[80] Such a sex-ratio was typical of these centres which were nominally mixed sex but predominantly girls' schools. Both the centres and the higher grade schools were considered to be providing secondary education and to do so increasingly for lower middle-class children which had not been the intention of the 1870 Act. As Wendy Robinson has identified, this concern about over-educating the working class, and especially the girls, was a factor in the decline of the pupil-teaching system, the development of secondary schools, the reinforcement of the segregation of social classes and the growing incursion of lower middle-class women into elementary school teaching. [81]

Moreover, whereas there had been glowing praise for the pupil-teacher centres in both the Cross and Bryce Commissions, the girls' curriculum at the end of the Victorian period was even more heavily weighted towards domestic subjects than at the beginning. Although this was considered essential to equip them to teach working-class girls, there was concern that such training was too narrowly based and that while due attention had to be paid to domestic skills, more was needed to raise the morals and manners of girls of the industrious classes. In this endeavour, the lower middle-class woman could add 'tone'. Wendy Robinson has set the rise of an exclusively college-based system of teacher training against the deliberate decline of pupil-teacher centres and the relocation of pupil teachers to secondary schools.[82] This development did not necessarily result in an increase in certificated teachers in elementary schools, however. Alec Ellis has recorded that in 1898 among elementary school teachers in England and Wales, 51 per cent of females and 29 per cent of males had not gained a certificate from a training college.[83] What it did do was further encourage lower middle-class women to become elementary school teachers, pushing out working-class girls whose parents could not afford secondary education, which many in any case did not consider useful for their daughters. Notwithstanding this change in the social composition of schoolmistresses, the feminization of elementary teaching generally was confirmed, and even extended, by the end of the Victorian period.

There was a similar development in Scotland. Whereas it had been the practice in parish schools since the Reformation to have a male teacher, even by the middle of the nineteenth century women were entering teaching in greater numbers, helped by the introduction of pupil teaching in 1846. Indeed this reflected the fact that Scotland's education system was coming under the increasing influence of the Treasury and of English practices, including not only the pupil-teacher system but also 'payment by results'. As previously noted, there was concern among Scottish educationalists that the former would undermine the position of the dominie, and that the latter would narrow the curriculum to the basics, emasculating the educational tradition of teaching higher (university) subjects in parish schools. In his report to the Argyll Commission, Assistant Commissioner Sellar advocated a combination of university education and normal school training for the male teacher, arguing that the former made the man, the latter the teacher. Sellar examined the normal schools in Glasgow and considered the education they provided as too narrowly professional for the male pupil teacher. In his view some university education would broaden it:

> unless we wish education in Scotland reduced to the same dead-level of quality, and our parish school system assimilated in all respects to the lower ideal of education existing in England, the teachers sent forth by the normal schools will fall below our former traditions and requirements.[84]

It was not proposed that every schoolmaster should attend university, but it was considered desirable that teachers in the rural parish schools and in the larger and more important schools in the towns should have the benefits of the general culture afforded by time at university. The idea of the schoolmistress attending university was not yet considered. Her place was in the normal school or training college, just like in the rest of the UK.

TEACHER TRAINING

The pupil-teacher system became the main point of entry into training colleges in the second half of the nineteenth century, but the beginnings of training for teachers of the poor in England may be seen almost half a century earlier in the monitorial system established by Joseph Lancaster and Andrew Bell, the former of the British and Foreign School Society (BFSS) and the latter the National School Society. Arguably monitorialism was more concerned with economy and discipline than teaching since one teacher was expected to supervise up to hundreds of children—Lancaster boasted even a thousand—with the help of monitors. Still, from the start Lancaster saw a need for training: at his Borough Road school from 1805, he had a number of young people who lived with him, while they served a short apprenticeship as monitors, and he trained them both in his methods and what he regarded as appropriate moral and behavioural standards.[85]

His methods of teaching and training teachers had international influence, while within the UK they were quickly adopted in Ireland. Indeed, Lancaster spent time travelling and lecturing there in 1806. The Kildare Place Society (1815) played a leading role in the development of teacher training, opening model schools in Dublin for men and, from 1829, for women. Like Lancaster's, the society's courses were brief—at first, around a month, then in 1822, two months. Throughout the UK establishments which adopted monitorialism were designed to produce teachers for elementary schools: by 'providing a minimum of education, the training colleges strove to impart to their students a level of academic knowledge just slightly above that of the students they would be teaching and a high degree of moral training'.[86] At first male students outnumbered female, while both students and the majority of staff were working class.

Whatever the attitude to training among the middle classes, as Jane Martin and Joyce Goodman have argued by the early nineteenth century, there were some professionalization strategies around 'spiritual motherhood or social maternalism', reflected in organisations such as the Ladies' Committee of the BFSS as well as female missionary societies.[87] The role of the Ladies' Committee (set up in 1813) was to superintend the affairs of the Female Department of the Borough Road School and Training Establishment and ensure that suitable young women were trained in the methods of the Lancaster system. The Ladies themselves did not run the training establishment on a daily basis; that was done by a woman, Ann Spring-man, who had already been trained by Joseph Lancaster. Such women were expected to dedicate themselves to teaching the poor, both in Britain and as foreign missionaries. Although the role of the Ladies' Committee became increasingly redundant due to the appointment of mixed committees, male inspectors (from both the society itself and the HMI), as well as the intro-duction of the Queen's Scholarship scheme in 1846, the BFSS continued to train female teachers throughout the Victorian period.[88]

The monitorial system persisted in Ireland, and indeed was extended in 1863. By 1831, the Commissioners of the Irish Education Inquiry had noted there were around 12,532 teachers in Ireland, of whom 2,380 (that is, 482 women and 1,898 men) had been trained in the Kildare Place model schools.[89] However, the Education Commission gave the same recogni-tion to monitors trained in large convent schools as to those in district model schools, which is seen as a factor in the feminization of the teaching workforce in Ireland, since the former trained many more teachers than the two colleges run by the Commissioners of National Education.[90] In contrast, in Wales it was not until 1872 that teacher training became avail-able for women with the opening of Swansea Training College by the BFSS, although a college for women only in Aberystwyth had been considered the year before. It was another 20 years before a day training college was opened at Aberystwyth for men and women, indicating that most students were local.[91]

While England and Ireland pioneered the monitorial system, in Scotland David Stow (1793–1864) disliked both it and the later pupil-teacher sys-tem, dependent as they were on children not much older than the ones they taught. The man responsible for the introduction of the pupil-teacher sys-tem, Kay-Shuttleworth, was also influenced by Stow's ideas, seeing the nor-mal school as forming the character of the schoolmaster.[92] Stow favoured trained adult teachers, both male and female, and although not the first, he is often seen as the inspiration for teacher training in Britain. He had looked to and borrowed from France's system of 'normal' schools, and he had been impressed by Samuel Wilderspin's programme of infant educa-tion. The relationship between Stow and Wilderspin (1791–1866) reflected the borrowing in the development of teacher education throughout the UK. Indeed, when Stow set up the Glasgow Infant School Society in 1827, he invited Wilderspin to advise it. Stow's teachers were trained first in the model school he attached to the society and then in the college affiliated to it, which was set up in 1837. However, whereas women soon predominated in elementary school teaching, especially of infants, the male domination of the profession in Scotland meant a slower rate of feminization than in the rest of the UK: in the first year of training at Stow's college only ten of the 96 teachers were female.[93]

Stow prioritised the moral over the intellectual benefits of schooling the poor, and while he was not the pioneer of teacher training, his method was regarded as the most systematic and very influential.[94] Thus, in his history of the teaching profession in England and Wales, Asher Tropp observed that training was particularly influenced by Stow's work, that demand grew for Stow's 'trainers', especially from his Normal Training Seminary at Glasgow, and that both the National Society and the BFSS sent deputations to study Stow's methods, while the Wesleyans sent their students to train in his seminary. Similarly, the Home and Colonial Society, founded in 1836 for training schoolmistresses and governesses, moved away from the monitorial system in its training college, embracing Pestalozzian theories.[95]

An early example of a Victorian woman teacher whose education and career incorporated both domestic and institutional schooling, reflecting the move of a minority of middle-class women from governessing to school teaching, was Jane Chessar (1835–1880). Born in Edinburgh, Jane's mother was widowed when her three daughters still required schooling. Jane's was a mixture of attendance at private schools and having lessons in her family home, which was typical for middle-class girls in Scotland, but in her case, the acknowledged aim was to prepare her to support herself as a teacher. To that end, she enrolled at the Home and Colonial College in London in 1851. Within a year, she was appointed as one of the organising mistresses who trained teachers, serving until the mid-1860s when illness forced her resignation, though she maintained her association with the college. She also continued to teach, notably at Frances Buss's North London School and became a member of Maria Grey's Teacher's Training and Registration Society, on whose council Frances Buss served.[96]

Once again, this highlights the importance of informal as well as formal networks for female teachers. Chessar, moreover, was part of a network of people who sought not only to promote the interests of particular teachers but also improvements in middle-class girls' education. An important figure here was Joseph Payne (1808–1876), who held that women and men were equal in mental capacities.[97] He had been a founder-member of the College of Preceptors in the same year as pupil teaching was adopted. A year later, he had become an examiner for the college's teachers' examination in the theory as well as practice of education. The college, however, was mainly concerned with the education of the middle class with the aim of improving the quality and raising the status of teachers, female as well as male. A Ladies' Department was quickly set up, reflecting a recognition that the college's certificates, which were for secondary, not elementary, education, conferred on their holders an aura of professionalism.[98] Payne was also associated with Maria Grey, being one of the first shareholders of the Girls' Public Day School Company and chairing its council in 1872, the year in which he also became chairman of the Women's Education Union (set up in 1871). Jane Chessar, too, served on the union's governing board.

Another woman who moved within this circle was Dorothea Beale who as we have seen had been a trenchant critic of middle-class girls' education. She had also long been an advocate of properly trained teachers, though in her view their training should differ from that of elementary schoolmistresses. She preferred 'in-house' training at her Cheltenham Ladies' College. Her counterpart in London Frances Buss preferred separate training institutions, including the Home and Colonial Institute and Maria Grey's Training College. Whatever the type of training establishment, they were from the 1860s catering for the increasingly professional mistresses who sought to carve a career for themselves in the new middle-class girls' schools.[99]

In addition, from the 1860s middle-class schoolmistresses began formally to associate together, such as in the London Schoolmistresses Association established by Emily Davies in 1866 and the prestigious Association of Headmistresses of Endowed and Proprietary Schools, founded by Frances Buss in 1874. Whereas male teachers' professionalism lay in their academic, especially university, education, and they resisted training unless they were teaching in elementary schools, women increasingly saw specialised training as a means of gaining professional status.[100]

True, the Bryce Commission into secondary education reported in 1895 that 'as a general rule there can be no doubt that women, like men, with good university qualifications can obtain employment without special professional preparation'. The introduction of public examinations in England since the 1840s, however, had gradually led to the construction of professional identity at least partially based on formal written examinations.[101] Even in the late Victorian period, there was considerable anxiety about the impact of this process, not only for female education, but notably over the issue of whether public examination would offer advancement to 'all sorts and conditions of men'. As Alice Cooper (1846–1917), headmistress of Edgbaston High School for Girls between 1873 and 1895, observed, examinations in schools should be 'the servants not the masters of the teachers'. Her concern was the girl who passed school examinations with honours, went on to university and then became a teacher, but who displayed 'sufficient brain power to get learning without much capacity for real culture'. Such a schoolmistress was, she contended, 'the last person one really needs for the proper education of girls'.[102] This concern was echoed by Lucy Soulsby (1856–1927), headmistresses of Oxford High School for girls between 1887 and 1897: 'book learning is but one of the many qualifications which are needed to make the real teacher. University honours are no guarantee for the moral thoughtfulness which is the main qualification.'[103] Still, Alice Cooper did promote the professional development of secondary schoolmistresses, suggesting to the Bryce Commission that there should be a year's training at university where the would-be mistress received lectures in theory, followed by the probationer's year in school.[104] Indeed, in 1897 she herself moved into teacher training at Oxford where she had been a member of the council for Somerville College since 1891.[105]

Thus, whereas Frances Buss was enthusiastic about public examinations, other headmistresses, including Dorothea Beale, were like Alice Cooper, at least at first, wary of the public examination of lady teachers (and pupils), suspicious of the element of competition and preferring to make their own arrangements, notably inviting the local university to inspect and examine in school.[106] That association of training with an acquired skill rather than with intellect and a liberal education persisted. Generally qualified elementary teachers were not accepted as genuine professionals but were caught somewhere between those and industrial workers. Besides the social hierarchy, Alison Prentice and Marjorie Theobald have argued that gender played a part too since most elementary school teachers were female: not only were the professions associated with middle-class men, but because schoolmistresses were in paid employment, they could not match the image of true womanhood.[107]

The College of Preceptors had opened its examination to women only three years after it was set up; by 1869, 88 of the 953 candidates were female. While male candidates always outnumbered female in the late Victorian period, the numbers of both grew until in 1893 there were 7,012 girls to 9,039 boys. As Andrea Jacobs has shown, the girls' examination results were better than the boys': in 1891 the average pass rate for boys was 59 per cent, whereas for girls it was 65.3 per cent.[108] In 1871 two prominent women campaigners for improvements in female education, Frances Buss and the Froebelian follower, Beate Doreck (1833–1875), were elected to the Council of the College of Preceptors, and two years later they became the first two women awarded fellowships by the college.[109]

These developments in teacher training reflected the growing view that it was considered no longer enough to teach through monitorial methods: rather than rote learning, the teacher was expected to raise the moral and cultural level of the pupils, to teach them both to know and to accept their place in society and to fill a useful role. For girls, the latter revolved around their domestic duties which ensured that the syllabus at teacher-training colleges was similarly gendered. Indeed, the teachers were also trained to accept their place and not to aspire to intellectual or professional advancement. However, as Frances Widdowson has pointed out, the increase in the numbers of lower middle-class girls going to these colleges from the 1860s led to pressure to reduce the vocational/domestic subjects and to raise the intellectual and cultural level of their education.[110]

TRAINING COLLEGES

Whereas school boards ran the pupil-teacher centres until 1890, teacher-training establishments were under the control of the churches. In England, the Anglican Church dominated—by 1887, 30 of the 44 residential training colleges were Church of England—though the state had significant influence since it doled out grants and enforced codes and inspections. Initially, many training schools and colleges were mixed sex, but they soon became single sex.[111] Kim Lowden's study of Anglican and Catholic contributions to women's teacher training in the nineteenth century noted that although convents attracted middle- and even upper-class women to the teaching profession, by the 1870s women who had experienced pupil-teacher apprenticeships made up the majority of Anglican training college staff. The training courses were two years in duration, but Lowden also records that such colleges run by formal religious orders offered a broader curriculum than that specified by government requirements.[112]

While as noted above, only a minority of Catholic girls became pupil teachers and fewer went on to training college, by the late nineteenth century, there was a chance for those able to stay on to obtain a post-elementary education, for example, with the establishment in Glasgow in 1894 of the first (in Scotland) Catholic teacher-training institution, Dowanhill College, run by the sisters of Notre Dame. It was for the training of schoolmistresses which confirmed the even greater dependence on female teachers in Catholic than in board schools, but it also gave those women an opportunity to enter a respected profession. Indeed, whereas the church had tried to attract men into its schools, it now accepted its reliance on women, not least because a training college for men would have been considerably more expensive. Reverend school-managers were particularly reliant on low salaried employees. Catholic schoolmistresses were paid less than both Catholic male teachers and female board teachers. In 1911, the average annual salary of male teachers in Catholic schools was £4 lower than their equivalents in board schools and that of Catholic women teachers was on average £7 lower than board schoolmistresses who in turn received on average around half the salary of their male counterparts.[113]

Whereas it was a religious order which ran Catholic training colleges, the majority of students were lay women, but that does not mean the religious who taught were untrained: before the establishment of Catholic training colleges religious congregations both trained those sisters who were directed to teaching in their own convent schools, and after 1856 Catholic training colleges supplied significant numbers of qualified schoolmistresses who entered religious life. Moreover, the Sisters of Notre Dame (at Mount Pleasant Training College, Liverpool, 1856) assured their students that they stood 'between the priests and the parents and like them derive authority from Almighty God'.[114] Whereas the clergy considered that the training the women received should essentially be limited to the narrow range of subjects they were expected to teach, the training received from the sisters included management not only of Irish parents who had to be dealt with firmly and professionally but also of priests. With the latter, tact rather than firmness was advised, but the teachers were reminded that they were the experts on 'professional educational issues'.[115]

Moreover, the first principal of Glasgow's Dowanhill College had come from Mount Pleasant College, and just as in Liverpool, where possible, she widened the curriculum beyond government requirements to include, for example, foreign and classical languages. According to Barbara Walsh, the records for the Sisters of Notre Dame de Namur at Liverpool reveal that in the late 1880s some sisters held teacher-training qualifications in advanced science long before those subjects were taught to girls. Walsh claims that teaching congregations led the way in opening up opportunities for girls to attain the highest degree of education by the end of the Victorian period, and similar claims are made for Scotland.[116] By the 1890s qualified Catholic schoolmistress were being encouraged to continue their education if at all possible, including taking the matriculation examinations for London University and the LLA from St Andrew's.[117] One example was Miss Mary Ginlay, headmistress of Holy Cross mixed-sex school in Glasgow, which had an all-female staff. She received the LLA in 1898. The HMI report for 1900 noted approvingly that she taught the most senior class:

> Nothing can have a more beneficial effect upon the older pupils and tend more to induce them to prolong their stay at school than the feeling that they are being directly taught and trained by the most highly qualified teacher.[118]

She was not unique among Catholic schoolmistresses: in 1893 it was reported that 'several' students at the Mount Pleasant College in Liverpool were preparing for the matriculation examination of London University for the first time, with the aim of raising the standard of education and 'mental cultivation' so that these women could in turn improve the education in Catholic schools, pupil-teacher centres and training colleges; ten years later, nine Dowanhill students registered at Glasgow University, while in 1906 the Notre Dame sisters were given permission to attend the University and take higher degrees.[119] These were not typical of the teaching force in Catholic schools, however. Even at the end of the Victorian period, two-thirds of female Catholic teachers (and one-half of males) were untrained.[120]

Indeed, since only a tiny minority of Catholic schoolmistresses was able to take advantage of such opportunities to further their professional development, HMI reports tended to highlight the lack of a serious intellectual education for the mostly unqualified teachers in Catholic schools. As one inspector reported in 1891, notwithstanding improvements there was a limit to what could be achieved with a still under-educated teaching force. In his view

> It is a deficiency which no industry of teachers, no skill of the managers, no stimulus of inspection can remedy, for it arises solely from the intellectual defects of a staff who have not received a regular and thorough training. By this I mean, not merely a training in the method of teaching, but a training in intellectual study. The good teacher must first of all be the good student.[121]

This reflects the long-standing belief in Scotland that the 'higher culture' gained at university which was not available in 'any institution devoted to purely professional training ... will greatly help in maintaining the high standard which has always been a traditional characteristic of Scottish education'.[122] This preponderance of teachers in Catholic schools without certificates was mirrored in the elementary schools of England: indeed, while females outnumbered males among elementary teachers, a higher proportion of the men held certificates by the 1890s. Thus in 1895, 67.26 per cent of the men and 47.04 per cent of the women had trained for two years, while 29.21 per cent of the men and 50.77 per cent of the women were untrained.[123]

In contrast to the churches in Britain holding sway over teacher training, Ireland at first had a non-denominational college, at Marlborough Street in Dublin (1833). This appeared to mark the demise of the Kildare Society's institution, but the Church of Ireland's decision to remain outside the national system led to its Education Society (1839) leasing the premises from the Kildare Society in 1855, including the model schools and training college. It ran both male and female departments, the latter always being the larger. Disestablishment hit this work very hard as the church found it increasingly difficult to finance the training college without government subsidy. Even the church's own schools could not afford to hire trained teachers. Nevertheless, the college attracted students from the north, and in the 1890s the female department developed significantly.[124]

However, only a minority of Catholic teachers trained there, and by the mid1870s religious orders were establishing training colleges: the Vincentian Fathers opened a training college for males in 1875 in Drumcondra, and two years later the Sisters of Mercy opened a new training school in Baggot Street, Dublin, which in 1883 was recognised by the government as a teacher-training college for women, Our Lady of Mercy College.[125] This was in line with the growing resistance to non-denominational education, but it was also official recognition of the key role played by female religious in the schooling of poor children in Ireland. While there have been similar claims for the religious teaching orders, especially the female ones, in Britain it was as noted above only in 1895 that a Catholic teacher-training college for women was opened in Scotland, while there was none in Wales. For most of the Victorian period, teaching qualifications were sought mainly in England, where a Catholic training college was set up for men in Hammersmith in 1850 and for women in Liverpool about five years later.[126] The majority of teachers in Catholic schools throughout the British Isles remained without certificates into the twentieth century.

Indeed, generally the demand for teachers in England and Wales after the 1870 Elementary Education Act led to great strain on the training colleges. Despite growth in numbers of certificate teachers and of pupil teachers in the elementary schools of England, un-certificated 'assistant' teachers (usually former pupil teachers who had not gone on to college) increased at a faster rate:

		1870	1895
Certificated Teachers:	Male	6395	21,223
	Female	6072	32,718
Assistant Teachers:	Male	487	5,047
	Female	775	22,914
Additional Teachers:	Male	6384	7,246
	Female	8228	26,757
Additional Teachers:	Female	-	11,678

Source: Tropp, *The School Teachers*, pp.114, 118. The 'additional' women teachers had no qualifications but had to be over 18 years of age, vaccinated and approved by the HMI.

According to Pamela Horn, by the eve of the First World War, 66 per cent of male and 32 per cent of female elementary school teachers were certificated. She drew attention to the sharp increase in the employment of women teachers not only without certificates but also without training, particularly in rural areas, from 13 per cent of the total employed in 1875 to 41 per cent in 1914.[127] In contrast, by that date the majority of women teachers in board schools in Scotland and just over half of elementary schoolmistresses in Wales were certificated and trained.[128] This reflected the higher status of teachers in Scotland and Wales, whereas in England the middle classes sneered at the 'pretensions' of elementary teachers.[129]

Yet despite the fact that the majority of students in colleges in Wales were Welsh, the Welsh language was not taught at Swansea until the twentieth century, though as noted in Chapter 2, this does not mean that the trainees were ignorant of the language since they were generally themselves Welsh, and outside of the classroom their social life was bound up with the chapel.[130] Of course, teaching in board schools was in English, but in the still popular Sunday schools Welsh remained the language of instruction. In recognition of the continuing prevalence of the Welsh language, it was introduced to elementary schools as a specific subject in 1888, as Gaelic had been in Scotland in 1886. In both cases, however, it was as a subject rather than a medium of education, with the language regarded as belonging in the home, not the school.

Still, there was growing recognition that teachers who knew only English were not sufficient in areas where it was not the first language. Thus, by the end of the century the Society in Scotland for Propagating Christian Knowledge was promoting post-elementary education, mainly but not only for boys. Two bursaries were offered to boys and two to girls who wanted to become teachers to enable them to enter a training college: in 1887, 20 boys and 17 girls competed for these. But Gaelic-speaking boys were offered more: four bursaries were offered to help them continue their education at secondary school, and four were awarded by competition to Gaelic-speaking young men about to enter university for the first time, with another four for students who had already attended two sessions at university.[131] Generally, however, the educational establishment and many teachers themselves regarded Gaelic and the Welsh language as inhibiting educational progress and tended to discourage its use.[132] Thus, English was the language of teacher training throughout the British Isles.

By this time, there was a growing tension between the low status of the elementary school teacher in England and the growing need of middle-class women to find respectable employment. As Elizabeth Edwards has pointed out, teaching the poor had been considered part of a middle-class lady's philanthropic duty, and even after the 1870 Act, there were 'lady visitors' who were meant to raise the cultural level of elementary schoolchildren, especially the girls.[133] This was the case throughout the UK: from the mid-nineteenth century philanthropists and feminists both sought to persuade the middle class of the propriety of doing such work full time and for a salary, not simply out of the necessity for increasing numbers of ladies to earn a living but also as a means of refining the manners of the poor, including the lower-class elementary schoolmistresses.[134]

Moreover, especially after the 1870 Education Act, there were opportunities for women to rise in the profession in England and Wales. Whereas men continued to dominate promoted posts in the teaching profession in Scotland even after the numbers of schoolmistresses outnumbered them by the later nineteenth century, in England the preference for single-sex schools gave scope for women to gain a headship.[135] However, although the lower middle class were persuaded, it proved much more difficult to win over the middle class who in any case generally lacked the training to cope with either the pupils or the staff in elementary schools. Eglantyne Jebb (1876–1928)—founder of the Save the Children Fund (1919) and author of the Declaration of the Rights of the Child (1924)—recorded in her diary her experience of work in an elementary school at the end of the nineteenth century. It was, she confided, like being on a 'treadmill': she found little sympathy among the staff who resented her as an 'Oxford lady' who would not stay the course—indeed who, unlike them, did not need to do so. As Linda Mahood has observed, Jebb herself had pity for, but little understanding of, the bright girls in her charge who were destined by poverty for lives of drudgery as 'washerwomen'. Jebb also met resistance among the mistresses themselves to what they saw as 'class missionaryism', a version of the philanthropy of their social superiors which they found so condescending.[136] As they expected, Jebb soon left, while more typically the middle class did not turn to elementary schools until the First World War.

SOCIAL CLASS, CURRICULUM AND A FEMINIZED PROFESSION

By the end of the Victorian period throughout the British Isles, lower middle-class and upper working-class women predominated in a numerically feminized profession. Dina Copelman's study of London women teachers between 1870 and 1930 shows that they did not consider employment as a feminist struggle or justify it in terms of separate spheres, as so many feminists did. Nor did the schoolmistresses fundamentally challenge gender roles. Rather, they manoeuvred within the spheres to achieve a degree of autonomy. Copelman argues that London's women teachers viewed teaching as a career and not simply as a staging-post to marriage, while they also prepared their daughters for a career, though not necessarily in teaching.[137]

Not all school boards, however, allowed married women to continue teaching: indeed, there was often an unspoken assumption that a schoolmistress resign on marriage. For example, in Tudhoe, County Durham, the school board agreed in 1885 that no married woman would henceforth be employed as a teacher; in Yorkshire a decade later, the Barnsley board passed a resolution which stated that any female teacher who married had to hand in her resignation and that while married schoolmistresses could continue to work for the board, no married woman would in future be employed.[138] Similarly in Glasgow, despite the absence of any statutory requirement for female teachers to give up their posts on marriage, there was no place in the board's workforce for married women. Hence Janet Anderson resigned in 1882 in anticipation of her marriage the following year. [139] Yet as a spinster-teacher, she had been able to resist male authority. Her headmaster complained in 1878 that she had 'altogether neglected the teaching of needlework to the female pupil teachers, which had been entrusted to her care', and he called on her to do her duty. The log book shows that not only did she not comply, but it was he, not she, who left the school soon after.[140]

Whether or not married women could continue teaching or return to it on widowhood, and despite the trend after 1870 for females to outnumber males in board schools, teacher training throughout the British Isles consolidated the gendered division of labour in the education of the poor, reflecting the notion of separate spheres for the sexes.[141] The increasing influence of the kindergarten movement also led to a growing demand for schoolmistresses. A decade earlier, training colleges had separate men's and women's training departments. Although the training of teachers was dominated by men, colleges also gradually employed more middle-class women whom it was felt would raise the cultural standards and manners of the students. Until the 1890s, the senior position among the female staff was that of Lady Superintendent whose duties were more moral and domestic than educational, but in the course of that decade more women were being employed in colleges as educators in their own right.[142] Indeed, the establishment of separate colleges for women and in particular the establishment of training departments attached to universities attracted increasing numbers of middle-class women to the sector. These brought higher status to teacher training but not yet to teaching in elementary schools. The universities of St Andrews and Edinburgh had pioneered the academic study of education by establishing chairs, with the appointments of John M.D. Meiklejohn

(1836–1902) to the former and Simon S. Laurie (1829–1909) to the latter in 1876. Yet it was only in the 1890s that universities became involved in training teachers in a significant way.

In the previous decade, the Cross Commission had enquired about the moral training in colleges, reflecting some concern that it was not as strong in day as it was in residential colleges. One witness, the Rev. T.W. Sharpe, who had been a school inspector since 1857, as well as an inspector of training colleges from 1875 for about a decade, displayed the English preference for residential, which contrasted with the Scottish preference for day. He admitted that he had 'no reason to suppose that the Scotch students are less moral than the English' but considered that training in a residential college was a 'certain guarantee for a good moral character'.[143] The Commission's Minority Report, however, was severely critical of the residential training colleges in England and Wales, and especially of their teaching staff. Indeed, both the Final and the Minority Reports recommended the extension of day colleges, though the latter was more enthusiastic about these. Day training colleges attached to universities and university colleges were rapidly opened across Britain between 1890 and 1901.[144]

Day colleges also provided job opportunities for middle-class women with a university education. As noted above, association with the universities was to give trainee-teachers a broader culture and more liberal education than the narrowly vocational training in pupil-teacher centres and denominational colleges. There was the example of the dominie in Scotland, continued under the school boards, who had been expected to have some experience of university education. Thus, the Cross Commission's Minority Report recommended that day training colleges should emulate the Scottish model where there was already a close relationship between the training colleges and the universities.[145] The importance of this development for female college staff is highlighted by Elizabeth Edwards:

> In the nineteenth century women staff in training colleges had normally received a vocational qualification only. By the early twentieth century, and with the encouragement of the Board of Education, women graduates were beginning in increasing numbers, to be appointed to training colleges. Their change in title from the nineteenth century's 'governess' to the twentieth century's 'lecturer' signalled this crucial development in training-college culture, while students were typically clever girls from the lower middle class, whose education had been in the state sector, the staff were now typically daughters of the professional middle class, who, after private schooling, had received a university or other form of tertiary education.[146]

Of course, this change did not undermine either the social or the gender hierarchies, while it consolidated the feminization of elementary school teaching. Still, in the Scottish mixed-sex board or public schools, the tradition of a university-educated teaching profession was, by the end of the Victorian period, beginning to open up to schoolmistresses, though as previously observed only in 1907 was formal permission granted to Catholic women, both lay and religious, to attend state universities.[147]

Not only, as noted above, had Catholic schools in Scotland depended on the colleges in England for qualified teachers until the last decade of the century, but before the first teacher-training college for women in Wales was opened in Swansea in 1872, Welsh board schools had had to depend on English and Scottish colleges for a supply of certificated teachers. This added to the difficulties in providing elementary schools with Welsh-speaking teachers, while the growing trend to employ unqualified and untrained teachers in Welsh elementary schools led to a call for the expansion of teacher-training colleges. Still, it was only in the last decade of the century that day training departments attached to the University Colleges of Cardiff (1890) were established at Aberystwyth (1892) and Bangor (1894), which, since the majority of teachers was female, was a significant development in women's education in Wales, and as in Scotland it provided a link between elementary schools and the universities.[148]

This development clearly went far beyond the thinking behind Kay-Shuttleworth's introduction of the pupil-teacher system a half century earlier. As noted above, he had deplored the low standards of housekeeping among poor females. In his explanation of the Minutes of 1846, he had proposed making the school itself a means of instructing and training girls in the 'arts' of domestic economy:

> It has been conceived that a considerable portion of the oral lessons given in the girls' school might be devoted to the subject of household management, and that if a wash-house and kitchen were connected with the school, they might by proper arrangements, receive a practical training in cottage cookery, and in the care of clothes of a labourer's family.[149]

Towards the end of the century, the prevailing notions of woman's place and fears for the health of the race led, as shown in Chapter 2, to an almost missionary zeal to raise standards of living and moral conduct by overcoming the assumed ignorance of working-class mothers. Initially it was sewing, and often just mending, which constituted the basis of the girls' domestic curriculum throughout Britain. However, before the 1860s when English influences on education really began to be felt, sewing was neglected in Scotland compared to the rest of the UK, unless female industrial departments were attached to parochial schools. In a late nineteenth-century study of female education in England and Scotland, G.W. Alexander, who was clerk to the school board of Glasgow, recorded that the first official recognition in Scotland of the education of girls, in the sense that it accepted the need for more gender-specific schooling for the working class, came with the Education Act of 1861. Needlework was made obligatory and 'special inducements' in the way of government grants were offered for teaching cookery, laundry work, and dairy work, as well as general domestic economy and hygiene'.[150]

This reflected not only the growing intervention of government in education but also the feminist strategy of championing gender differences in education as a means of providing middle-class women with career opportunities which men could not claim and which would bring the woman teacher both status and influence in public life as the domestic science teacher. Generally men agreed, although in Scotland there was considerable resistance from the male educational establishment to such an increase in domestic training at the expense of a more traditional academic curriculum. Nevertheless, the government grants noted by Alexander led to increases in the number of girls studying domestic economy as well as the numbers of specialist teachers.

Sewing could be taught by the elementary school mistress, indeed, it was expected that she do so; but domestic economy became a much broader subject with certain aspects of it requiring specialist skills. In 1878 it became compulsory for all girls in board schools who wanted to take a specific subject. That decade saw the establishment of cookery schools in major cities of Britain opening, for example, in London and Leeds in 1874, Liverpool and Edinburgh in 1875 and Glasgow in 1876, while two decades later schools were opened in Bath, Cardiff, Newcastle and Preston.[151] Tom Begg's history of the Edinburgh School of Cookery places the efforts of the domestic science movement in the late nineteenth-century context of concern with public health and improvements in sanitation.[152] The Edinburgh School's experience was similar to that of other British domestic science schools which by the last decade of the century had changed from offering classes to working-class mothers, to targeting their daughters by training cookery teachers for board schools and to providing residential accommodation for middle-class students. One result was that the cookery school became a post-school institution for the daughters of the prosperous classes. Thus, since domestic subjects were deemed inappropriate for middle-class girls' education in the nineteenth century, the domestic economy teacher received her training after her experience of school, in specially established cookery schools. For her, it was an academic subject which opened up careers, notably in teaching, including from the end of the Victorian period as school inspectors of domestic subjects.

As recorded in Chapter 3, England led the way here with the appointment of a 'Directress' of Needlework in 1883 and an 'Inspectress' of Cookery and Laundry in 1890, though at first both were temporary. In Scotland, the first appointment of a woman inspector of domestic economy was not until 1902 and Jane Crawford (1864–1947) who was a lecturer at the Edinburgh School of Cookery. The Cross Commission cautioned that the appointment of lady inspectors of domestic subjects was often resented by the board schoolmistresses (another aspect of perceived social class 'missionaryism', perhaps), and also expressed concerns that the ladies would be required to travel a lot.[153] For working-class girls, no such career ladder was envisaged. Indeed, many who argued in favour of domestic economy playing a large part in their schooling referred to widespread complaints about the lack of skills of domestic servants. Lindy Moore suggests that in contrast to England, domestic economy was not generally seen as training for domestic service in Scotland, though it shared the common goal of imparting vocational skills to equip the girls as efficient housewives.[154]

Helen Corr sees irony in the dynamic role played by an elite group of female educationalists in reinforcing gender divisions in the teaching profession through promoting domestic economy as an academic subject for girls and a specialism for schoolmistresses.[155] Of the home economics movement in the USA in the same period, Sarah Stage concludes that it 'constitutes a classic case of the interplay of politics and domesticity in women's history', that it 'politicized domesticity by urging women to use their skills in "that larger household, the city", beginning as part of the broader movement for progressive reform'.[156] As in Britain, the context was also the nineteenth-century movement for professionalization, which was profoundly gendered and largely excluded women. Thus, middle-class, college-educated women 'developed parallel tracks to career and sought to upgrade, standardize and professionalize the fields in which they worked in an attempt to be competitive for jobs and resources and to gain legitimacy'.[157]

Similarly, Dina Copelman has observed of the relationship between gender, class and feminism in London between 1870 and 1930 that feminist campaigns for female education were part of a broader trend to consolidate a middle-class identity.[158] Middle-class feminists thus sought to carve out a professional niche for schoolmistresses based on social class divisions which were shaped by gender assumptions and to convince their male peers of its worth. To achieve that, home economists argued in conventionally gendered terms and so never escaped gender stereotypes. As in the USA, home economics in the UK never won parity of esteem with the male professions, nor, in the nineteenth century at least, with the feminized teaching profession who resented the 'pretensions' of cookery teachers who tended to be their social superiors.[159] Indeed, in Scotland the desire for professional status for the teaching of domestic economy was seen as a threat to the national tradition of an intellectual curriculum in parish schools. To a considerable degree, that had changed by the end of the Victorian period, under the influence of eugenicist ideas bringing Scotland into line with the rest of the UK.

CONCLUSION

There were, then, significant differences in the experience of training between middle- and working-class teachers in the nineteenth century. The former sought professional status, but whereas their male counterparts regarded training as generally unnecessary, the women increasingly sought formal qualifications as proof of their professionalism. Still, they steered clear of training colleges until the end of the century when those offered both links to the universities and posts for university-educated ladies. Before then, the education which they received was seen to be sufficient to equip them as teachers in the schools for the daughters of their own class, whereas the task of the trainers of elementary teachers was not to stretch them academically or intellectually but to turn them into efficient practitioners who could impart basic skills to their pupils and instil in them an acceptance of the established order and their place within it. As the educational reformer Emily Shirreff (1814–1897) remarked in 1877, 'teachers of elementary schools are taken in general from the wholly uneducated classes; and apart from what the training colleges have given, possess no culture at all'.[160]

There were differences, for example, in the higher status of teaching in Ireland, Scotland and Wales than in England and in the role of religious orders in training, notably in Ireland and of Catholics in Britain. Throughout the British Isles, the churches dominated teacher training and, though in a minority among teachers, men monopolized the promoted posts, notably in Scotland with its tradition of mixed-sex schools and university-educated masters. At the same time, the construction of femininity through the gendered curriculum was common to all parts of the UK, as were the efforts of social reformers and feminists to gain professional status for the female teacher. Perhaps above all, whatever the social hierarchy, women not only accepted but promoted the gendered division of labour.

There were, too, centralizing pressures which pushed for conformity in elementary schools. From the early 1860s Robert Lowe's Revised Code was imposed on English and Welsh elementary schools, instituting a system of payment by results which focused on the 'three Rs'. Despite resistance to this practice, the principles behind it and system of inspection were in place in Ireland and Scotland by the 1870s. As we have seen, one impact on the training of teachers was the narrowing of the normal school curricula. Although in Scotland this discouraged men from entering the profession, the educational tradition which insisted on the need for teachers with a university education persisted. Thus the First Annual Report of the Board of Education for Scotland (1873) accepted that teacher training promoted 'dexterity' in the management of schools but insisted that it also exercised an 'injurious influence on the mental rigour and learning of the members of the profession'. The report reflected concerns that the training of pupil teachers was not sufficiently intellectual, which it acknowledged was not an issue in England and that the central place of the dominie would be weakened by the increased employment of women.[161]

Their numbers continued to increase, but even the development of higher grade schools from the 1880s did not upset the gendered hierarchy. As

Wendy Robinson noted of London, whereas higher grade schools provided one of the few routes through which lower class women could gain financial and social independence, they also perpetuated limited opportunities for them: even in the late nineteenth century, the elementary school teacher occupied the bottom rung of the educational hierarchy, with little if any chance of improving her position.[162] In fact, Pamela Horn pointed to a dilution of the formal academic standards of school teachers in England: in 1875, certificated teachers had represented 70 per cent of the males and 57 per cent of the females employed in elementary schools, whereas in 1914 their shares had fallen to 66 per cent of the men and 32 per cent of the women; the situation was worse in rural areas.[163] June Purvis also shows that the rise in un-certificated male teachers was not so great: in 1875, only nine per cent of men and 13 per cent of women elementary teachers were without certificates; by 1914, it was 12 per cent of men but 41 per cent of women.[164] This was in the same period as a rise in the academic qualifications of Irish and Scottish schoolmistresses, though in Scotland's mixed-sex board schools few achieved headships. A notable exception was Mrs Isabella Skea (1845–1914), who trained in Edinburgh and taught in Aberdeen, becoming head teacher of St Paul Street School in 1868, and when it was extended in 1896, she became the first female head of a large (1,000 pupils) mixed-sex board school from which she retired in 1908.[165]

While the Scottish tradition privileged men, even where single-sex schooling was preferred, women teachers did not achieve parity with men in pay or promotion, even where, as in Ireland, the women tended to be better educated and were more likely to have a training certificate by the end of the century. Moreover, schoolmistresses in England argued against co-education not only because it led to fewer career opportunities for women but also because it was 'unnatural' and even 'un-English'.[166] The opening up of alternative teaching appointments by the late Victorian period eased the plight of the governess since competition was less fierce; her continuing employment also reflected the fact that many middle-class girls continued to be taught in the home. Still, from the 1870s middle-class women across the UK were drawn to training as teachers of domestic subjects, especially cookery, further strengthening social divisions since domestic subjects were not taught in private or high schools for girls. The Association of Headmistresses sought to ensure a career structure for the middle-class female teacher, with public school headmistresses emulating their male counterparts.[167] As June Purvis has pointed out, the new girls' public schools, modeled on Cheltenham Ladies' College, emphasised their elite status, and while high schools were more socially mixed, they remained middle-class institutions. Generally, university-educated women stayed aloof from working-class elementary school teaching, but Anne Jemima Clough encouraged elementary schoolmistresses to spend part of their summer holiday at Newnham College.[168]

Ironically, it was the improvements in girls' secondary education in the later nineteenth century which led to a growing interest among middle-class women in elementary teaching as a career, thus blocking the social mobility of working-class and lower middle-class women who could not afford the secondary school fees. Dina Copelman has argued that at the end of the nineteenth century, elementary school teachers in London had moved closer to the middle-class, feminist advocacy of a gender-specific education for working-class girls. At the same time she identified a deterioration in their career prospects: they were barred from inspectorships (unless of needlework); their share of headships declined as boys' and girls' departments were amalgamated under a single and, as in Scotland, usually male head teacher; and also as infants' and girls' departments were combined, with the loss of one headship for a woman.[169] Indeed, for reasons of economy mixed-sex schooling was increasing in London and other major urban centres in England by the later nineteenth century, and, as in Scotland, it privileged men in the profession.

5 Conclusion

Writing in 1822 on female education among the 'cultivated ranks of society', Harriet Martineau complained that so much of a young lady's time was spent on 'light accomplishments' that her desire for knowledge was subdued. She was not, she added, claiming that 'the natural powers of women were equal to those of men' but rather that 'if fair play has been given to the faculties' then the female mind may be compared to the male:

> If she wants his enterprising spirit, the deficiency is made up by perseverance in what she does undertake; for his ambition, she has a thirst for knowledge; and for his ready perception, she has unwearied application.[1]

Martineau went on to reassure her readers that woman's pursuit of knowledge would not result in the neglect of her 'appropriate duties and peculiar employments'. Woman was 'formed to be a domestic companion', but she could not fulfil that role if she was kept ignorant; a woman could not carry out her duties as the 'guardian and instructress of infancy' if she was not enlightened; and if a lady remained single (as Martineau did) then 'liberal pursuits were absolutely necessary to preserve [her] from the faults so generally attributable to that state'.[2]

It is striking how early in her writing career Martineau accepted that women had a subordinate role in society, while claiming that they could not live up to what was expected of that role unless they had a serious education. At the same time, she was not suggesting that such an education for a woman would be an end in itself; instead, it was a means to an end, for the good of her family and of society. Moreover, as female education improved, Martineau observed, the 'odious pedantry of the "blue-stockings" would disappear'.[3] Deirdre David has written of this manoeuvring within a patriarchal society, arguing that Martineau's career 'is defined by her auxiliary usefulness to a male-dominated culture': on the one hand, Martineau 'embraces her subordinate status', while on the other, she aligns it 'with her forthright, courageous and life-long feminism'.[4] Martineau seems to believe in the sexes as equal but different, a feminism which was both empowering (facilitating a public role for women) and constraining (reinforcing conventional gender stereotypes, if diluting patriarchal authority). It was also a feminism which was firmly entrenched in the established social hierarchy. What this study of female education shows is that there was no 'equal but different' in the relationship of Martineau's class of women to their social inferiors: however, much the ladies may have sympathised with and sought to ameliorate and improve the conditions of the working classes, they carved a public role for themselves on the basis of a domesticated life for their lower-class 'sisters'.

Still, what they had in common was that they were to be educated for the good of others. Both classes of women were to ensure a virtuous society, but poor women were to do that in their own homes, while middle-class ladies had a much broader domestic sphere which encompassed public duties. It helped that the housekeeping skills which the daughters of the poor were taught in school would not only bring comfort to their future family but also contribute to the public health of the imperial nation. Thus, theirs was essentially a home-based domestic role. Working-class women entered the public sphere from necessity, while there were middle-class fears that the virtue of such women could only be ensured if it was tied to the domestic. As a counter-balance, middle-class women had a moral duty to 'police' the public, to ensure social purity and rescue 'fallen' women, if possible before their loss of virtue.[5]

While the ideal was to keep the working-class woman in her home, her middle-class 'saviours' recognised that many had to spend some time in paid work, though their preference was that it be in domestic service, which as the biggest employer of girls and women in the Victorian period also called for a schooling in the household skills.[6] Job opportunities for working-class girls increased in the later Victorian period, partly related to their improved levels of education. Yet the former remained limited (especially in mining areas or in agriculture in England), while the latter remained basic due to continuing problems over school attendance. Their paid work was determined more by the local economy than their educational achievements. Moreover, whatever the growth of the retail and service sectors, women workers' wages remained low, and there were few incentives or opportunities to raise the level of their skills.

Improvements in education, therefore, had to take account of that home-centred role, and by the end of the nineteenth century, the curriculum for working-class girls across the UK was heavily weighted with domestic subjects. This was not just a case of the condescension of one class to another; working-class girls' education did improve, yet their lives remained almost as constricted as that of their Victorian mothers and grandmothers. It has been noted how few lower-class women wrote memoirs but one who did reveals how limited their opportunities remained. Jean Rennie was born in Greenock five years after the death of Queen Victoria. Jean attended a board school, and at 13 years of age she passed the 'qualifying' examination for the local high school, leaving it four years later with honours and a scholarship to Glasgow University. Because of her father's unemployment, however, she was unable to pursue her studies. In 1924 Jean went into service as a third housemaid in Argyllshire at £18 a year. She wrote

> I can only vaguely imagine what my mother must have felt. All that time, and all those books, and all my education—I know she was inarticulate—but I can see now the hurt in her eyes, that after all that, her daughter, her eldest, gawky, clever, talented daughter, was going 'into service', as she herself had done at the age of twelve—without an education.[7]

The tone of regret at not being able to continue her education and fulfil her mother's unspoken aspirations is palpable, indeed painful. Certainly, it was circumstances which prevented her taking advantage of the scholarship. Jonathan Rose has shown that at the end of the Victorian period, parents took as great if not a greater interest in the education of their daughters as in their sons, while in contrast to Jean's mother 'it was not unusual to find working-class families where the women were better read than the men'. Whereas Jean had had parental support in her school education, Rose has also observed that so many lower working-class parents discouraged their children even from reading: the girls because it distracted them from their domestic chores and the boys because it was unmanly to indulge in such a 'useless' pastime.[8]

The example of Jean Rennie is from the Scottish Lowlands, and whereas the educational tradition there valued academic subjects above vocational, the curriculum she experienced, particularly in the board school, would have been gendered with the emphasis on domestic subjects for girls, just as it was throughout the UK. Very few working-class children, boys or girls, would have had the opportunity to continue their schooling after the age of 12 or 13. True, by the end of the Victorian period there were qualifying examinations and scholarships, but they were for a tiny minority only, while as we have seen it was feared that a scholarship girl would miss out on the essential schooling in domestic skills.

Jean had been one of the very few to have had the prospect of a university education: she was indeed a 'lass of parts' but one whose poverty cut her education short. As Robert Anderson has shown, the pathway for most of such talented females was a narrow one, leading to the teacher-training college rather than the university.[9] Certainly, schoolteaching was seen as a mark of respectability for women, particularly compared to factory work, and even at the elementary level it was held in relative esteem in Ireland, Scotland and Wales; and however patronized the elementary schoolmistress was in England for her social pretensions and lack of cultivation, it was nevertheless a post which was recognised as crucial for ensuring a stable society, not least in the inculcation of gender roles.

By the end of the Victorian period, the emphasis in the schooling of the poor was on domestic 'efficiency' as well as subservience: it was not enough for a girl to know her place; she was expected to fulfil its functions to a degree judged satisfactory by her social superiors. While it was thought that boys need be taught only basic vocational skills in school since they would go on to learn 'on the job', for their sisters the school curriculum would have to impart domestic skills for her assumed future as wife and mother, since these could not be left to the inefficient mother in the home. Such criticisms of working-class mothers never changed over the Victorian period; indeed, they intensified in the late nineteenth century as Britain's imperial power came under threat. No matter how weighted down their daughters' curriculum was by domestic subjects, there were always calls for more time to be spent on them.

Stephen Heathorn points out that apart from this gender difference the staple reading materials in elementary schools for girls as well as boys consisted of historical, geographical and literary readers. Whereas it has been seen that the readers produced for use in the national schools in Ireland did not have specifically Irish themes and could be used throughout the UK and the Empire, Heathorn argues that readers used in English elementary schools portrayed the English as not just the dominant but also the superior nationality making up the imperial race.[10] This, not surprisingly, was resented by the smaller parts of the Union, and efforts of the governing elite to centralize power at Westminster were resisted. In terms of the education of the lower orders, Ireland, Scotland and Wales sought to show their superiority to the English either through a distinctive national tradition (as in Presbyterian Scotland) or by their superior virtues (ensured by Catholicism in Ireland, Nonconformity in Wales) which were seen to be bound up in the morals of their women. Yet underlying all this insistence on national difference, there was agreement on gender roles.

Thus, the elementary school readers for girls in all parts of the UK emphasised domestic and family themes, upholding the consensus on gender roles and separate spheres for the sexes.[11] Heathorn underplays the gendered aspect of the assumption of English superiority which mainly applied to boys and men: those traits of 'heroism, justice and glory' in the elementary school readers were above all masculine. It was English*men* who were cast as the carriers of law and order and progress; women more generally were portrayed in supportive roles, usually in the background, their duties, as Heathorn acknowledges, bound up with motherhood.[12] Whereas, as noted earlier, each nation within the Union assumed its women either were, or ought to be, the most virtuous, there was no disagreement on the female role. Indeed, as seen in the Welsh reaction to the English criticism of female morality in the Blue Books of 1847, there was an even stronger insistence on a domestic education for girls as proof of their virtue. Across the UK, whatever the religious or national differences, all reading books aimed at the elementary sector displayed the same image of the domesticated girl.

The stereotype of the virtuous lady was similar in its gendered restraints, but the improvements in their education sought by campaigners, including feminists, held out the prospect of a much more varied domestic role for them, one which embraced the public sphere. It was still assumed that a lady who did not need to work for a living would not do so, but that did not prevent her from performing unpaid public work, through for example, philanthropy or taking on what were effectively full-time positions, as Grace Paterson did in the role of 'honorary secretary' of the Glasgow School of Cookery for 30 years.[13] Through such dedicated service women like Paterson achieved a degree of personal autonomy as well as a respected place in their local communities, recognised as experts in female education. Thus, as has been seen, middle-class women benefited not only from reforms which improved their own education but also from the superior position they assumed over women of the lower classes. This was not only in terms of philanthropy; reforms to female education at all levels opened up respectable career opportunities for middle-class women, notably in teaching but also in public health and welfare.

England's dominant position in the Union ensured that it influenced female education in other parts of the UK, notably in the gendered curriculum. In Scotland, the introduction of such English policies as pupil teaching provided opportunities for women to secure a place within the traditionally male-dominated teaching profession. That a tiny minority of female board teachers in Scotland had the opportunity of a university education by the end of the Victorian period—indeed that their Catholic counterparts were also attending university classes by 1898—may be seen as a means of teaching retaining (or regaining) its traditional professional status, however much that focused on men.[14] Yet being dominated by the dominie did not mean patriarchy in education was stronger in Scotland than in England.[15] Rather it reflected the higher status of the teacher within Scotland, which was also the case in Ireland and Wales, compared to England. The professions generally were a masculine preserve, and indeed the Victorian period saw professional men closing ranks in the face of women who clamoured for entry: hence, the attempts to establish women-only professions or particular specialisms for women within a male profession.[16] Throughout the UK the female model of professionalization was rooted as much in social class as in gender, with feminist efforts to distinguish between not only the schooling of working and middle-class girls but also the training and education of their mistresses.[17] The main efforts expended by feminists across the UK concerned with education and achieving professional status was to focus on the teaching of girls and within that to carve out spaces for women who specialised in domestic subjects and infant schooling. Indeed, teaching remained the key profession for women—even at the end of the Victorian period, women were a tiny fraction of what were regarded as the higher professions.[18] Hence, when universities accepted female students (by the end of the Victorian period their numbers, though still small, were rising faster in Scotland and Wales than in England or Ireland), it was primarily to produce well-educated schoolmistresses.[19]

In a previous examination of the schooling of working-class girls in Victorian Scotland, I concluded that it was subject to the interaction of nationality with class and gender.[20] This comparison of female education across the UK, however, points to more similarities than differences between the constituent parts of the Union. This is also seen in the feminist campaigns for improvements to middle-class girls' education, and confirms the point made earlier about the predominantly Protestant nature of British feminism which alienated Catholic women. Megan Smitley has shown that among British feminists a 'philosophy of sisterhood—reinforced by common parliamentary agitation—minimized attention to "racial" or ethnic difference'; like Margaret Ward, she sees Victorian feminism as bound up with the Union and, implicitly, Protestantism. Also like Ward, she points to Edinburgh-born, Belfast-based staunch Presbyterian Isabella Tod as the most prominent representative of Ireland in the English feminist press. Tod declared in 1892 that as 'a worker for women who believes that there is no government on the face of the earth so favourable to the full freedom and dignity of women as the Imperial Parliament, I work for the maintenance of the union'.[21]

Whereas there were differences in middle-class girls' education across the UK, and feminism was much more prominent in the campaigns for reform in England, Ireland and Wales than in Scotland, reformers in all the constituent parts of the Union agreed on the need for a broadly based, liberal education on a par with their male peers. The young lady, Harriet Martineau had written in 1822, ought not to be ignorant of

> the Evidence and Principles of her Religious belief, of Sacred History, of the outline at least of General History, of the elements of the Philosophy of nature and of the Human Mind; and to those should be added the knowledge of such living languages, and the acquirement of such accomplishments, as situation and circumstances may direct'.[22]

While Catholic women stayed aloof from such campaigns, the growing Catholic middle class also sought improvements and put pressure on the Church hierarchy to provide their daughters with a similar education to their Protestant counterparts. Thus, religion, often intertwined with national identity, was clearly a key influence on education. At the same time, all denominations agreed that women's role was primarily domestic. Even within sects such as the Unitarians and Quakers which had progressive ideas on female education, the position of women was still 'auxiliary' to men, and they too accepted social differences in education.

Clearly, then gender was a major factor influencing education, but it was also always mediated by social class, while national, regional and local conditions had more of an effect on working-class than on middle-class girls' schooling. Girls of the lower ranks of society by the end of the Victorian period received an education in domesticity which focused narrowly on the practical skills of housewifery. Of course, women who advocated such a class-based education for their social inferiors were not simply handmaidens to patriarchy. It has been observed that feminists preferred to manipulate rather than directly challenge the ideology of domesticity as a means of domesticating the public sphere, while middle-class women in general had more room to manoeuvre within and extend the scope of the—or more precisely *their*—domestic sphere.[23] In the process of claiming for themselves a public role based on a service-orientated ideal, however, they both increased the constraints on working-class women and reinforced the notion of separate spheres for men and women.

Education, then, was increasingly seen as necessary for girls in the Victorian period, but it was not about transforming their lives in ways which would contest the social or gender hierarchies. For a tiny minority it was a liberating experience, allowing some women, especially if university educated, to step on to the lower rungs of a narrow ladder of limited career opportunities.[24] Feminists were aware both of the need for reform and of how much had to be done. Writing nearly four decades after that article on female education, Harriet Martineau was still urging that

> we must improve and extend education to the utmost; and then open a fair field to the powers and energies we have educed. This will secure our welfare, nationally and in our homes, to which few elements can contribute more vitally and more richly than the independent industry of our countrywomen.[25]

Despite the reservations discussed above, we should not underestimate the gains educational reforms brought to Victorian girls, especially the middle class but including those working-class girls like Jean Rennie whose talents had a chance to thrive even if only during their school years. Moreover, however tedious the emphasis on domestic subjects in their schooling, this gendered curriculum and the associated developments in the further education of specialist teachers in home economics kept the 'private' sphere in the public eye: housework was a political issue and a civic responsibility. Nor should we underestimate the pride working-class women had in their domestic skills.[26] Indeed, as (mainly) middle-class women became more involved in local government in the later nineteenth century, 'municipal housekeeping' became a public concern. In her study of women in English local government Patricia Hollis argued that 'local government touches the lives of women in at least three ways. It employs women; it provides services for women; and it is a place of political power and public advancement for women'. She quoted from the Conservative [and Unionist] Party handbook for 1975, which could have been written a century before: 'Women are extremely well-equipped for local government. They have a vested interest in, and immediate knowledge of, the schools, services, housing, care of children, and the environment, which are the responsibilities of local authorities.'[27]

As that quotation implies and this study has argued female education was concerned with gender formation, mediated by social class distinctions, not just between the classes but within them. For working-class girls generally, it was to prepare them above all for a domestic future. For middle-class girls, it was to make them suitable companions for a husband and to fit them, single or married, for a socially useful adulthood, whether in philanthropy or paid employment. Women had a civilizing mission, but the working-class version was much more narrowly conceived: hence, the restricted and highly gendered curriculum. A lady's duty encompassed the wider moral sphere, with the emphasis on her responsibility to act for the public good: hence, the need for a curriculum which was more broadly based on academic rather than vocational subjects, similar to that of their male peers but graced by the accomplishments to preserve their femininity and ward off the charge of being one of Martineau's 'odious' bluestockings.

Yet despite these differences, female education was, as noted above, always meant to benefit others rather than the girls themselves. Still, while Victoria's daughters were taught to know their place and to fulfil the gender and social roles allotted to them, they were not simply passive recipients: non-attendance by working-class girls was not just a mark of their usefulness in the home but a criticism of their schooling; and while elementary schoolmistresses were expected to teach the domestic subjects, they did not always accept that role with good grace.[28] Above all, while only a minority of middle-class girls benefited from the new high schools and the opening of the universities, the feminists who campaigned for such reforms recognised the potential of such an education not just for Victoria's daughters but their granddaughters.

Notes

NOTES TO CHAPTER 1

1. See, for example, Margaret Bryant, *The Unexpected Revolution: A Study in the History of the Education of Women and Girls in the Nineteenth Century* (London: University of London Institute of Education, 1979); Joan Burstyn, *Victorian Education and the Ideal of Womanhood* (London: Croom Helm, 1980); Sheila Fletcher, *Feminists and Bureaucrats: A Study in the Development of Girls' Education in the Nineteenth Century* (Cambridge: Cambridge University Press, 1980); Felicity Hunt (ed.), *Lessons for Life: The Schooling of Girls and Women 1850–1950* (Oxford: Basil Blackwell, 1987); June Purvis, *History of Women's Education in England* (Milton Keynes: Open University Press, 1991); Deirdre Raftery & Susan M. Parkes, *Female Education in Ireland 1700–1900: Minerva or Madonna?* (Dublin: Irish Academic Press, 2007); Mary Cullen (ed.), *Girls Don't Do Honours: Irish Women in Education in the Nineteenth and Twentieth Centuries* (Dublin: Women's Education Bureau, 1987); Fiona M.S. Paterson & Judith Fewell (eds.), *Girls in Their Prime: Scottish Education Revisited* (Edinburgh: Scottish Academic Press, 1990); W. Gareth Evans, *Education and Female Emancipation: The Welsh Experience, 1847–1914* (Cardiff: University of Wales Press, 1990); Helen Corr, *Changes in Educational Policies in Britain, 1800–1920: How Gender Inequalities Reshaped the Teaching Profession* (Lampeter: Edwin Mellen Press, 2008).
2. Jane McDermid, *The Schooling of Working-Class Girls in Victorian Scotland: Gender, Education and Identity* (Abingdon: Routledge, 2005).
3. See, for example, Jane McDermid, 'Women and Education', pp.107–130 in June Purvis (ed.), *Women's History: Britain, 1850–1945* (London: Routledge, 1995), which surveyed Britain but not Ireland. See pp.129–130 for a brief discussion of the literature on female education.
4. Deirdre Raftery, Jane McDermid & Gareth Elwyn Jones, 'Social Change and Education in Ireland, Scotland and Wales: Historiography on Nineteenth-Century Schooling', *History of Education* (September, 2007), vol.36, nos.4–5, pp.447–463: 452. For the ESRC seminar series, see Gary McCulloch, Joyce Goodman & William Richardson, 'Social Change in the History of Education: An ESRC Seminar Series', *History of Education Researcher* (2005), no.75, pp.1–13. See also their edited collection, *Social Change in the History of Education* (Abingdon: Routledge, 2008).
5. George E. Davie, *The Democratic Intellect: Scotland and Her Universities in the Nineteenth Century* (Edinburgh: Edinburgh University Press, 1961). See also Robert D. Anderson, *Education and the Scottish People, 1750–1918* (Oxford: Clarendon Press, 1995), pp.18–23.

6. Lindy Moore, 'Invisible Scholars: Girls Learning Latin and Mathematics in the Elementary Public Schools of Scotland before 1872', *History of Education* (June, 1984), vol.13, no.2, pp.121–137.
7. See Ian J. Simpson, *Education in Aberdeenshire before 1872* (London: University of London Press, 1947); John S. Smith & David Stevenson, *Aberdeen in the Nineteenth Century* (Aberdeen: Aberdeen University Press, 1988).
8. That has persisted: see, for example, Margaret Macintosh, 'The Gender Imbalance in Scottish Education', *Scottish Affairs* (Autumn, 1993), no.5, pp.118–123.
9. Helen Corr, 'Teachers and Gender: Debating the Myths of Equal Opportunities in Scottish Education 1800–1914', *Cambridge Journal of Education* (November, 1997), vol.27, no.3, pp.355–363.
10. Lesley Anne Orr Macdonald, *A Unique and Glorious Mission: Women and Presbyterianism in Scotland 1830–1930* (Edinburgh: John Donald, 2000), p.282.
11. See, for example, Jane McDermid, '"Intellectual Instruction Is Best Left to a Man": The Feminisation of the Scottish Teaching Profession in the Nineteenth Century', *Women's History Review* (1997), vol.6, no.1, pp.95–114; Jane McDermid, 'Handmaiden to a Patriarchal Tradition? The Schoolmistress in Victorian Scotland', *Études écossaises* (Winter, 2003–2004), vol. 9, pp.43–57.
12. Jonathan Rose, *The Intellectual Life of the British Working Classes* (New Haven: Yale University Press, 2001), p.2. See also David Vincent, *Bread, Knowledge and Freedom: A Study of Nineteenth-Century Working-Class Autobiography* (London: Europa, 1981), pp.90–91 for the 'silence of women' in this genre.
13. Barbara Taylor, *Eve and the New Jerusalem: socialism and feminism in the nineteenth century* (London: Virago, 1983), pp.230–237. See also June Purvis, *Hard Lessons: The Lives and Education of Working-Class Women in Nineteenth-Century England* (Cambridge: Polity Press, 1989).
14. Gayle Graham Yates (ed.), *Harriet Martineau on Women* (New Brunswick, NJ: Rutgers University Press, 1985), p.117.
15. June Purvis, *A History of Women's Education in England* (Milton Keynes: Open University Press, 1991), pp.11–33 for working-class girls' education and pp.34–63 for working-class women's education. See also W.B. Stephens, *Education in Britain 1750–1914* (Basingstoke: Macmillan, 1998), pp.1–20. For a list of significant interventionist measures in education between 1833 and 1870, see Eric J. Evans, *The Forging of the Modern State: Early Industrial Britain, 1783–1870* (2nd ed., London: Longman, 1996), p.410.
16. Thomas Kelly, *A History of Adult Education in Great Britain from the Middle Ages to the Twentieth Century* (Liverpool: Liverppool University Press, 1992), pp.128, 153–57; Malcolm Chase, *Chartism: A New History* (Manchester: Manchester University Press, 2007), p.144 for the quotation and pp.144–145, 168–171, 186–191 for Chartist educational initiatives.
17. See Eileen Yeo, 'Robert Owen and Radical Culture', pp.84–114 in Sydney Pollard & John Salt (eds.), *Robert Owen, Prophet of the Poor* (London: Macmillan, 1971), pp.97, 111 (Note 45); Purvis, *Hard Lessons*, pp.153–156 for women lecturers; Chase, *Chartism*, pp.23–25, 27–29, 186, 324 for female Chartist speakers.
18. See Purvis, *Hard Lessons*, pp.99–160 for women and the Mechanics' Institutes.
19. Ibid., p.234.
20. See Patricia Hollis (ed.), *Pressure from Without in Early Victorian England* (London: Edward Arnold, 1974), especially Brian Harrison, 'State

Intervention and Moral Reform in Nineteenth-Century England', pp.289–
322. See also John T. Wards (ed.), *Popular Movements 1830–1850* (London:
Macmillan, 1970); Edward Royle, *Radical Politics, 1790–1900: Religion
and Unbelief* (London: Longman, 1971); John Belchem, *Popular Radicalism
in Nineteenth-Century Britain* (London: Macmillan, 1995).

21. Calum Brown, *The Social History of Religion in Scotland since 1730* (London: Methuen, 1987), p.12.

22. Paul O'Leary, *Immigration and Integration: The Irish in Wales, 1798–1922* (Cardiff: University of Wales Press, 2000), p.10; James J. Smyth, *Labour in Glasgow 1896–1936: Socialism, Suffrage, Sectarianism* (East Linton: Tuckwell Press, 2000), p.127.

23. The 1801 Act of Union resulted in the proportion of non-English seats in the House of Commons rising to about 25 per cent, of which the highest number came from Ireland: Evans, *The Forging of the Modern State*, p.401.

24. Dudley Baines, *Emigration from Europe, 1815–1930* (Basingstoke: Macmillan, 1991), p.441, table 6.1.1. See also T.M. Devine, *The Scottish Nation* (London: Allen Lane, 1999), pp.468–485. There was also a significant rate of return (around a third): M. Anderson and D.J. Morse, 'The People', pp.8–45 in W. Hamish Fraser & R.J. Morris (eds.), *People and Society in Scotland. Volume ll, 1830–1914* (Edinburgh: John Donald, 1990), p.16.

25. Keith Robbins, *Great Britain: Identities, Institutions and the Idea of Britishness* (London: Longman, 1998), p.274.

26. Mary Carpenter, 'The Application of the Principles of Education to Schools for the Lower Orders of Society', *Transactions of the N.A.P.P.S.* (London, 1862), p.348; 'Mary Carpenter on *The Education of Pauper Girls* (1862)', pp.50–57 in Dale Spender (ed.), *The Education Papers: Women's Quest for Equality in Britain 1850–1912* (London: Routledge & Kegan Paul, 1987), p.52. See also Ruth Watts, 'Mary Carpenter: Educator of the Children of the "Perishing and Dangerous Classes"', pp.39–51 in Mary Hilton & Pam Hirsch (eds.), *Practical Visionaries: Women, Education and Social Progress 1790–1930* (Harlow: Longman, 2000); Jacob Middleton, 'The Cry for Useless Knowledge: Fear of Over-Education in Late Nineteenth-Century England', *History of Education Researcher* (2005), no.76, pp.91–99.

27. See Raftery, McDermid & Jones, 'Social Change and Education in Ireland, Scotland and Wales', p.452.

28. Quoted in Prys Morgan, 'Early Victorian Wales and Its Crisis of Identity', pp.93–109 in Laurence Brockliss & David Eastwood (eds.), *A Union of Multiple Identities: The British Isles, c.1750–c.1850* (Manchester: Manchester University Press, 1997), p.99.

29. See Gwyneth Tyson Roberts, *The Language of the Blue Books: The Perfect Instrument of Empire* (Cardiff: University of Wales Press, 1998).

30. Robert Anderson, 'In Search of the "Lad of Parts": The Mythical History of Scottish Education', *History Workshop* (Spring, 1985), no.19, pp. 82–104.

31. J. Stuart MacLure (ed.), *Educational Documents England and Wales 1816 to the Present Day* (5th ed., London: Methuen, 1985), pp.79–82. The Revised Code was not introduced into Ireland and Scotland until 1872.

32. W. Gareth Evans, 'The Welsh Intermediate and Technical Education Act of 1889: A Centenary Appreciation', *History of Education* (September, 1990), vol.19, no.3, pp.195–210.

33. John Roach, *Secondary Education in England, 1870–1902: Public Activity and Private Enterprise* (London: Routledge, 1991), pp.83, 182.

34. For the importance of local government, see Alice Brown, David McCrone & Lindsay Paterson, *Politics and Society in Scotland* (Basingstoke: Macmillan,

1996), pp.3, 5, 48; Richard J. Finlay, *A Partnership for Good? Scottish Politics and the Union Since 1800* (Edinburgh: John Donald, 1997), p.24.

35. Colin Matthew (ed.), *The Nineteenth Century: The British Isles, 1815–1901* (Oxford: Oxford University Press, 2000), p.12.

36. George Combe, *Lectures on Popular Education, Delivered to the Edinburgh Philosophical Association in April and November 1833* (Edinburgh: Maclachlan, Stewart & Co., 1848), pp.50–52. For Simpson, see his pamphlet *Necessity of Popular Education, as National Object* (Edinburgh: Adam & Charles Black, 1834), p.183.

37. See Ruth Watts, *Women in Science: A Social and Cultural History* (London: Routledge, 2007), pp.113–114.

38. Linda Colley, *Britons: Forging the Nation, 1707–1837* (New Haven: Yale University Press, 1992), p.23.

39. Michael Hechter, *Internal Colonialism: The Celtic Fringe in British National Development, 1536–1966* (London: Routledge & Kegan Paul, 1975), p.122; Linda Colley, 'Whose Nation? Class and National Consciousness in Britain, 1750–1830', *Past & Present* (November, 1986), no.113, pp.97–117: 111.

40. Colley, *Britons*, pp.237–273.

41. Benedict Anderson, *Imagined Communities* (London: Verso, 1983).

42. See Colin Matthew, 'The Union and the Nations', pp.104–106 in Matthew (ed.), *The Nineteenth Century*; Eric Evans, 'Englishness and Britishness: National Identities, c.1790–1870', pp.223–243 in Alexander Grant & Keith J. Stringer (eds.), *Uniting the Kingdom? The Making of British History* (London: Routledge, 1995).

43. In 1868, around 80 per cent of the population in Ireland was Catholic: Evans, *The Forging of the Modern State*, p.379. Linda Colley has little to say about Ireland in *Britons*, though she acknowledges (p.322) that 'there was not even the possibility of Ireland being permanently reconciled to direct rule from Westminster unless its predominantly Catholic population was granted wider civil rights'. Eric Evans, however, pointed out that even Catholic Emancipation (1829) did not reconcile the majority of Irish to the Union: Evans, *The Forging of the Modern State*, p.103.

44. Richard J. Evans, *The Feminists* (London, 1977), p.32.

45. Anne Stott, *Hannah More: The First Victorian* (Oxford: Oxford University Press, 2003), pp.327–328; Barbara Caine, *English Feminism 1780–1980* (Oxford: Oxford Univesity Press, 1997), p.125; Sally Mitchell, 'From Winter into Summer: The Italian Evolution of Frances Power Cobbe', *Women's Writing* (2003), vol.10. no.2, pp.343–351: 344.

46. Margaret Ward, 'Gendering the Union: Imperial Feminism and the Ladies' Land League', *Women's History Review* (2001), vol.10, no.1, pp.71–92: 73, 86; Antoinette Burton, *Burdens of History: British Feminists, Indian Women and Imperial Culture, 1865–1915* (Chapel Hill: University of North Carolina Press, 1994), p.123.

47. Paul Ward, 'Nationalism and National Identity in British Politics, c.1880s to 1914', pp.223–241 in Helen Brocklehurst & Robert Phillips (eds.), *History, Nationhood and the Question of Britain* (Basingstoke: Palgrave Macmillan, 2004), pp.215, 220.

48. Mary J. Hickman, 'Alternative Historiographies of the Irish in Britain: A Critique of the Segregation/Assimilation Model', pp.236–253 in Roger Swift & Sheridan Gilley (eds.), *The Irish in Victorian Britain: The Local Dimension* (Dublin: Four Courts Press, 1999), p.247.

49. O'Leary, *Immigration and Integration*, p.240; S. Karly Kehoe, *Creating a Scottish Church: Catholicism, Gender and Ethnicity in Nineteenth-Century Scotland* (Manchester: Manchester University Press, 2010), pp.110–143.

50. See J.H. Treble, 'The Development of Roman Catholic Education in Scotland, 1878–1978', *The Innes Review* (1978), vol.29, no.2, pp.111–139. See also Marie McClelland, 'Catholic Education in Victorian Hull', pp.101–121 in Swift & Gilley (eds,), *The Irish in Victorian Britain.*

51. See Simon Morgan, *A Victorian Woman's Place: Public Culture in the Nineteenth Century* (London: Taurus, 2007), p.37.

52. Harriet Martineau, 'The Governess. Her Health', *Once a Week* (1 September 1860), vol.3, pp.267–272: 261, 271.

53. See Trygve R. Tholfsen, 'Moral Education in the Victorian Sunday School', *History of Education Quarterly* (Spring, 1980), vol. 20, no.1, pp.77–99. For upper-class women's role in Sunday and charity schools, see Kim D. Reynolds, *Aristocratic Women and Political Society in Victorian Britain* (Oxford: Clarendon Press, 1998), pp.91–100; Rosalind K. Marshall, *Virgins and Viragos: A History of Women in Scotland from 1080 to 1980* (Chicago: Academy Chicago, 1983), pp.252–256.

54. See, for example, John Dwyer, *Virtuous Discourse: Sensibility and Community in Late Eighteenth Century Scotland* (Edinburgh: John Donald, 1987); Christopher J. Berry, *Social Theory of the Scottish Enlightenment* (Edinburgh: Edinburgh University Press, 1997), especially pp.109–113. These writers were not all Scottish and not all based in Edinburgh: for example, a key figure, Francis Hutcheson (1694–1746), a professor of moral philosophy at Glasgow University, was from Ulster. See Karen O'Brien, *Women and Enlightenment in Eighteenth-Century Britain* (Cambridge: Cambridge University Press, 2009), pp.68–109; Jane Rendall, *The Origins of Modern Feminism: Women in Britain, France and the United States, 1780–1850* (London: Macmillan, 1985), pp.7–32. See also Pam Perkins, *Women Writers and the Edinburgh Enlightenment* (New York: Rodopi, 2010), especially pp.13–53 on 'Excellent Women and Not Too Blue'.

55. See Elizabeth Eger, *Bluestockings: Women of Reason from Enlightenment to Romanticism* (Basingstoke: Palgrave Macmillan, 2010).

56. O'Brien, *Women and Enlightenment*, p.81.

57. Leonore Davidoff & Catherine Hall, *Family Fortunes: Men and Women of the English Middle Class, 1780–1850* (2nd ed., London: Routledge, 2002), see pp.xiii–l for the authors' response to the debate on separate spheres stimulated by the first edition (1987) of their work.

58. Jane Rendall, 'Women and the Public Sphere', *Gender and History* (November, 1991), vol.11, no.3, pp.475–488: 478.

59. William Stafford, *English Feminists and Their Opponents in the 1790s: Unsex'd and Proper Females* (Manchester: Manchester University Press, 2002), p.173. See also Sylvana Tomiselli, 'The Most Public Sphere of All: The Family', pp.239–256 in Elizabeth Eger, Charlote Grant, Cliona O Gallchoir & Penny Warburton (eds.), *Women, Writing and the Public Sphere 1700–1830* (Cambridge: Cambridge University Press, 2001).

60. Mary Wollstonecraft, *A Vindication of the Rights of Women* (1792: A Norton Critical Edition, edited by Carol H. Postan, 2nd ed., New York, 1988); Hannah More, *Strictures on the Modern System of Female Education* (2 vols., 8th ed., London: T. Cadell & W. Davies, 1800). See also Joyce Goodman, 'Undermining or Building Up the Nation? Elizabeth Hamilton (1758–1816), National Identities and an Authoritative Role for Women Educationists', *History of Education* (1999), vol.28, no.3, pp.279–296.

61. According to her biographer she was more flexible than this suggests and did support female activism, notably in her later years: Stott, *Hannah More*, p.329. See also Hannah Guest, *Small Change: Women, Learning, Patriotism, 1730–1810* (Chicago: University of Chicago Press, 2000), p.325.

62. Maurice J. Quinlan, *Victorian Prelude* (London: Cass, 1941), p.159.
63. See Ruth Watts, *Gender, Power and the Unitarians in England, 1760–1860* (Harlow: Longman, 1998); Kathryn Gleadle, *The Early Feminists: Radical Unitarians and the Emergence of the Women's Rights Movement, c.1831–1851* (Basingstoke: Macmillan, 1999); Joyce Goodman & Camilla Leach, '"At the Centre of a Circle Whose Circumference Spans All the Nations": Quaker Women and the Ladies Committee of the British and Foreign School Society, 1813–1837', pp.53–70 in Sue Morgan (ed.), *Women, Religion and Feminism in Britain, 1750–1900* (Basingstoke: Palgrave Macmillan, 2002).
64. Morgan (ed.), *Women, Religion and Feminism*, p.15.
65. Rebecca Rogers, 'Learning to Be Good Girls and Women: Education, Training and Schools', pp.93–133 in Deborah Simonton (ed.), *The Routledge History of Women in Europe since 1700* (Abingdon: Routledge, 2006), p.93.
66. Anne Stott, '"A Singular Injustice towards Women": Hannah More, Evangelicalism and Female Education', pp.23–38 in Morgan (ed.), *Women, Religion and Feminism*, p.34.
67. Mary Hilton, *Women and the Shaping of the Nation's Young: Education and Public Doctrine in Britain 1750–1850* (Aldershot: Ashgate, 2007), p.2.
68. Kenneth O. Morgan, *Rebirth of a Nation: Wales 1880–1980* (Oxford: Clarendon Press, 1981), p.105.
69. Michèle Cohen, 'Gender and the Private/Public Debate on Education in the Long Eighteenth Century', pp.15–35 in Richard Aldrich, *Public or Private? Lessons from History* (London: Woburn, 2004), p.34 (Note 85).
70. Deirdre Raftery, 'Educational Ideologies and Reading for Girls in England, 1815–1915', *History of Education Society Bulletin* (Spring, 1997), no.59, pp.4–11:.8.
71. Carol Dyhouse, *Girls Growing Up in Late Victorian and Edwardian England* (London: Routledge & Kegan Paul, 1981).
72. Susan Williams, 'Domestic Science: The Education of Girls at Home', pp.116–126 in Aldrich (ed.), *Public or Private Education?* p.118.
73. See, for example, Donald H. Akenson, *The Irish Education Experiment: The National System of Education in the Nineteenth Century* (London: Routledge & Kegan Paul, 1970), p.217.
74. Georgina Brewis, 'From Working Parties to Social Work: Middle-Class Girls' Education and Social Service 1890–1914', *History of Education* (November, 2009), vol.38, no.6, pp.761–777.
75. For middle-class daughters whose fathers have died and left them penniless, see Martineau, 'The Governess. Her Health', p.271. For Wollstonecraft's sisters, see Ruth Brandon, *Other People's Daughters: The Life and Times of the Governess* (London: Weidenfeld & Nicolson, 2008), p.3.
76. See, for example, Anderson, *Education and the Scottish People*, pp.125, 234. The 1870 Act gave school boards the power to introduce byelaws to make attendance compulsory: see, for example, David Rubinstein, *School Attendance in London, 1870–1904: A Social History* (New York: A.M. Kelley, 1969). See also Susan Williams, *The Children of London: Attendance and Welfare at School, 1870–1990* (London: Institute of Education, 2001).
77. Jane Humphries, *Childhood and Child Labour in the British Industrial Revolution* (Cambridge: Cambridge University Press, 2010), pp.31, 310, 370. As in the studies of David Vincent and Jonathan Rose (see Note 12), the majority of autobiographers consulted by Humphries were male.
78. Keith Snell, 'The Sunday-School Movement in England and Wales: Child Labour, Denominational Control and Working-Class Culture', *Past & Present* (August, 1999), no.164, pp.122–168: 140.

79. Hugh Cunningham, 'The Employment and Unemployment of Children in England, c.1680–1851', *Past & Present* (February, 1990), no.126, pp.115–150: 141, 144, 145.
80. Richard Aldrich, 'Elementary Education, Literacy and Child Employment in Mid-Nineteenth-Century Bedfordshire: A Statistical Study', pp.87–99 in Giovanni Genovesi *et al* (eds.), *History of Elementary School Teaching and Curriculum* (Hildesheim: International Series for the History of Education, 1990), pp.97–98.
81. Pamela Sharpe, 'The Women's Harvest: Straw-Plaiting and Labouring Women's Employment, 1793–1885', *Rural History* (1994), vol.5, no.2, pp.129–142.
82. Dot Jones, 'Counting the Cost of Coal: Women's Lives in the Rhondda, 1881–1911', pp.109–133 in Angela V. John (ed.), *Our Mothers' Land: Chapters in Welsh Women's History 1830–1939* (Cardiff: University fo Wales Press, 1991). See also Ellen Jordan, 'The Exclusion of Women from Industry in Nineteenth-Century Britain', *Comparative Studies in Society and History* (1989), vol.31, no.2, pp.273–296.
83. James Pressley, 'Childhood, Education and Labour: Moral Pressure and the End of the Half-Time system', PhD, Lancaster University, 2000, p.11.
84. See Angela V. John, *By the Sweat of Their Brow: Women Workers at Victorian Coal Mines* (London: Croom Helm, 1980); Eve Hostettler, 'Labouring Women: A Reply to Eric Hobsbawm', *History Workshop Journal* (Autumn, 1979), no.8, pp.174–182: 75–76.
85. Women's seasonal labour in English agriculture, however, notably in Norfolk where there was little alternative work for them, tended to be under-recorded: Nicola Verdon, 'The Employment of Women and Children in Agriculture: A Reassessment of Agricultural Gangs in Nineteenth-Century Norfolk', *Agricultural History Review* (2001), vol.49, no.1, pp.41–55. See also Nicola Verdon, *Rural Women Workers in Nineteenth-Century England: Gender, Work and Wages* (Woodbridge: Boydell Press, 2002); David Fitzpatrick, 'The Modernization of the Irish Female', pp.162–180 in Patrick O'Flannagan, Paul Ferguson & Kevin Whelan (eds.), *Rural Ireland: Modernization and Change 1600–1900* (Cork: Cork University Press, 1987); Barbara W. Robertson, 'In Bondage: The Female Farm Worker in South-East Scotland', pp.117–135 in Eleanor Gordon & Esther Breitenbach (eds.), *The World Is Ill Divided: Women's Work in Scotland in the Nineteenth and Early Twentieth Centuries* (Edinburgh: Edinburgh University Press, 1990).
86. McDermid, *The Schooling of Working-Class Girls in Victorian Scotland*, pp.86–113.
87. Janet Howarth, 'Gender, Domesticity and Sexual Politics', pp.163–193 in Matthew (ed.), *The Nineteenth Century*, p.171.
88. John Williams, *Was Wales Industrialised? Essays in Modern Welsh History* (Llandysul: Gomer, 1995), pp.58–78: 67.
89. Anderson, *Education and the Scottish People*, p.134.
90. Sara Horrell & Jane Humphries, 'Women's Labour Force Participation and the Transition to the Male-Breadwinner Family', *The Economic History Review* (February, 1995), vol.48, no.1, pp.89–117; Pamela Sharpe, 'Continuity and Change: Women's History and Economic History in Britain', *The Economic History Review* (May, 1995), vol.48, no.2, pp.353–369.
91. Edward Higgs, 'Women, Occupations and Work in the Nineteenth-Century Censuses', *History Workshop Journal* (Spring, 1978), no.23, pp.59–80: 76.
92. Williams, *Was Wales Industrialised?* pp.14–34.
93. *The Aberdeen Journal*, 15 May 1867.

94. Sydney & Olive Checkland, *Industry and Ethos: Scotland 1832–1914* (2nd ed., Edinburgh: Edinburgh University Press, 1989), pp.13, 34, 41, 43, 46.
95. See, for example, Heather Holmes, *'As Good As a Holiday': Potato Harvesting in the Lothians from 1870 to the Present* (East Linton: Tuckwell press, 2000).
96. The last two reveal the growing importance of tourism and gentlemanly leisure pursuits to the local economy. See McDermid, *The Schooling of Working-Class Girls*, pp.98–105.
97. Malcolm Gray, *The Highland Economy 1750–1850* (Edinburgh: Oliver & Boyd, 1957), p.80; John F. McCaffrey, *Scotland in the Nineteenth Century* (Basingstoke: Macmillan, 1998), p.9.
98. See Ian Carter in *Farmlife in Northeast Scotland 1840–1914: The Poor Man's Country* (Edinburgh: John Donald, 1979).
99. John Coolahan, *Irish Education: Its History and Structure* (Dublin: Institute of Public Administration, 1981), p.30.
100. Sean Farren, *The Politics of Irish Education* (Belfast: Institute of Irish Studies Queen's University, 1995), p.9.
101. John (ed.), *Our Mothers' Land*, p.2.
102. John Butt, 'The Changing Character of Urban Employment 1901–1981', pp.212–235 in George Gordon (ed.), *Perspectives of the Scottish City* (Aberdeen: Aberdeen University Press, 1985), p.213–215.
103. Paul Thompson, 'Women in the Fishing: The Roots of Power between the Sexes', *Comparative Studies in Society and History* (January, 1985), vol.27, no.1, pp.3–32: 9. See also T.M. Devine, 'Migration and the Scottish Highlands in the Nineteenth Century', *The Economic History Review* (August, 1979), vol.32, no.3, pp.344–359: 353–355.
104. David Fitzpatrick, 'A Share of the Honeycomb: Education, Emigration and Irishwomen', *Continuity and Change* (1986), vol.1, no.2, pp.217–234.
105. Farren, *The Politics of Irish Education*, p.10.
106. For Scotland, see Devine, 'Temporary Migration and the Scottish Highlands in the Nineteenth Century'; Charles W.J. Withers & Alexandra J. Watson, 'Stepwise Migration and Highland Migration to Glasgow, 1852–1898', *Journal of Historical Geography* (1991), vol.17, no.1, pp.35–55. For Ireland, see Fitzpatrick, 'The Modernization of the Irish Female'.
107. See, for example, 'Wilena Hitching, *Home Management* (1910)', pp.311–315 in Spender (ed.), *The Education Papers*.
108. Carol Dyhouse, 'Good Wives and Little Mothers: Social Anxieties and the Schoolgirl's Curriculum, 1890–1920', *Oxford Review of Education* (1977), vol.3, no.1, pp.21–35.
109. Edinburgh Central Library, YL343 Edinburgh School Board Minute Book, 13 June 1877.
110. R. Rodger, 'Employment, Wages and Poverty in the Scottish Cities 1841–1914', pp.25–63 in Gordon (ed.), *Perspectives of the Scottish City*, p.35. See also Siân Reynolds, *Britannica's Typesetters. Women Compositors in Edwardian Edinburgh* (Edinburgh: Edinburgh University Press, 1989), p.97.
111. Elizabeth Sanderson, *Women and Work in Eighteenth-Century Edinburgh* (Basingstoke: Macmillan, 1996), pp.87–91.
112. Lynn M. Alexander, *Women, Work and Representation: Needlewomen in Victorian Art and Literature* (Athens, Ohio: Ohio University Press, 2003), pp.28, 209–228. See also T.J. Edelstein, 'They Sang "The Song of the Shirt": The Visual Iconology of the Seamstress', *Victorian Studies* (1980), vol.23, no.2, pp.183–210; Sheila C. Blackburn, '"Princesses and Sweated-Wage Slaves Go Well Together": Images of British Sweated Workers, 1843–1914' *International Labor and Working-Class History* (2002), vol.61, pp.24–44.

113. Domestic economy became compulsory for girls taking specific subjects in 1878, and after 1893 it became a class subject, again for girls only. See Carol Dyhouse, 'Towards a "Feminine" Curriculum for English Schoolgirls: The Demands of Ideology, 1870–1963', *Women's Studies International Quarterly* (1978), vol.1, no.4, pp.297–311: 297–301.

114. Jones, 'Counting the Cost of Coal'. See also Michael R. Haines, 'Fertility, Nuptiality, and Occupation: A Study of Coal Mining Populations and Regions in England and Wales in the Mid-Nineteenth Century', *The Journal of Interdisciplinary History* (Autumn, 1977), vol.8, no.2, pp.265–280: 279.

115. See, for example, Jane Martin, '"Hard-Headed and Large-Hearted": Women and the Industrial Schools, 1870–1885', *History of Education* (1991), vol.20, no.3, pp.187–201.

116. See, for example, Linda Mahood, *Policing Gender, Class and Family: Britain, 1850–1914* (London: UCL Press, 1995); Maria Luddy, 'Prostitution and Rescue Work in Nineteenth-Century Ireland', pp.51–84 in Maria Luddy & Cliona Murphy (eds.), *Women Surviving: Studies in Irish Women's History in the Nineteenth and Twentieth Centuries* (Dublin: Poolbeg Press, 1990); Linda Mahood, 'Family Ties: Lady Child-Savers and Girls of the Street, 1850–1925', pp.42–64 in Esther Breitenbach & Eleanor Gordon (eds.), *Out of Bounds Women in Scottish Society 1800–1945* (Edinburgh: Edinburgh University Press, 1992); Paula Bartley, 'Preventing Prostitution: The Ladies' Association for the Care and Protection of Young Girls in Birmingham, *Women's History Review* (1998), vol.7, no.1, pp.37–60; Joyce Goodman, 'Sex and the City: Educational Initiatives for "Dangerous" and "Endangered" Girls in Late Victorian and Early Edwardian Manchester', *Paedagogica Historica* (2003), vol.39, no.1, pp.75–84.

117. Farren, *The Politics of Irish Education*, p.10.

118. Lindy Moore, 'Educating for the "Woman's Sphere": Domestic Training versus Intellectual Discipline' pp.10–41 in Breitenbach & Gordon (eds.), *Out of Bounds*, pp.31–32.

119. See, for example, McDermid, *The Schooling of Working-Class Girls in Victorian* Scotland, pp.69–70, 82, 122. For histories of cookery schools, see, for example, Tom Begg, *The Excellent Women: The Origins and History of Queen Margaret College* (Edinburgh: John Donald, 1994); Ellice Miller, *Century of Change 1875–1975: One Hundred Years of Training Home Economics' Students in Glasgow* (Glasgow: Queen's College Centenary Pamphlet, c.1975); Margaret E. Scott, *The History of F.L. Calder College of Domestic Science, 1875–1965* (Liverpool: Calder College of Education for Domestic Science, 1967). See also Annmarie Turnbull, 'Women, Education and Domesticity: A Study of the Domestic Subjects Movement, 1870–1914', PhD, Polytechnic of the Southbank, 1983.

120. See Elizabeth Bird, '"High Class Cookery": Gender, Status and Domestic Subjects', *Gender and Education* (1998), vol.10, no.2, pp.117–131.

121. Helen Corr, '"Home Rule" in Scotland: The Teaching of Housework in Scottish Schools 1872–1914', pp.38–53 in Judith Fewell & Fiona Paterson (eds.), *Girls in Their Prime: Scottish Education Revisited* (Edinburgh: Scottish Academic Press, 1990), p.39.

122. Barbara Bodichon, *Reasons For and Against the Enfranchisement of Women* (London: National Society for Women's Suffrage, 1869), p.6.

123. Eileen Janes Yeo (ed.), *Radical Femininity: Women's Self-Representation in the Public Sphere* (Manchester: Manchester University Press, 1998), p.8.

124. For the 'set of uneasy compromises' in education over the course of the nineteenth century, 'mainly involving the major churches and the country's

British controlled administration', see Farren, *The Politics of Irish Education*, pp.1–14.

125. Maria Luddy, 'Women and Charitable Organisations in Nineteenth Century Ireland', *Women's Studies International Forum* (1988), vol.11, no.4, pp.301–305: 304.

126. See Angela John for two examples, Lady Charlotte Guest and Mrs Rose Crawshay, of whom the latter went on to sit on school boards: 'Beyond Paternalism: The Ironmaster's Wife in the Industrial Community', pp.43–68 in John (ed.), *Our Mothers' Land*.

127. See Joyce Goodman, 'Committee Women: Women School Governors in Early Nineteenth-Century England', *History of Education Society Bulletin* (Autumn, 1995), no.56, pp.48–57; Peter Gordon, *The Victorian School Manager: A Study in the Management of Education, 1800–1902* (London: Woburn, 1974), pp.181–189.

128. Patricia Hollis, *Ladies Elect: Women in English Local Government, 1865–1914* (Oxford: Clarendon Press, 1987), p.97.

129. Jane Martin, *Women and the Politics of Schooling in Victorian and Edwardian England* (Leicester, 1999). See also Jane Martin & Joyce Goodman, *Women and Education, 1800–1980: Educational Change and Personal Identities* (Basingstoke: Palgrave Macmillan, 2004), p.90.

130. Jane McDermid, 'School Board Women and Active Citizenship in Scotland, 1873–1919', *History of Education* (May, 2009), vol.38, no.3, pp.333–347: 340. See also Anna Davin, 'Imperialism and Motherhood', *History Workshop Journal* (Spring, 1978), no.5, pp.9–65.

131. Hollis, *Ladies Elect*, pp.112, 135.

132. See, for example, Jane McDermid, 'Blurring the Boundaries: School Board Women in Scotland, 1872–1919', *Women's History Review* (July, 2010), vol.19, no.3, pp.357–373: 360.

133. Hollis, *Ladies Elect*, p.136; McDermid, 'School Board Women and Active Citizenship', pp.339–340.

134. Brockliss & Eastwood (eds.), *A Union of Multiple Identities*, pp.1, 9. By the early twentieth century, there was some questioning of the centralized nature of the Union. Thus Mary Burton, who served four terms on the Edinburgh Board from 1885, bequeathed £100 to the Edinburgh Women's Suffrage Association in 1908 'to be expended in any movement which may be made for the admission of women to sit as members of parliament, either at Westminster or in a Scottish Parliament'. See McDermid, 'School Board Women and Active Citizenship in Scotland', p.340.

135. Ibid., p.340.

136. See Seth Koven and Sonya Michel (eds.), *Mothers of a New World: Maternalist Politics and the Origins of Welfare States* (London: Routledge, 1993), p.3.

137. *The Dundee Advertiser*, 18 February 1872. For Dundee as a 'woman's town', see Christopher A. Whatley, David B. Swinfen & Annette M. Smith (eds.), *The Life and Times of Dundee* (Edinburgh: John Donald, 1993), especially Jan Merchant, '"An Insurrection of Maids": domestic servants and the agitation of 1872', pp.104–121: p.113.

138. Martin, *Women and the Politics of Schooling*, p.1 (see also p.12 for the names of the female members); Anderson, *Education and the Scottish People*, p.170; Hollis, *Ladies Elect*, pp.130, 133.

139. However, in elections to the local education authorities in Scotland after the 1918 Education Act, some women candidates stood as representatives of churches: see McDermid, 'Blurring the Boundaries', p.367.

140. Ryland Wallace, *Organise! Organise! Organise! A Study of Reform Agitations in Wales, 1850–1886* (Cardiff: University fo Wales Press, 1991), p.167.

Angela John notes that Mrs Crawshay appears to have been the only woman in the nineteenth century who simultaneously sat on two school boards (she was also elected to the Merthyr Tydfil school board in 1871): John (ed.), *Our Mothers' Land*, p .59.
141. McDermid, 'Blurring the Boundaries', p.368.
142. Gordon, *The Victorian School Manager*, p.182.
143. See Jane McDermid, 'Place the Book in their Hands: Grace Paterson's Contribution to the Health and Welfare Policies of the School Board of Glasgow, 1885–1906', *History of Education* (November, 2007), vol.36, no.6, pp.697–713. See also Hollis, *Ladies Elect*, p.153.
144. *The Ardrossan & Saltcoats Herald*, 26 March 1897, p.1.
145. Quoted in Wallace, *Organise! Organise! Organise!*, p.165. See also John (ed.), *Our Mothers' Land*, pp.60–61 for the scope of Rose Crawshay's involvement in the curriculum.
146. Hollis, *Ladies Elect*, pp.86, 144, 157; McDermid, 'School Board Women and Active Citizenship in Scotland', p.342. See also Vanessa Heggie, 'Domestic and Domesticating Education in the Late Victorian city', *History of Education* (May, 2011), vol.40, no.3, pp.273–290, which looks at the Manchester and Salford boards; Joan E. Parker, 'Lydia Becker's "School for Science"', *Women's History Review* (2001), vol.10, no.4, pp.629–650.
147. Neil Daglish, *Educational Policy-Making in England and Wales: The Crucible Years, 1895–1911* (London: Woburn, 1996), p.34.
148. John Wolffe, *God and Greater Britain: Religion and National Life in Britain and Ireland, 1843–1945* (London: Routledge, 1994), pp.140–141. See also Gordon W. Roderick & David Allsobrook, 'Welsh Society and University Funding, 1860–1914', *The Welsh History Review* (June, 2000), vol.20, no.1, pp.34–61.
149. Anderson, 'In Search of the "Lad of Parts"', p.84.
150. McDermid, 'Place the Book in Their Hands', p.711.
151. Gordon, *The Victorian School Manager*, p.184.
152. See Joyce Goodman, 'Women School Board Members and Women School Managers: The Structuring of Educational Authority in Manchester and Liverpool, 1870–1903', pp.59–77 in Joyce Goodman & Sylvia Harrop (eds.), *Women, Educational Policy-Making and Administration in England: Authoritative Women since 1880* (London: Routledge, 2000), p.71.
153. See Edward L. Edmonds , *The School Inspector* (London: Routledge & Kegan Paul, 1962), pp.154–172; Joyce Goodman & Sylvia Harrop, '"The Peculiar Preserve of the Male Kind": Women and the Education Inspectorate, 1893 to the Second World War', pp.137–155 in Goodman & Harrop (eds.), *Women, Educational Policy-Making and Administration in England*, p.139.
154. Begg, *The Excellent Women*, p.100.
155. Lindy Moore, 'Women in Education', pp. 316–343 in Heather Holmes (ed.), *Scottish Life and Society, Volume 11: Institutions of Scotland: Education* (East Linton: Tuckwell Press, 2000), p.331.
156. Hollis, *Ladies Elect*, p.153.
157. Lindsay Paterson, *The Autonomy of Modern Scotland* (Edinburgh: Edinburgh University Press, 1994), pp.65–66, 70.
158. *The Educational News*, 6 May 1876.
159. See Alison Prentice & Marjorie R. Theobald (eds.), *Women Who Taught* (Toronto: University of Toronto Press, 1991), p.7; Carolyn Steedman, '"The Mother Made Conscious": The Historical Development of a Primary School Pedagogy', *History Workshop Journal* (Autumn, 1985), no.20, pp.149–163: 156.

160. Hollis, *Ladies Elect*, pp.128–131; McDermid, 'School Board Women and Active Citizenship in Scotland', p.341.
161. Martin & Goodman, *Women and Education, 1800–1980*, pp.1, 86.
162. Frances Widdowson, *Going Up Into the Next Class: Women and Elementary Teacher Training, 1840–1914* (London: Hutchinson, 1980), p.46.
163. 'Dorothea Beale *Address to the National Association for the Promotion of Social Science* (1865)', pp.123–139 in Spender (ed.), *The Education Papers*, p.126.
164. See Purvis, *Hard Lessons*, pp.161–220; Watts, *Women in Science*, pp.99–103. See also John F.C Harrison, *Learning and Living, 1790–1960* (London: Routledge & Kegan Paul, 1961); Anthony Cooke, *From Popular Enlightenment to Lifelong Learning: A History of Adult Education in Scotland 1701–2005* (Leicester: NIACE, 2006).
165. Kathryn Hughes, *The Victorian Governess* (London: Hambledon, 2001), p.200.
166. See John. T. Smith, *'A Victorian Class Conflict?' Schoolteaching and the Parson, Priest and Minister, 1837–1902* (Portland, Oregon: Sussex Academic Press, 2009).
167. Beale in Spender (ed.), *The Education Papers*, p.123.

NOTES TO CHAPTER 2

1. See, for example, Donald H. Akenson, *The Irish Education Experiment: The National System of Education in the Nineteenth Century* (London: Routledge & Kegan Paul, 1970).
2. Roger Webster, 'Education in Wales and the Rebirth of a Nation', *History of Education* (September, 1990), vol.19, no.3, pp.183–194: 189. See also Deirdre Raftery, Jane McDermid & Gareth Elwyn Jones, 'Social Change and Education in Ireland, Scotland and Wales: Historiography on Nineteenth-Century Schooling', *History of Education* (July, 2007) vol.36, no.4, pp.447–463.
3. H.G. Williams, '"Learning Suitable to the Situation of the Poorest Classes": The National Society and Wales, 1811–1839', *The Welsh History Review* (June, 1998), vol.19, no.3, pp.425–452: 428.
4. Webster, 'Education in Wales and the Rebirth of the Nation', p.184.
5. See Bryn L. Davies, 'An Assessment of the Contribution of Sir Hugh Owen to Education in Wales', PhD, University of Bangor, 1971.
6. *Report of the Commission of Inquiry into the State of Education in Wales* [Blue Books] (1847), part 1, p.xxvii. See also David Jones, *The Last Rising: The Newport Chartist Insurrection of 1839* (Cardiff: University of Wales Press, 1999).
7. *Reports of the Commissioners of Board of Education in Ireland. First Report* [Free Schools], *Second Report* [Schools of Private Foundation], *Third Report* [Protestant Charter Schools] (1809), Third Report, pp.16, 61.
8. Ibid., p. 63.
9. Ibid., p. 61.
10. *Report of the Royal Commission on Irish Education* (1825), First Report, Appendix 9, p.44.
11. Ibid., p.23.
12. Ibid., Appendix 263, p.840.
13. Ibid., pp.23, 86–89.
14. Education Commission (Scotland), *Report on the State of Education in Glasgow* by James Grieg and Thomas Harvey (Edinburgh, 1866), p.84. See also Thomas A. Fitzpatrick, 'Catholic Education', pp.435–456 in Heather

Holmes (ed.), *Scottish Life and Society. A Compendium of Scottish Ethnology. Volume 11, Institutions of Scotland: Education* (East Linton: Tuckwell Press, 2000).

15. *Royal Commission on Irish Education*. First Report, p.840. For the Kildare Place society, see Harold Hislop, 'The Management of the Kildare Place School System, 1811–1831', *Irish Educational Studies* (Spring, 1992), vol.11, no.1, pp.52–71.

16. *Reflections of an Irish Protestant on the Measure of Roman Catholic Emancipation, Addressed to the Yeomanry of England* (Special Collections, Hartley Library Southampton University, WP 946/14).

17. Akenson, *The Irish Educational Experiment*, pp.199–217.

18. Ibid., p.199.

19. See MichaelW. de Nie, *The Eternal Paddy: Irish Identity and the British Press, 1798–1882* (Madison, Wisconsin: University of Wisconsin Press, 2004).

20. Leslie Wynne Evans, *Education in Industrial Wales 1700–1900* (Cardiff: Avalon Books, 1971), p.iii.

21. *Report of the Commissioners into the State of Popular Education in England and Wales* [Newcastle Commission] (1861), vol.2, p.188.

22. *Report of the Commission of Inquiry into the State of Education in Wales*, part 1, p.50.

23. Ibid., part 2, p.66.

24. Ibid., part 1, pp.3, 28.

25. Ibid., part 2, p.16.

26. Newcastle Commission, vol.2, p.449.

27. Penny Fielding, *Writing and Orality: Nationality, Culture and Nineteenth Century Scottish Fiction* (Oxford: Clarendon Press, 1996), p.23.

28. P.J. Dowling, *The Hedge Schools of Ireland* (Cork: P. Talbot, 1931); Antonia McManus, *The Irish Hedge School and its Books, 1605–1831* (Dublin: Four Courts Press, 2002); J.R.R. Adams, 'Swine-Tax and Eat-Him-All-Magee: The Hedge Schools and Popular Education in Ireland', pp.97–117 in James S. Donnelly & Kerby A. Miller (eds.), *Irish Popular Culture 1650–1850* (Dublin: Irish Academic Press, 1998).

29. Declan Kiberd, 'Irish Literature and Irish History', pp.275–337 in Roy Foster (ed.), *The Oxford History of Ireland* (Oxford: Oxford University Press, 1992), pp.251–252; Maria Yolanda Fernández-Suárez, 'An Essential Picture in a Sketch-book of Ireland: The Last Hedge Schools', *Estudios Irlandeses* (2006), no.1, pp.45–57: 48.

30. See, for example, *The New Statistical Account of Scotland* (15 vols., Edinburgh: William Blackwood & Sons, 1845), vol.14, p.213; Education Commission (Scotland), *Report on the State of Education in the Hebrides* by Alexander Nicolson (Edinburgh, 1866), p.24.

31. Donald J. Withrington, '"Scotland A Half-Educated Nation" in 1845? Reliable Critique or Persuasive Polemic?' pp.55–74 in W.M. Humes & H.M. Paterson (eds.), *Scottish Culture and Scottish Education 1800–1980* (Edinburgh: John Donald, 1983).

32. See, for example, National Archives of Scotland (NAS), GD95/9/1, SSPCK Records, Minutes of General Meetings, vol.4, 1 January 1736–15 November 1759, p.17.

33. Education Commission (Scotland), *Report on the State of Education in the Hebrides*, by Alexander Nicolson (Edinburgh, 1866), p.27.

34. Ibid., p.122.

35. Lynn Abrams, *Myth and Materiality in a Woman's World: Shetland 1800–2000* (Manchester: Manchester University Press, 2005), pp.6, 163.

36. See, for example, W. Gareth Evans, 'The "Bilingual Difficulty": HMI and the Welsh Language in the Victorian Age', *The Welsh Historical Review* (December, 1993), vol.16, no.4, pp.494–513: 506, 509.

37. Maureen Langan-Egan, *Galway Women in the Nineteenth Century* (Dublin: Four Courts Press, 1999), p.99.

38. Deirdre Raftery, 'The Academic Formation of the Fin De Siècle Female-Schooling for Girls in Late Nineteenth Century Ireland', *Irish Educational Studies* (Spring, 2001), vol.20, no.1, pp.321–334: 372; David Fitzpatrick, 'A Share of the Honeycomb: Education, Emigration and Irishwomen', *Continuity and Change* (1986), vol.1, no.2, pp.217–234; Janet Nolan, 'The National Schools and Irish women's Mobility in the Late Nineteenth and Early Twentieth Centuries', *Irish Studies Review* (Spring, 1997), vol.5, no.18, pp.23–28: 25.

39. *Report on the State of Education in the Hebrides*, pp.13–14.

40. See Mary J. Hickman, *Religion, Class and Identity: The State, the Catholic Church and the Education of the Irish in Britain* (Aldershot: Avebury, 1995).

41. Martin Mitchell, *The Irish in the West of Scotland, 1797–1848* (Edinburgh: John Donald, 1988), p.2: between four-fifths and two-thirds of these Irish migrants were Catholics.

42. Brian Titley, *Church, State and the Control of Schooling in Ireland 1900–1944* (Kingston, Ontario: McGill Queen's University Press, 1983), pp.156–157.

43. Catherine Mary Keane (Sr. M. Vincent), 'A History of the Foundation of the Presentation Convents in the Diocese of Kerry and their Contribution to Education during the Nineteenth Century', M.Ed., Trinity College Dublin, 1976, p.161.

44. Paula Coonerty, 'The Presentation Order and the National School System in Limerick, 1837–1870', *North Munster Antiquarian Journal* (1988), vol.30, pp.29–34; John Logan, 'The Dimensions of Gender in Nineteenth-Century Schooling', pp.36–49 in Margaret Kelleher & James H. Murphy (eds.), *Gender Perspectives in Nineteenth-Century Ireland* (Dublin: Irish Academic Press, 1997), p.36.

45. Denis Mclaughlin, 'The Irish Christian Brothers and the National Board of Education: Challenging the Myths', *History of Education* (January, 2008), vol.37, no.1, pp.43–70: 47–52.

46. Jane McCarthy, 'Contribution of the Sisters of Mercy to West Cork Schooling, 1844–1922', M.Ed. Dissertation, University College Cork, 1979, p.185.

47. See Tony Fahey, 'Nuns in the Catholic Church in Ireland in the Nineteenth Century', pp.7–29 in Mary Cullen (ed.), *Girls Don't Do Honours: Irish Women in Education in the 19th and 20th Centuries* (Dublin: Women's Education Bureau, 1987), p.22. Because the female religious orders who taught refused to enter the system of teacher classification operated by the National Board, they (or the Church) received considerably less than a teacher's salary and so, however much inspectors praised their work, the sisters were a cheap source of labour: Deirdre Raftery & Catherine Nowlan-Roebuck, 'Convent Schools and National Education in Nineteenth-century Ireland: Negotiating a Place within a Non-Denominational System', *History of Education* (May, 2007), vol.36, no.3, pp.353–365: 361.

48. Seosamh Mac Suibhne, *Oblivious to the Dawn: Gender Themes in Nineteenth-Century National School Reading Books, Ireland 1831–1900* (Sligo: F.R.D., 1996), pp.viii, 42, 78. See also J.M. Goldstrom, *The Social Content of Education 1808–1870: A Study of the Working-Class School Reader in England and Ireland* (Shannon: Irish University Press, 1972); Lorcan Walsh,

'Images of Women in Nineteenth Century Schoolbooks', *Irish Educational Studies* (1984), vol.4, no.1, pp.73–87.

49. Commissioners of the Board of Education in Ireland, Third Report (1809), p.101. See also Revel Guest & Angela V. John, *Lady Charlotte: An Extraordinary Life* (2nd ed., London: Weidenfeld & Nicolson, 2007), especially pp.72–81.
50. See, for example, Educational Commission (Scotland), *Second Report* (Edinburgh, 1867), p.xxxvii.
51. Education Commission (Scotland), *Report on the Sate of Education in the Country Districts* by A.C. Sellar and C.F. Maxwell (Edinburgh, 1866), p.98.
52. Newcastle Commission, vol.2, p.183.
53. See A.F.B. Roberts, 'A New View of the Infant School Movement', *British Journal of Educational Studies* (June, 1972), vol.20, no.2, pp.154–164. See also Phil Gardner, *The Lost Elementary Schools of Victorian England: The People's Education* (London: Croom Helm, 1984); Phillip McCann, *Popular Education and Socialization in the Nineteenth Century* (London: Methuen, 1977).
54. See J.H. Higginson, 'Dame Schools', *British Journal of Educational Studies* (1974), vol.22, no.2, pp.166–181; D.P Leinster-Mackay, 'Dame Schools: A Need for Review', *British Journal of Educational Studies* (1976), vol.24, no.1, pp.33–48.
55. Maria Hull, 'A Derbyshire Schooling: 1884–1893', *History Workshop Journal* (Spring, 1988), vol.25, no.1, pp.166–170: 168, 170. See also Colin Griffin, 'Learning to Labour: Elementary Education in the Leicestershire and South Derbyshire Coalfields c.1840–1870', *History of Education* (2002), vol.31, no.2, pp.95–116: 114–15.
56. Newcastle Commission, vol.3, p.358.
57. Minutes of the Committee of Council on Education, 1859–1860, p.273.
58. Christina S. Bremner, *Education of Girls and Women in Great Britain* (London: Swan Sonnenschein, 1897), p.233.
59. *Report on the State of Education in the Hebrides*, p.118; Minutes of the Committee of Council on Education, 1851–1852, p.1016.
60. Report on the State of Education in the Country Districts, p.125.
61. Minutes of the Committee of Council on Education, 1851–1852, p.1016; *Report on the State of Education in the Hebrides*, p.118.
62. Minutes of the Committee of Council on Education, 1852–1853, pp.806–807.
63. Minutes of the Committee of Council on Education, 1852–1853, pp.1092–1093; 1854–1855, pp.405–408.
64. *Report of the Commission of Inquiry into the State of Education in Wales*, part 3, p.65.
65. The exception might be grocers: see Troy Bickham, 'Eating the Empire: Intersections of Food, Cookery and Imperialism in Eighteenth-Century Britain', *Past & Present* (February, 2008), vol.198, no.1, pp.71–109.
66. See Gwyneth Tyson Roberts, *The Language of the Blue Books: The Perfect Instrument of Empire* (Cardiff: University of Wales Press, 1998).
67. The Blue Books, part 1, p.7. For a discussion of the construction of the Celtic stereotype and associated Anglo-Saxon superiority, see Roberts, *The Language of the Blue Books*, p.231.
68. The Blue Books, part 2, p.66.
69. Ibid., part 1, p.32.
70. Newcastle Commission, vol.2, pp.248–249.
71. The Blue Books, part 1, p.17.

72. Newcastle Commission, vol.1, p.89.
73. Gareth Elwyn Jones, *The Education of a Nation* (Cardiff: University of Wales Press, 1997), p.13. See also Frank Price Jones, 'The Blue Books of 1847', pp.127–144 in Jac L. Williams & Gwilym Rees Hughes (eds.), *The History of Education in Wales* (Swansea: C. Davies, 1978); Gwyneth Tyson Roberts, *The Language of the Blue Books*.
74. See W. Gareth Evans, *Education and Female Emancipation: The Welsh Experience, 1847–1914* (Cardiff: University of Wales, 1990), pp.46–49.
75. *Report on the State of Education in the Country Districts of Scotland* by A.C. Sellar and C.F. Maxwell (Edinburgh, 1866), pp.132–133.
76. Ibid., p.146. See also Lindy Moore, 'Invisible Scholars: Girls Learning Latin and Mathematics in the Elementary Public Schools of Scotland before 1872', *History of Education* (June, 1984), vol.13, no.2, pp.121–137.
77. *Report on the State of Education in the Country Districts*, p.131.
78. Education Commission (Scotland). *First Report by Her Majesty's Commissioners, Oral Evidence* (Edinburgh, 1865), p.18.
79. Education Commission (Scotland) *Third Report of Her Majesty's Commissioners, Burgh and Middle-Class Schools* by T. Harvey & A. Sellar (Edinburgh, 1868), vol.1, p.ix.
80. [George Lewis], *Scotland A Half-Educated Nation both in the Quality and Quantity of her Educational Institutions* (Glasgow: William Collins, 1834).
81. See Lindsay Anderson, *The Autonomy of Modern Scotland* (Edinburgh: Edinburgh University Press, 1994), pp.66–67.
82. *Report on the State of Education in the Country Districts of Scotland*, p.98.
83. Ibid., p.67.
84. *Third Report of Her Majesty's Commissioners, Burgh and Middle-Class Schools*, p.139.
85. T.M. Devine, *The Scottish Nation 1700–2000* (London: Allen Lane, 1999), pp.533–534; William W. Knox, *Industrial Nation. Work Culture and Society in Scotland, 1800–Present* (Edinburgh: Edinburgh University Press, 1999), p.58.
86. Evans, *Education in Industrial Wales*, pp.204–205.
87. Ibid., p.ii.
88. Kenneth O. Morgan, *Rebirth of a Nation: Wales 1880–1980* (Oxford: Clarendon Press, 1981), p.5.
89. The Blue Books, part 1, p.20.
90. Paul O'Leary, *Immigration and Integration: The Irish in Wales, 1789–1922* (Cardiff: University of Wales Press, 2000), pp.3–4.
91. The Blue Books, part 1, p.21.
92. Ibid., p.22. See also pp.217, 219; and part 2, p.57. For the defence of the moral character of Welsh womanhood, see Sian R. Williams, 'The True Cymraes: Images of Women in Women's Nineteenth-Century Periodicals', pp.69–91 in Angela V. John (ed.), *Our Mothers' Land: Chapters in Welsh Women's History* (Cardiff: University of Wales Press, 1991).
93. The Blue Books, part 3 [872], p.64.
94. Ibid., part 2, p.275.
95. Ibid., part 2, p.275.
96. See pp.35–59 on education in Glamorgan since 1780 in Jones, *The Education of a Nation*.
97. The Blue Books, part 1, p.60.
98. Ibid., part 2, p.50.
99. Evans, *Education in Industrial Wales, 1700–1900*, chapter 4.

100. Royal Commission on Irish Education, *First Report* (1825), p.840.
101. Quoted in O'Leary, *Immigration and Integration*, p.62.
102. Ibid., p.63.
103. Morgan, *Rebirth of a Nation*, p.22.
104. Jones, 'The Blue Books of 1847', p.127.
105. Newcastle Commission, vol.1, p.89.
106. John J. Bagley & Alexander J. Bagley, *The State and Education in England and Wales, 1833–1968* (London: Macmillan, 1969), p.16.
107. Newcastle Commission, vol.2, p.149.
108. Ibid., p.176.
109. Ibid., p.190.
110. Ibid., p.176. See also Adrian Elliott, 'The Bradford School Board and the Department of Education, 1870–1902: Areas of Conflict', *Journal of Educational Administration and History* (July, 1981), vol.13, no.2, pp.18–23.
111. Gerald Ashton Banks, 'The Provision of Elementary Education in Liverpool 1861–1870', M.Ed. Dissertation, University of Liverpool, 1981, pp.27–28.
112. Newcastle Commission, vol.2, pp.287, 348.
113. Colin Griffin, 'Learning to Labour: Elementary Education in the Leicestershire and South Derbyshire Coalfield c.1840–1870', *History of Education* (2002), vol.3.1, no.2, pp.95–116: 100.
114. W.B. Stephens, *Education in Britain 1750–1914* (Basingstoke: Macmillan, 1998), p.37.
115. Ibid.
116. Meg Gomersall, 'Education for Domesticity? A Nineteenth-Century Perspective on Girls' Schooling and Education', *Gender and Education* (1999), vol.6, no.3, pp.235–247: 239.
117. Meg Gomersall, 'Ideas and Realities: The Education of Working-Class Girls, 1800–1870,' *History of Education* (March, 1988), vol.17, no.1, pp.37–54: 41.
118. Newcastle Commission, vol.2, pp.145–148. For a Scottish example of boys employed as grouse beaters, see Glasgow City Archives (GCA), SR10/3/1069/1/1, Lanark County, Dolphinton Public School, log book entries for 11/11.1877; 18/1/1884, 3/11/1893.
119. Jane McDermid, *The Schooling of Working-Class Girls in Victorian Scotland: Gender, Education and Identity* (Abingdon: Routledge, 2005), p.80.
120. Newcastle Commission, vol.2, p.149; *Argyll Commission Second Report: Elementary Schools*, p.cxxxv.
121. McDermid, *The Schooling of Working-Class Girls in Victorian Scotland*, pp.71, 77. For Lancashire, see Meg Gomersall, *Working-Class Girls in Nineteenth-Century England: Life, Work and Schooling* (London: Macmillan, 1997), p.58.
122. H.G. Williams, 'Elementary Education in Caernarvonshire, 1839–1902', PhD, University of Bangor, 1981, p.438.
123. L.J. Williams & Dot Jones, 'Women at Work in Nineteenth-Century Wales', *Llafur: The Journal of the Society of Welsh Labour History* (1983), vol.3, no.3, pp.20–32: 23.
124. Deirdre Beddoe, 'Images of Welsh Women', pp.227–238 in Tony Curtis (ed.), *Wales: The Imagined Nation. Studies in Cultural and National Identity* (Bridgend: Poetry Wales Press, 1986), p.230.
125. Williams & Jones, 'Women at Work in Nineteenth-Century Wales', p.24.
126. John, *Our Mothers' Land*. See also Michael Roberts, 'Gender, Work and Socialization in Wales c.1450–c.1850', pp.15–54 in Sandra Betts (ed.), *Our Daughters' Land: Past and Present* (Cardiff: University of Wales Press, 1996).

127. Newcastle Commission, vol.2, p.149.
128. *Report on the State of Education in the Country Districts*, p.111.
129. *The Scotsman*, 20 January 1864.
130. Newcastle Commission, vol.2, pp.323–324.
131. Ibid., p.364.
132. See Robert A. Houston, *Scottish Literacy and Scottish Identity: Illiteracy and Society in Scotland and Northern England 1600–1800* (Cambridge: Cambridge University Press, 1985).
133. Newcastle Commission, vol.3, p.521.
134. Ibid., p.247.
135. Ibid., p.511.
136. *Report on the State of Education in the Hebrides*, pp.52, 56, 92. See also Robert E. Tyson, 'The Economy of Aberdeen', pp.9–21 in John S. Smith & David Stevenson (eds.), *Aberdeen in the Nineteenth Century* (Aberdeen: Aberdeen University Press, 1988).
137. See, for example, A.M. Davies, *The Barnsley School Board 1871–1903* (Barnsley, 1965), p.53: boys in Barnsley also found work in the glass-making industry.
138. See Eleanor Gordon, *Women and the Labour Movement in Scotland 1850–1914* (Oxford: Oxford University Press, 1991).
139. Christopher A. Whatley, David B. Swinfen & Annette M. Smith, *The Life and Times of Dundee* (Edinburgh: John Donald, 1993), pp.114–115; *Report of the State of Education in Glasgow*, Education Commission (Scotland), p.116.
140. Pamela Horn, 'Child Workers in the Pillow Lace and Straw Plait Trades of Victorian Buckinghamshire and Bedfordshire', *The Historical Journal* (1974), vol.17, no.4, pp.79–96: 795.
141. Helen Corr, *Changes in Educational Policies in Britain, 1800–1920: How Gender Inequalities Reshaped the Teaching Profession* (Lampeter: Edwin Mellen Press, 2008), pp.186–187.
142. Jane McDermid, 'Catholic Working-Class Girls' Education in Lowland Scotland, 1872–1900', *The Innes Review* (Spring, 1996), vol.47, no.1, pp.69–80:73.
143. *Report of the Royal Commission Appointed to Inquire into the Working of the Elementary Education Acts, England and Wales* [Cross Commission] (1888), pp.142–143.
144. Robert Smith, *Schools, Politics and Society: Elementary Education in Wales, 1870–1902* (Cardiff: University of Wales Press, 1999), p.143.
145. Ibid., p.138.
146. *Report of the Committee of Council on Education in Scotland for 1886–1887* (London, 1887), p.174.
147. Hull, 'A Derbyshire Schooling: 1884–1893', pp.168, 170.
148. For examples from Lanarkshire, see Mary MacKintosh, 'Education in Lanarkshire: A Historical Survey Up to the Act of 1872, from Original and Contemporary Sources', PhD, Glasgow University, 1968, p.479 (for 1861); Samuel Cooper, *The 1872 Education Act in Lanarkshire* (Hamilton: Hamilton College of Education, 1973), p.6 (for 1884).
149. Jane Martin, '"To Blaise the Trail for Women to Follow Along": Sex, Gender and the Politics of Education on the London School Board, 1870–1904', *Gender and Education* (2000), vol.12, no.2, pp.165–181: 174.
150. GCA, T-HH4/1/1, Hill & Hogan Bequest, Sederunt Book of Directors of the Glasgow School of Cookery, 19 February 1892, 27.
151. Martin, *Women and the Politics of Schooling in Victorian and Edwardian England*, pp.79–84.

152. Edinburgh City Library (ECL), Edinburgh School Board Press Cuttings, vol.1, p.22: *The Scotsman*, 6 December 1877.
153. Ibid., p.199 for *The Scotsman* 21 January 1888.
154. For example, see Andrew Bain, *Ancient and Modern. A Comparison of the Social Composition of the Burgh School Boards of Stirling and Falkirk from 1873 to 1919* (Polmont: Falkirk Education Services, 2006), pp.55–61.
155. McDermid, *The Schooling of Working-Class Girls in Victorian Scotland*, p.69.
156. Jenny Zmroczek, 'The Education and Employment of Girls in Norwich, 1870–1939', PhD, University of East Anglia, 2004, Abstract and p.355.
157. Quoted in Keane, 'A History of the Foundation of the Presentation Convents in the Diocese of Kerry and Their Contribution to Education during the Nineteenth Century', p.162. See also Jane Barnes, *Irish Industrial Schools 1868–1908: Origins and Development* (Dublin: Irish Academic Press, 1980), pp.47, 118–122.
158. Mary Daly, *Social and Economic History of Ireland since 1800* (Dublin: Educational Company, 1981), p.105.
159. Langan-Egan, *Galway Women in the Nineteenth Century*, p.91.
160. Fitzpatrick, '"A Share of the Honeycomb"', p.223. See also Joanna Bourke, '"The Health Caravan": Domestic Education and Female Labour in Rural Ireland, 1890–1914', *Eire/Ireland* (Winter, 1989), no.24, pp.21–38.
161. See Séamas Ó. Buachalla, 'Educational Policy and the Role of the Irish Language 1831–1981', *European Journal of Education* (1984), vol.19, no.1, pp.75–92.
162. See, for example, the *Third Annual Report of the Board of Education for Scotland* (Edinburgh, 1876), p.xxv.
163. *Fourth Annual Report of the Board of Education for Scotland* (Edinburgh, 1877), p.xvii.
164. *Report of the Committee of Council on Education in Scotland for 1886–1887* (London, 1887), p.xx.
165. This did not mean that there were no higher grade schools in Wales: see, for example, E. John Davies, 'The Origins and Development of Secondary Education in the Rhondda Valleys (1878–1923)', M.A. Dissertation, 1965, University of Wales, pp.41–41, 55; John Fletcher, 'The Influence of the Welsh Intermediate Education Act of 1889 on Technical Education', PhD, University of Wales, 1982, pp.107, 110 for higher grade schools in Swansea and Cardiff.
166. Gareth Elwyn Jones, *Controls and Conflicts in Welsh Secondary Education 1889–1944* (Cardiff: University of Wales Press, 1982), p.7.
167. Deborah James, '"Teaching Girls": Intermediate Schools and Career Opportunities for Girls in the East Glamorgan Valleys of Wales, 1896–1914', *History of Education* (2001), vol.30, no.6, pp.513–526.
168. Gordon Roderick, 'Social Class, Curriculum and the Concept of Relevance in Secondary Education: Industrial Glamorgan, 1889–1914', *The Welsh History Review* (1998), vol.19, no.2, pp.289–318: 309–310.
169. W. Gareth Evans, 'The Welsh Intermediate and Technical Education Act of 1889: A Centenary Appreciation', *History of Education* (September, 1990), vol.19, no.3, pp.195–210:199, 207.
170. Kenneth David Evans, 'The Development of Secondary Education in South Pembrokeshire, 1889–1939', M.A. Dissertation, University of Wales, 1970, pp.68–70.
171. Robert D. Anderson, *Education and the Scottish People 1750–1918* (Oxford: Clarendon Press, 1995), pp.190–92.
172. Jones, *Controls and Conflicts in Welsh Secondary Education*, p.8; Smith, *Schools, Politics and Society*, pp.154, 156.

173. It did increase proportionately higher than in England in the first decade of the twentieth century, though the spread of occupations was more limited than in England, while there was considerable regional variation within Wales: see Williams & Jones, 'Women at Work in Nineteenth Century Wales', p.28.

174. Jacob Middleton, 'The Cry for Useless Knowledge', *History of Education Researcher* (November, 2005), no.76, pp.91–99. See also Joyce Goodman for technical education for girls which went beyond domestic subjects: 'Social Investigation and Economic Empowerment: Trade Schools for Girls, 1892–1914', *History of Education* (1998), vol.27, no.3, pp.297–314.

175. *Report of the Royal Commission on Secondary Education* [Bryce Commission] (1895), vol.1, p.77.

176. Ibid., pp.12–15, 77.

177. Ibid., p.297.

178. Ibid., vol. 6, p.252.

179. Ibid., vol.5, p.88.

180. Richard Aldrich, 'Educating Our Mistresses', *History of Education* (1983), vol.12, no.2, pp.93–102: 93–94, 96.

181. See, for example, Stephens, *Education in Britain 1750–1914*, especially Chapter 1 on 'Elementary Education to the 1860s, pp.1–20, and the tables on attendance in Chapter 2, pp.22–39: 22, 24, 29, 30.

182. See Joyce Elizabeth Livingstone, 'Pauper Education in Victorian England: Organization and Administration within the New Poor Law, 1834–1880', PhD, London Guildhall University, 1993.

183. Quoted in Dale Spender (ed.), *The Education Papers: Women's Quest for Equality in Britain 1850–1912* (London: Routledge & Kegan Paul, 1987), pp.50–57: 54.

184. Barnes, *Irish Industrial Schools 1868–1908*, p.139.

NOTES TO CHAPTER 3

1. See 'The Old Adam and the New Man: Emerging Themes in the History of English Masculinities, 1750–1850', pp.61–82 in John Tosh, *Manliness and Masculinities in Nineteenth-Century Britain* (Harlow: Pearson Education, 2005); Robert B. Shoemaker, *Gender in English Society 1650–1850: The Emergence of Separate Spheres?* (Harlow: Longman, 1998).

2. Trevor May, *The Victorian Public School* (Oxford: Shire, 2009); Thomas W. Bamford, *Rise of the Public Schools: A Study of Boys' Public Boarding Schools in England and Wales from 1837 to the Present Day* (London: Nelson, 1967).

3. J.A. Mangan, *Athleticism in the Victorian and Edwardian Public School: The Emergence and Consolidation of the Educational Ideology* (Cambridge: Cambridge University Press, 1982) and *The Games Ethic and Imperialism: Aspects of the Diffusion of an Ideal* (London, 1986).

4. John Tosh, *A Man's Place: Masculinity and the Middle-Class Home in Victorian England* (London: Yale University Press, 1999), pp.102–122.

5. See Sara Delamont & Lorna Duffin (eds.), *The Nineteenth-Century Woman: Her Cultural and Physical World* (London: Croom Helm, 1978); Joan Burstyn, *Victorian Education and the Ideal of Womanhood* (London: Croom Helm, 1980).

6. Maria Edgeworth & Richard Lowell Edgeworth, *Practical Education* (2nd ed., 3 vols., London: J. Johnson, 1801), vol.3, p.6.

7. 'Dorothea Beale, *Address to the National Association for the Promotion of Social Science* (1865)', pp.123–139 in Dale Spender (ed.), *The Education*

   Papers: Women's Quest for Equality in Britain 1850–1912 (London: Routledge & Kegan Paul, 1987), p.123.
8. Ibid., p.130.
9. Andrea Jacobs & Joyce Goodman, 'The Music Teacher in English Girls' Secondary Schools before 1939', *Women's History Magazine* (Spring, 2007), no.55, pp.12–20; Paula Gillett, *Musical Women in England, 1870–1914: 'Encroaching on All Man's Privileges'* (Basingstoke: Macmillan, 2000), pp.9–11 for women as music teachers and daily governesses.
10. Ellen Jordan, *The Women's Movement and Women's Employment in Nineteenth-Century Britain* (London: Routledge, 1999), pp.113–114.
11. For Harrow, see *Report of the Public Schools Commission* [Clarendon Commission] (1864) vol.1, p.13.
12. Samuel Whyte on 'Feminine Education' (May, 1772), quoted in Robert E. Ward, *An Encyclopedia of Irish Schools, 1500–1800* (Lampeter: Edwin Mellen Press, 1995), pp.233–235: 234.
13. Christine de Bellaigue, *Educating Women: Schooling and Identity in England and France 1800–1867* (Oxford: Oxford University Press, 2007), p.173.
14. Marjorie R. Theobald, 'The Accomplished Woman and the Propriety of Intellect: A New Look at Women's Education in Britain and Australia, 1800–1850', *History of Education* (March, 1988), vol.17, no.1, pp.21–35.
15. See Colin Shrosbree, *Public Schools and Private Education: The Clarendon Commission, 1861–1864, and the Public School Acts* (Manchester: Manchester University Press, 1988).
16. Michael McCram, *Thomas Arnold, Headmaster: A Reassessment* (Oxford: Oxford University Press, 1989).
17. Ruth Watts, *Women in Science: A Social and Cultural History* (Abingdon: Routledge, 2007), pp.112–114.
18. George Combe, *Lectures on Popular Education Delivered to the Edinburgh Philosophical Association in April and November 1833* (3rd ed., Edinburgh: Maclachlan, Stewart & Co., 1848), pp.50–58.
19. Watts, *Women in Science*, pp.112–114. Camilla Leach found that the 'provision of science education within Quakerism does not appear to have been differentiated by gender': 'Religion and Rationality: Quaker Women and Science Education 1790–1850', *History of Education* (2006), vol.35, no.1, pp.69–90: 76.
20. Burstyn, *Victorian Education and the Ideal of Womanhood*, p.32.
21. Brian Simon & Ian C. Bradley (eds.), *The Victorian Public School* (Dublin: Gill & Macmillan, 1975), p.143.
22. Norman Vance, *The Sinews of the Spirit: The Ideal of Christian Manliness in Victorian Literature and Religious Thought* (Cambridge: Cambridge University Press, 1985), pp.134–160.
23. Peter Searby (ed.), *Educating the Victorian Middle Class* (Leicester: History of Education Society, 1982).
24. W.B. Stephens, *Education in Britain 1750–1914* (Basingstoke: Macmillan, 1998), p.115. Working-class men also took advantage of these classes: Sheila Rowbotham, 'Travellers in a Strange Country: Responses of Working-Class Students to the University Extension Movement, 1873–1910', *History Workshop Journal* (1981), no.12, pp.62–95: see p. 71 for working-class women and the movement.
25. Christina S. Bremner, *Education of Girls and Women in Great Britain* (London: Swan Sonnenschein, 1897), p.159.
26. See Carol Dyhouse, 'Miss Buss and Miss Beale: Gender and Authority in the History of Education', pp.2–39 in Felicity Hunt (ed.), *Lessons for Life: The*

Schooling of Girls and Women 1850–1950 (Oxford: Basil Blackwell, 1987); for Emily Davies, see pp.133–165 in Margaret Forster, *Significant Sisters: The Grassroots of Active Feminism 1839–1939* (London: Penguin, 1986).

27. Tosh, *A Man's Place*, pp.172–174
28. *Report of the Schools Inquiry Commission* [Taunton Commission] (1868), vol.1, p.2.
29. Ibid., vol.1, p.546.
30. Ibid., vol.8, p.46.
31. Ibid., vol.7, p.212.
32. Ibid., vol.8, no.41.
33. Ibid., vol.8, p.41; vol.6, p.21.
34. Ibid., vol.8, pp.471–479; *Report of the Royal Commission on Secondary Education* [Bryce Commission] (1895), vol.6, p.311.
35. Donald H. Akenson, *The Irish Education Experiment: The National System of Education in the Nineteenth Century* (London: Routledge & Kegan Paul, 1970), p.217.
36. John Roach, 'Boys and Girls at School, 1800–1870', *History of Education* (1986), vol.15, no.3, pp.147–159: 158.
37. Anne V. O'Connor, 'Influences Affecting Girls' Secondary Education in Ireland, 1860–1910', *Archivium Hibernicum* (1986), vol.41, pp.83–98: 85. O'Connor records that of the 62 convent boarding schools founded in Ireland in the nineteenth century, only six were by Irish religious orders.
38. Barbara Walsh, *Roman Catholic Nuns in England and Wales, 1800–1937: A Social History* (Dublin: Irish Academic Press, 2002), p.37. For an example of a Quaker boarding school which offered sports such as cricket and lessons in horse-riding, see William E. Marsden, *Unequal Educational Provision in England and Wales: The Nineteenth-Century Roots* (London: Woburn, 1987), p.245.
39. Susan O'Brien, '"Terra Incognita": The Nun in Nineteenth-Century England', *Past & Present* (1989), no.121, pp.110–140. See also Carmen M. Mangion, '"Good Teacher" or "Good Religious"? The Professional Identity of Catholic Women Religious in Nineteenth-Century England and Wales', *Women's History Review* (2005), vol.14, no.2, pp.223–242.
40. Susan O'Brien, 'French Nuns in Nineteenth-Century England', *Past & Present* (February, 1997), no.154, pp.142–180: 179 and footnote 115.
41. Janet Howarth, 'The Church of England and Women's Higher Education, c.1840–1914', pp.153–170 in Peter Ghosh & Lawrence Goldman (eds.), *Politics and Culture in Victorian Britain: Essays in Memory of Colin Matthew* (Oxford: Oxford University Press, 2006), p.156.
42. Walsh, *Roman Catholic Nuns in England and Wales*, p.79.
43. S. Karly Kehoe, *Creating a Scottish Church: Catholicism, Gender and Ethnicity in Nineteenth-Century Scotland* (Manchester: Manchester University Press, 2010), p.80 and pp.118–120 for the geographical spread of female religious communities.
44. Taunton Commission, vol.1, p.548.
45. Ibid., vol.7, pp.208, 493.
46. Ibid., vol.9, p.282.
47. Marsden, *Unequal Educational Provision*, p.240; Joyce Senders Pedersen, 'The Reform of Women's Secondary and Higher Education: Institutional Change and Social Values in Mid and Late Victorian England', *History of Education Quarterly* (Spring, 1979), vol.19, no.1, pp.61–91: 63.
48. Taunton Commission, vol.5, p.241.
49. Ibid., p.631.
50. Ibid., pp.251, 254.

51. Ibid., p.707.
52. Ibid., vol.7, p.53.
53. Marjorie Cruickshank, 'The Argyll Commission Report 1865–1868: A Landmark Review in Scottish Education', *British Journal of Educational Studies* (June, 1967), vol.15, no.2, pp.133–147.
54. *Report on the State of Education in the Burgh and Middle-Class Schools in Scotland* by Thomas Harvey & A.C. Sellar [Argyll Commission] (2 vols., Edinburgh, 1868), vol.2, pp.10, 179, 227, 295.
55. Ibid., vol.1, p.295.
56. Ibid., p.x.
57. Taunton Commission, vol.5, p.59.
58. Ibid., vol.6, pp.7–21.
59. Harvey & Sellar, Argyll Commission, vol.1, p.139.
60. Taunton Commission, vol.6, pp.57–58.
61. Harvey & Sellar, Argyll Commission, vol.1, pp.84–85.
62. Taunton Commission, vol.5, p.83; de Bellaigue, *Educating Women*, p.143.
63. Lindy Moore, 'Young Ladies' Institutions: The Development of Secondary Schools for Girls in Scotland, 1833–c. 1870', *History of Education* (May, 2003), vol.32, no.3, pp.249–272: 249–250.
64. Ibid., p.258.
65. de Bellaigue, *Educating Women*, p.13.
66. Pedersen, 'The Reform of Women's Secondary and Higher Education', p.63.
67. Moore, 'Young Ladies' Institutes', p.251; Mary Macdonald with Ann Hope, 'The Scottish Institution: A Pioneer Venture', *History of Education Society Bulletin* (Autumn, 1993), no.52, pp.49–55.
68. Grainne O'Flynn, 'Some Aspects of the Education of Irish Women through the Years', *Capuchin Annual* (1971), pp.164–179: 17–75.
69. Maria Luddy, *Women and Philanthropy in Nineteenth-Century Ireland* (Cambridge: Cambridge University Press, 1995), p.13.
70. O'Connor, 'Influences Affecting Girls' Secondary Education in Ireland'.
71. Anne V. O'Connor on Jellicoe in Mary Cullen & Maria Luddy (eds.), *Women, Power and Consciousness in Nineteenth-Century Ireland: Eight Biographical Studies* (Dublin: Attic Press, 1995), pp.134–140.
72. Alison Jordan, '"Opening the Gates of Learning": The Belfast Ladies' Institute, 1867–1897', pp.33–57 in Janice Holmes & Diane Urquhart (eds.), *Coming into the Light: The Work, Politics and Religion of Women in Ulster 1840–1940* (Belfast: Institute of Irish Studies Queen's University, 1994), pp.35–39. Queen's College Belfast admitted women to its arts classes in 1882, Queen's College Cork followed suit in 1885 and Queen's College Galway in 1888, though few women attended the colleges until the establishment of the National University of Ireland in 1908: Alan Hayes & Diane Urquhart (eds.), *The Irish Women's History Reader* (London: Routledge, 2001), p.46; Margaret Ó hÓgartaigh, 'Emerging from the Educational Cloisters: Educational Influences on the Development of Professional Women', *PaGes* (1996), vol.3, pp.113–123: 118.
73. Luddy, *Women and Philanthropy in Nineteenth-Century Ireland*, p.13.
74. E. Brian Titley, *Church, State and the Control of Schooling in Ireland, 1900–1944* (Kingston, Ontario: McGill-Queen's University Press, 1983), pp.7, 12.
75. For these women see Cullen & Luddy (eds.) *Women, Power and Consciousness in Nineteenth-Century Ireland*: in 1884 Alice Oldham was one of the first female graduates of the Royal University of Ireland.
76. O'Flynn, 'Some Aspects of the Education of Irish Women through the Years', p.176.

77. See Marsden, *Unequal Educational Provision*, p.237 for an advertisement for a 'first-class school for the daughters of gentlemen' boasting extensive grounds facing the sea, tennis courts, hockey, archery, a 'cycle stable' and gymnasium.
78. Deirdre Raftery, 'The Academic Formation of the Fin De Siècle Female-Schooling for Girls in Late Nineteenth Century Ireland', *Irish Educational Studies* (Spring, 2001), vol.20, no.1, pp.321–334: 329.
79. W. Gareth Evans, *Education and Emancipation*, pp.37–38.
80. Ibid., pp.39–40.
81. W. Gareth Evans, 'The Welsh Intermediate and Technical Education Act 1889 and the Education of Girls', *The Welsh History Review* (1991), vol.15, no.3, pp.183–217: 186.
82. Kenneth David Evans, 'The Development of Secondary Education in South Pembrokeshire 1889–1939', M.A. Dissertation, University of Wales, 1970, pp.1–2.
83. Malcolm Seaborne, *Schools in Wales 1500–1900: A Social and Architectural History* (Denbigh: Gee & Son, 1992), pp.163–165. The staff at the Howell's schools but not the pupils had to be Church of England.
84. *Report of the Committee Appointed to Inquire into the Condition of Intermediate and Higher Education in Wales* [Aberdare Report] (1881), pp.lii–liii.
85. W. Gareth Evans, *Perspectives on a Century of Secondary Education in Wales 1889–1999* (Aberystwyth: University College of Wales, 1990), p.35.
86. Gordon Roderick, 'Social Class, Curriculum and the Concept of Relevance in Secondary Education: Industrial Glamorgan, 1889–1914', *The Welsh History Review* (1998), vol.19, no.2, pp.289–318: p.297.
87. Aberdare Report, p.856.
88. Roderick, 'Social Class, Curriculum and the Concept of Relevance in Secondary Education', p.295.
89. Ibid., p.300.
90. Aberdare Report, p.xliii.
91. Roderick, 'Social Class, Curriculum and the Concept of Relevance in Secondary Education', p.308.
92. Evans, 'The Development of Secondary Education in South Pembrokeshire 1889–1939', p.68.
93. Deborah James, '"Teaching Girls": Intermediate Schools and Career Opportunities for Girls in the East Glamorgan Valleys of Wales, 1890–1914', *History of Education* (2001), vol.30, no.6, pp.513–526.
94. Roderick, 'Social Class, Curriculum and the Concept of Relevance in Secondary Education', p.309.
95. Geoffrey Walford (ed.), *The Private Schooling of Girls Past and Present* (London: Woburn, 1993), p.21; Sheila Fletcher, *Feminists and Bureaucrats: A Study in the Development of Girls' Education in the Nineteenth Century* (Cambridge: Cambridge University Press, 1980), p.13.
96. Some Church of England clergymen helped promote GPDSC schools: Howarth, 'The Church of England and Women's Higher Education, c.1840–1914', p.163.
97. Fletcher, *Feminists and Bureaucrats*, pp.3, 100, 151, 171. Mary Cathcart Borer records that there were 34 GPDSC schools by 1890, but four closed 'mainly because they were in districts from which the middle-class population was moving away'; by 1901 another four had been added: *Willingly to School: A History of Women's Education* (London: P. Lutterworth, 1976), p.287. Rosemary Annette Thynne suggests that the GPDSC had closed six schools by the end of the 1890s and had 33 schools in 1900: 'The Girls' High

Schools 1872–1914 and the shaping of a new generation of middle-class girls', PhD, Royal Holloway College, London, 2005, p.221. The difference may be that a number of those accredited to the GPDSC were founded by what Thynne terms 'individual enthusiasts' or local branches of the Women's Educational Union: she gives (p.6) a total of 46 high schools based on the GPDSC model. The Church School Society had 24 girls' high schools, but these had less funding and poorer facilities and were smaller than either endowed or GPDSC schools.

98. Thynne, 'The Girls' High Schools 1872–1914', pp.7, 124–125.
99. Janet Howarth, 'Public Schools, Safety-Nets and Educational Ladders: The Classification of Girls' Secondary Schools, 1880–1914', *Oxford Review of Education* (1985), vol.11, no.1, pp.59–71: 66.
100. Moore, 'Young Ladies' Institutes', p.267.
101. Gillian Avery *'The Best Type of Girl': A History of Girls' Independent Schools* (London, 1991), pp.73–74.
102. Carol Dyhouse, 'Good Wives and Little Mothers: Social Anxieties and the Schoolgirl's Curriculum, 1890–1920', *Oxford Review of Education* (1977), vol.3, no.1, pp.21–35: 21.
103. Josephine Kamm, *Hope Deferred: Girls' Education in English History* (London: Methuen, 1965), p.217; Borer, *Willingly to School*, p.286; Bremner, *Education of Girls and Women in Great Britain*, pp.92, 95.
104. de Bellaigue, *Educating Women*, p.138. See also Joyce Senders Pedersen, *The Reform of Girls' Secondary Education in Victorian England: A Study of Elites and Educational Change* (New York: Garland, 1987).
105. Joyce Goodman, 'Constructing Contradiction: The Power and Powerlessness of Women in the Giving and Taking of Evidence in the Bryce Commission', *History of Education* (1997), vol.26, no.3, pp.287–306: 287.
106. *Reports from the Commissioners, Inspectors and Others into Secondary Education* [Bryce Commission] (1895), vol.6, p.vii.
107. Ibid., vol.7, p.111.
108. Ibid., vol.1, pp.1–12. Bryce considered that Bedford College, London, had 'attained a rank equal to that of these five (university colleges)'.
109. Ibid., p.76.
110. Ibid., p.159.
111. Ibid., vol.6, p.viii.
112. Ibid., p. 294.
113. Ibid., pp.88–94.
114. Ibid., p.104.
115. Ibid., vol.7, p.29.
116. Ibid., p.105.
117. Ibid., vol.6, pp.258–259, 272–274.
118. Ibid., vol.7, p.29.
119. Watts, *Women in Science*, pp.116, 120.
120. Bremner, *Education of Girls and Women in Great Britain*, p.180.
121. Walford, *The Private Schooling of Girls*, pp.71–72.
122. Juliet Stevenson, 'A Neglected Issue in the History of Education and Training: Women Students of University College London and the Polytechnic at Regent Street, c.1870–1930', PhD, Thames Valley University, London, 1996. UCL first admitted women as undergraduates in 1878; Regent Street Polytechnic admitted women almost from its establishment in 1838, setting up a separate women's college in 1888.
123. Joyce Goodman, 'Social Investigation and Economic Empowerment: The Women's Industrial Council and the LCC Trade Schools for Girls, 1892–1914', *History of Education* (1998), vol.27, no.3, pp.297–314.

124. Bremner, *The Education of Girls and Women in Great Britain*, pp.188–214.
125. Goodman, 'Social Investigation and Economic Empowerment', pp.313–334.
126. Bryce Commission, vol.6, pp.285–287.
127. Jordan, '"Opening the Gates of Learning"', p.37; Sarah Burstall, *The Story of Manchester High School for Girls 1871–1911* (Manchester, 1911), p.13.
128. Bryce Commission, vol.7, p.289.
129. Ibid., vol.7, p.40.
130. Ibid., pp.105–107.
131. Ibid., vol.6, p.vii.
132. Gareth Elwyn Jones, *Controls and Conflicts in Welsh Secondary Education 1889–1944* (Cardiff: University of Wales Press, 1982), pp.5–8.
133. Bryce Commission, vol.6, pp.290–292.
134. Ibid., vol.1, p.77.
135. Aberdare Report, p.lxiii.
136. John Fletcher, 'The Influence of the Welsh Intermediate Education Act of 1889 on Technical Education', PhD, University of Wales, 1982, pp.227–235.
137. E. John Davies, 'The Origins and Development of Secondary Education in the Rhondda Valleys (1878–1923)', M.A. Dissertation, University of Wales, 1965, p.41.
138. Bryce Commission, vol.7, p.305.
139. Combe, *Lectures on Popular Education*, p.58.
140. Taunton Commission, vol.5, p.735.
141. Ibid., vol.2, p.128.
142. Ibid., vol.9, p.825.
143. See, for example, Erasmus Darwin, *A Plan for the Conduct of Female Education in Boarding Schools* (London: J. Johnson, 1797), pp.9–12, 68–70.
144. *The English Woman's Journal* (May 1858), vol.1, no.3, pp.189–190: 150.
145. de Bellaigue, *Educating Women*, pp.12–13, 21.
146. Bryce Commission, vol.7, p.320.
147. *The English Woman's Journal*, (May 1858), vol.1, no.3, pp.189–190.
148. Taunton Commission, vol.1, p.552.
149. Ibid., vol.5, p.265, vol.9, p.299; Spender (ed.), *The Education Papers*, p.137.
150. Henry Maudsley, 'Sex in Mind and Education', *Fortnightly Review* (January–June 1874), vol.15, pp.466–483.
151. See Elizabeth Garrett Anderson, 'Sex in Mind and Education: A Reply', ibid., pp.582–594. See also Bessie Rayner Parkes, *Remarks on the Education of Girls* (London: John Chapman, 1854).
152. Kathleen E. McCrone, *Sport and the Physical Emancipation of English Women, 1870–1914* (London: Routledge, 1988), p.279.
153. See Neil Daglish, *Educational Policy-Making in England and Wales: The Crucible Years, 1895–1911* (London: Woburn, 1996), Chapter 11; Anna Davin, 'Imperialism and Motherhood', *History Workshop Journal* (Spring, 1978), no.5, pp.9–65.
154. Kathleen E. McCrone, '"Playing the Game" and "Playing the Piano": Physical Culture and Culture at Girls' Public Schools', c.1850–1914', pp.33–55 in Walford, *The Private Schooling of Girls*.
155. Jennifer A. Hargreaves, 'Victorian Familism and the Formative Years of Female Sport', pp.130–144 in J.A. Mangan & Roberta J. Park (eds.), *From 'Fair Sex' to Feminism: Sport and the Socialization of Women in the Industrial and Post-Industrial Era* (London: Cass, 1987), p.141.
156. Taunton Commission, vol.1, p.522.

157. Kathleen E. McCrone, '"Play Up! Play Up! And Play the Game!" Sport at the Late Victorian Girls' Public Schools', pp.97–129 in Mangan & Park, *From 'Fair Sex' to Feminism*, p.116.
158. Taunton Commission, vol.2, p.52.
159. J.S. Howson, 'On Schools for Girls of the Middle Class', *Transactions of the National Association for the Promotion of Social Science* (London, 1859), p.316.
160. Kelvin John Street, 'Female Culture in Physical Training Colleges 1885–1918', PhD, De Montfort University, 1999, p.15.
161. Catriona M. Parrat, 'Athletic "Womanhood": Exploring Sources for Female Sport in Victorian and Edwardian England', *Journal of Sport History* (Summer, 1989), vol.16, no.2, pp.140–157:152. See also Ina Zweiniger-Bargielowska, *Managing the Body: Beauty, Health and Fitness in Britain, 1880–1939* (Oxford: Oxford University Press, 2010), pp.109–115.
162. McCrone, *Sport and the Physical Emancipation of English Women*, p.18.
163. Bryce Commission, vol.7, no.320.
164. Ibid., vol. 6, p.259.
165. McCrone, *Sport and the Physical Emancipation of English Women*, p.70.
166. Jennifer A. Hargreaves 'Playing Like Gentlemen While Behaving Like Ladies: Contradictory Features of the Formative Years of Women's Sport', *British Journal of Sports History* (1985), vol.2, no.1, pp.40–52. See also J.A. Mangan, 'The Social Construction of Victorian Femininity: Emancipation, Education and Exercise', *International Journal of the History of Sport* (1989), vol.6, no.1, pp.19.
167. Pauline Bell, 'A History of Physical Education in Girls' Public Schools, 1870–1920', M.Ed. Dissertation, Manchester University, 1978. St Leonards (1877) was the first girls' boarding school to be run on the house system of the boys' public schools. Its first headmistress, Louisa Lumsden (1840–1935), had been one of the first six women to attend Hitchen College and had previously taught classics at Cheltenham Ladies' College from 1867: Louisa Lumsden, *Yellow Leaves: Memories of a Long Life* (Edinburgh: Blackwood, 1933).
168. See Paul Atkinson, 'Fitness, Feminism and Schooling', pp.92–133 in Sara Delamont & Lorna Duffin (eds.), *The Nineteenth-Century Woman: Her Cultural and Physical World* (London: Croom Helm, 1978), p.93.
169. Sheila Fletcher, *Women First: The Tradition in English Physical Education 1880–1980* (London: Athlone, 1984), p.20. By this time, boys were also being taught gymnastics in the board's schools.
170. Fletcher, *Women First*, pp.23, 27. Bergman-Österberg continued the work of Concordia Löfving who had worked since 1879 as inspector of physical education in girls' schools under the London School board and also taught and examined the board's mistresses. See Else Trangbæk, 'One System, Several Cultures: A Comparative Study of Swedish Gymnastics for Women', *International Sports Studies* (2000), vol.22, no.2, pp.43–56: 54 (note 14).
171. Richard Holt, *Sport and the British: A Modern History* (Oxford: Oxford University Press, 1989), p.119.
172. The *English Woman's Journal* (May 1858), vol.1, no.3, p.157.
173. Michèle Cohen, 'Language and Meaning in a Documentary Source: Girls' Curriculum from the Late Eighteenth Century to the Schools Inquiry Commission, 1868', *History of Education* (January, 2005), vol.34, no.1, pp.77–93: 93.
174. Sarah J. Smith, 'Retaking the Register: Women's Higher Education in Glasgow and Beyond, c.1796–1845', *Gender & History* (July, 2000), vol.12, no.2, pp.310–335; Lindy Moore, 'The Scottish Universities and Women Students', pp.138–146 in Jennifer J. Carter & Donald J. Withrington (eds.), *Scottish Universities* (Edinburgh: John Donald, 1990).

175. Watts, *Women in Science*, pp.112–114.
176. Penelope J. Corfield, *Power and the Professions in Britain 1700–1850* (London: Routledge, 1995), pp.33–34.
177. Christine de Bellaigue, 'The Development of Teaching as a Profession for Women before 1870', *The Historical Journal* (2001), vol.44, no.4, pp.963–988: 964–965.
178. Bremner, *Education of Girls and Women in Great Britain*, p.157.
179. Carol Dyhouse, *No Distinction of Sex? Women in British Universities 1870–1939* (London: UCL Press, 1995), p.17.
180. Hayes & Urquhart (eds.), *The Irish Women's History Reader*, p.47.
181. Judith Harford, 'The Movement for the Higher Education of Women in Ireland: Gender Equality or Denominational Rivalry?', *History of Education* (September, 2005), vol.34, no.5, pp.497–516. See also her *The Opening of University Education to Women in Ireland* (Dublin: Irish Academic Press, 2008).
182. Jordan, *The Women's Movement*, pp.206–207.
183. Bremner, *Education of Girls and Women in Great Britain*, p.163.
184. Burstyn, *Victorian Education and the Ideal of Womanhood*, p.37.
185. Spender (ed.), *The Education Papers*, p.137.
186. George J. Romanes, 'Mental Differences between Men and Women (1887)', pp.10–31 in Spender (ed.), *The Education Papers*; Joan N. Burstyn, 'Education and Sex: The Medical Case against Higher Education for Women in England, 1870–1900', *Proceedings of the American Philosophical Society* (April, 1973), vol.117, no.2, pp.79–89.
187. Howarth, 'The Church of England and Women's Higher Education, c.1840–1914', pp.153–54, 170. Howarth points out (p.154) that although intended to be non-denominational, Royal Holloway opened in 1886 with a board of governors which was wholly Anglican; it took over a decade for this to be changed.
188. Eibhlin Breathnach, 'A History of the Movement for Women's Higher Education in Dublin, 1860–1912', M.A. Dissertation, University College Dublin, 1981, p.56.
189. See Daphne Bennett, *Emily Davies and the Liberation of Women, 1830–1921* (London, 1990); Gillian Sutherland, *Faith, Duty and the Power of the Mind: The Cloughs and Their Circle 1820–1960* (Cambridge: Cambridge University Press, 2006), pp.84–109.
190. See Christina Hunt Mahony, 'Women's Education, Edward Dowden and the University Curriculum in English Literature: An Unlikely Progression', pp.195–202 in Margaret Kelleher & James H. Murphy (eds.), *Gender Perspectives in Nineteenth-Century Ireland* (Dublin: Irish Academic Press, 1997): 196–197.
191. Dyhouse, *No Distinction of Sex?* pp.13–17.
192. Emily Davies, 'Some Account of a Proposed New College for Women', *Contemporary Review* (December, 1868), 9, pp.540–557: 550.
193. Julia Bush, '"Special Strengths for Their Own Special Duties": Women, Higher Education and Gender Conservatism in Late Victorian Britain', *History of Education* (July, 2005), vol.34, no.4, pp.387–405.
194. See Dyhouse, *No Distinction of Sex?* pp.45–48 for the controversy at King's College for Women and the attempt to introduce a course in 'home science' in 1908. See also 'Margaret A. Gilland, *Home Arts* (1911)', pp.316–324 and 'L.M. Faithfull, *Home Science* (1911)', pp.325–327 in Spender (ed.), *The Education Papers*.
195. See Catherine Manthorpe, 'Science or Domestic Science? The Struggle to Define an Appropriate Science for Girls in Early Twentieth-Century England',

History of Education (1986) vol.15, no.3, pp.195–213. Manthorpe notes (p.195) the lack of precision in terms used, including 'home economics', 'domestic science', 'household science' and 'domestic economy'.

196. Margaret Burney Vickery, *Buildings for Bluestockings: The Architecture and Social History of Women's Colleges in Late Victorian England* (London: Associated University Presses, 1999), pp.143, 148.

197. Jane McDermid, 'Place the Book in Their Hands: Grace Paterson's Contribution to the Health and Welfare Policies of the School Board of Glasgow, 1885–1906', *History of Education* (November, 2007), vol.36, no.6, pp.697–713: 705.

198. Annemarie Turnbull, 'An Isolated Missionary: The Domestic Subjects Teacher in England, 1870–1914', *Women's History Review* (1994), vol.3, no.1, pp.81–100.

199. Dyhouse, *No Distinction of Sex?* p.12. She renders LLA as 'Lady Literate in Arts', as does Lesley A. Orr Macdonald in *A Unique and Glorious Mission: Women and Presbyterianism in Scotland 1830–1930* (Edinburgh: John Donald, 2000), p.277; but whether the first 'L' means 'Lady' was never entirely clear. The second 'L' is also referred to as 'Licentiate'. See Robert Bell & Malcolm Tight, *Open Universities: A British Tradition* (Buckingham: Open University Press, 1993), p.78; Lindy Moore, 'Women in Education' pp.316–343 in Heather Holmes (ed.), *Scottish Life and Society Volume 11: Institutions of Scotland: Education* (East Linton: Tuckwell Press, 2000), p.320.

200. Bell & Tight, *Open Universities*, p.74.

201. Lynn Patricia Edwards, 'Women Students at the University of Liverpool: Their Academic Careers and Postgraduate Lives 1833–1937', PhD, University of Liverpool, 1999, pp.18, 35. Established (1880) as a federal institution, Victoria University's charter placed women and men on an equal footing: Mabel Tylecote, *The Education of Women at Manchester University, 1883 to 1933* (Manchester: Manchester University Press, 1941), pp.1–31.

202. Sheila Hamilton, 'Women and the Scottish Universities circa 1869–1939', PhD, University of Edinburgh, 1987, p.176.

203. Robert D. Anderson, *Universities and Elites in Britain since 1800* (Basingstoke: Macmillan, 1992), p.23.

204. Lindy Moore, *Bajanellas and Semilinas: Aberdeen University and the Education of Women, 1860–1920* (Aberdeen: Aberdeen University Press, 1991), pp.120, 122, 134.

205. Lindy Moore, 'Women in Education', p.325.

206. See Deirdre Raftery, 'The Higher Education of Women in Ireland, 1860–1904', pp.5–18 in Susan M. Parkes (ed.), *A Danger to the Men? A History of Women in Trinity College Dublin, 1904–2004* (Dublin: Lilliput Press, 2004), p.14. Bell & Tight, *Open Universities*, record (p.60) that many Catholic women took immediate advantage of the opportunity to sit the Royal University's examinations and note (p.73) that the Royal University forbade the entry of women to both the lectures of its Fellows and the same examination rooms as men into the first decade of the twentieth century.

207. Trinity College did not run local examinations for boys. It admitted women in 1904 but with significant restrictions: Lucinda Thompson, 'The Campaign for Admission, 1870–1904', pp.19–54 in Parkes (ed.), *A Danger to the Men?* p19. Thompson points out (p.53) that the motives for admitting women to Trinity were due to 'fear that Irish Protestant women would "go elsewhere" and fall under the influence of a new national university of Ireland'.

208. Ellen Jordan, '"The Great Principle of English Fair-Play": The Admission of Women to the Pharmaceutical Society of Great Britain', *Women's History*

Review (September, 1998), vol.7, no.3, pp.381–409. Women were admitted to the Irish Pharmaceutical Society in 1878.

209. See Sophia Jex-Blake, *Medical Women: A Ten Year's Retrospect* (Edinburgh: Oliphant, Anderson & Ferrier, 1886); Enid Moberly Bell, *Storming the Citadel: The Rise of the Woman Doctor* (London: Constable, 1953). For local examples, see Isabel Thorne, *Sketch of the Foundation and Development of the London School of Medicine for Women* (London: Women's Printing Society, 1915); Wendy Alexander, 'Early Glasgow Women Medical Graduates', pp.49–94 in Eleanor Gordon & Esther Breitenbach, *The World Is Ill Divided: Women's Work in Scotland in the Nineteenth and Early Twentieth Centuries* (Edinburgh: Edinburgh University Press, 1990); Mary S.T. Logan, 'The Centenary of the Admission of Women Students to the Belfast Medical School', *The Ulster Medical Journal* (October, 1990), vol.59, no.2, pp.200–203.

210. Elizabeth Garrett Anderson, 'Medical Education of Women', *The British Medical Journal* (7 September, 1895), vol.2, no.18110, pp.608–609: 608.

NOTES TO CHAPTER 4

1. Mary Wollstonecraft, *Vindication of the Rights of Woman* (1792: Norton Critical 2nd ed., Carol H. Poston (ed.), New York, 1988), p.22. Michèle Cohen has challenged this assumption of a lack of method in middle-class girls' education: 'Gender and "Method" in Eighteenth-Century English Education', *History of Education* (September, 2004), vol.33, no.5, pp.585–595. For an interesting case study, see Penny Russell, 'An Improper Education? Jane Griffin's Pursuit of Self-Improvement and "Truth", 1811–1812', *History of Education* (May, 2004), vol.33, no.3, pp.249–265.
2. See Janet Todd, *Mary Wollstonecraft: A Revolutionary Life* (London: Weidenfeld & Nicolson, 2000), pp.79–116.
3. Maria and Richard Edgeworth, *Practical Education* (2nd ed., 3 vols., London: J. Johnson, 1801), vol.3, p.48.
4. Hannah More, *Strictures on the Modern System of Female Education* (2 vols., London: T. Cadell & W. Davies, 1800), vol.2, p.12.
5. See Marjorie Theobald, *Knowing Women: Origins of Women's Education in Nineteenth-Century Australia* (Cambridge: Cambridge University Press, 1996), p.45.
6. Thomas Gisborne, *An Enquiry into the Duties of the Female Sex* (London: T. Cadell jun. & W. Davies, 1797), p.58.
7. Erasmus Darwin, *A Plan for the Conduct of Female Education in Boarding Schools* (London: J. Johnson, 1797), pp.10–11.
8. John Gregory, *A Father's Legacy to His Daughters* (London: T. Cadell, 1774), pp.50–51.
9. Darwin, *A Plan for the Conduct of Female Education in Boarding Schools*, pp.11–41; Gregory, *A Father's Legacy to His Daughters*, pp.57–58.
10. Edgeworth, *Practical Education*, vol.3, p.50.
11. *Some Account of the Life and Writings of Mrs Trimmer* (2 vols., London: Rivington, 1816), vol.1, p.38.
12. M.A. Stodart, *Principles of Education* (London: Seeley, 1844), pp.9–14.
13. P.M. Heath, *The Works of Mrs Trimmer (1741–1810)* (Saarbrücken: Lambert Academic Publishing, 2010), pp. 237–39, 282.
14. See, for example, Helena Wells, *Letters on Subjects of Importance to the Happiness of Young Females* (London: L. Peacock, 1799) and Anon., *A Word to a Young Governess by an Old One* (Bath: A.W. Bennet, 1860).

15. *The Complete Governess: A Course of Mental Instruction for Ladies: With a Notice of the Principal Female Accomplishments. Intended to Facilitate the Business of Public Establishments, and Abridge the Labour of Private Education, by an Experienced Teacher* (London: Ibotson & Palmer, 1826), p.2.
16. Ibid., p.3.
17. Ibid., pp.469–475
18. Anne Stott, *Hannah More: The First Victorian* (Oxford: Oxford University Press, 2003), p.10.
19. Lindy Moore, 'Young Ladies' Institutions: The Development of Secondary Schools for Girls in Scotland, 1833–c.1870', *History of Education* (May, 2003), vol.32, no.3, pp.249–272: 249–250.
20. Priscilla Wakefield, *Reflections on the Present Condition of the Female Sex; with Suggestions for its Improvement* (2nd ed., London: J. Johnson, 1817), pp.49–50. By the Victorian period, some women were so accomplished in art and music that they could become professional tutors to wealthy young ladies: Ruth Watts gives the example of Marianne North (1830–1890) whose own artistic skills helped advance botanical research, notably on fungi. Ruth Watts, *Women in Science: A Social and Cultural History* (Abingdon: Routledge, 2007), p.106.
21. See Bridget Hill, *Women Alone: Spinsters in England 1660–1850* (New Haven: Yale University Press, 2001), pp.54–66.
22. See, for example, [An Anxious Observer], *Hints on Education; or Directions to Mothers in the Selection and Treatment of a Governess* (London: H. Rowe, 1821), p.7; Margaret Thornley, *The True End of Education, and the Means Adapted to It; in a Series of Familiar Letters to a Lady Entering on the Duties of Her Profession as Private Governess* (Edinburgh: T. & T. Clark, 1846), pp.3–4.
23. See, for example, George B. Bennett, *The Christian Governess: A Memoir and a Selection of the Correspondence of Miss Sarah Bennett, Late of Melton Mowbray* (London: J. Nisbet & Co., 1862).
24. Jane McDermid, 'Home and Away', *History of Education Quarterly* (February, 2011), vol.51, no.1, pp.28–48.
25. The quotation is from the Reverend David Esdaile of the Church of Scotland, explaining why he had opened a College for the Daughters of Ministers and Professors in the 1860s: see Lesley A. Orr Macdonald, *A Unique and Glorious Mission: Women and Presbyterianism in Scotland 1830–1930* (Edinburgh: John Donald, 2000), p.270. The Esdaile Trust continues to provide grants to assist in the education of daughters and deaconesses of the Church of Scotland.
26. Joanna Martin (ed.), *A Governess in the Age of Jane Austen: Letters and Journals of Miss Agnes Porter Dated from 1788–1814* (London: Hambledon Press, 1988).
27. Clara Reeve, *Plans of Education* (London: T. Hookam & J. Carpenter, 1792), pp.145–156.
28. Kathryn Hughes, *The Victorian Governess* (London: Hambledon Press, 2001), pp.38–40. For the Cork Seminary see John Logan, 'Governesses, Tutors and Parents: Domestic Education in Ireland 1700–1880', *Irish Educational Studies* (1988), vol.7, no.2, pp.1–19: 4. Deirdre Raftery, in 'Home Education in Nineteenth-Century Ireland: The Role and Status of the Governess', *Irish Educational Studies* (Spring, 2000), vol.19, no.1, pp.308–317: 312, notes that this seminary was more concerned with securing respectable employment for its trainees than with preparing them to teach. See also Maria Luddy, *Women in Ireland, 1800–1918* (Cork: Cork University Press, 1995), pp.121–122.

29. Report of the Schools Inquiry Commission [Taunton] (1868), vol.1, Chapter 6, 'Girls Schools', p.562.
30. See Jeanne Peterson, 'The Victorian Governess: Status Incongruence in Family and Society', pp.3–19 in Martha Vicinus (ed.), *Suffer and Be Still: Women in the Victorian Age* (Bloomingon, Indiana: Indiana University Press, 1972).
31. Trev Broughton & Ruth Symes (eds.), *The Governess: An Anthology* (Stroud: Sutton, 1997), pp.33–35.
32. Thornley, *The True End of Education*, p.9. For an example of a school in Edinburgh offering classes on teaching methods to potential governesses, see Moore, 'Young Ladies' Institutions', p.253.
33. Susan Skedd, 'Women Teachers and the Expansion of Girls' Schooling in England, c.1760–1820', pp.101–125 in Hannah Barker & Elaine Chalus, *Gender in Eighteenth-Century England: Roles, Representations and Responsibilities* (London: Routledge, 1997), p.125.
34. Broughton & Symes, *The Governess*, p.14. For the More sisters' school, see Stott, *Hannah More*, pp.9–10. For examples of boarding schools run by sisters in Hanoverian England, see Skedd, 'Women Teachers and the Expansion of Girls' Schooling in England, c.1760–1820', p.113. For examples in Wales as well as England, see William E. Marsden, *Unequal Educational Provision in England and Wales: The Nineteenth-Century Roots* (London, 1987), pp.240–245.
35. Quoted in W. Hamish Fraser & Irene Maver (eds.), *Glasgow, vol.2, 1830–1912* (Manchester, 1996), pp.270–271. See also Sarah Tytler, *Three Generations: The Story of a Middle-Class Scottish Family* (London: John Murray, 1911).
36. Martin, *A Governess in the Age of Jane Austen*, p.39.
37. Edward Hall (ed.), *Miss Weeton: Journal of a Governess, Volume 1, 1807–1811, Volume 2, 1811–1825* (London: Oxford University Press, 1936), vol.2, p.205.
38. Harriet Martineau, 'The Governess. Her Health', *Once a Week* (1 September 1860), vol.3, pp.267–272: 270. See also Peterson, 'The Victorian Governess', p.8; Hill, *Women Alone*, p.63. Deirdre Raftery, 'Home Education in Nineteenth-Century Ireland', p. 310, cites the average salary for a resident governess in Ireland in the mid-nineteenth century as between £40 and £60 'from which deductions were made to cover the cost of laundry and candles', but Raftery points out that nursery governesses were often paid as little as £20 a year and daily governesses as little as a pound a month.
39. Hall (ed.), *Miss Weeton*, vol.2, p.62.
40. See *The Dundee Advertiser*, 9 July 1872, where this Institution boasted 'Efficient Masters and Governesses'.
41. McDermid, 'Home and Away', p.35
42. Hughes, *The Governess*, pp.184–187. However, concern for governesses had been reflected in a few charitable institutions at the start of the Victorian period, such as the Asylum for Aged Governesses in Dublin, established by a small committee of Protestant men and women in 1838. Deirdre Raftery notes that in the first half of the nineteenth century, governesses in Ireland were most likely to be employed by the aristocratic and upper middle classes which meant dependence on a small and largely Protestant section of the population. See Raftery, 'Home Education in Nineteenth Century Ireland', pp.309–310. That changed with the growth of a Catholic middle class, while advertisements at the end of the century indicated a decline in residential and an increase in day governesses. John Logan points out, however, that the success of the Association for Promoting the Higher Education of Ladies

as Teachers, or the Governesses Association of Ireland, after 1869 may have contributed to a decline in demand for governesses: Logan, 'Governesses, Tutors and Parents', p.13.

43. Christine de Bellaigue, 'The Development of Teaching as a Profession for Women before 1870', *The Historical Journal* (2001), vol.44, no.4, pp.963–988: 966–970. See also her *Educating Women: Schooling and identity in England and France 1800–1867* (Oxford, 2007).

44. Theobald, *Knowing Women*, pp.40–43.

45. See Moore, 'Young Ladies' Institutions'.

46. *The Largs and Millport Weekly News*, 30 May 1877.

47. de Bellaigue, 'The Development of Teaching as a Profession for Women before 1870', pp.996–970.

48. See M.J. Illing, 'Pupil-Teachers and the Emancipation of Women, 1870–1905', MPhil, King's College London, 1978; J. Waugh, 'Aspects of Policy-Making in Teacher-Training and the Teachers' Struggle for Professional Status, 1895–1910', MLitt, Oxford University, 1993.

49. See Hughes, *The Victorian Governess*, pp.43, 66, 79, 115 and 195 for the experience of May Pinhorn, the governess employed by his son in 1895.

50. Richard Aldrich, *Education for the Nation* (London, 1996), pp.27, 66, 70.

51. Trygve R. Tholfsen (ed.), *Sir James Kay-Shuttleworth on Popular Education* (New York: Teachers' College Press, 1974), p.166.

52. *First Report of the Royal [Cross] Commission Appointed to Inquire into the Working of the Elementary Education Acts, England and Wales* (1886), p.288.

53. Wendy Robinson, 'In Search of a "Plain Tale": Rediscovering the Champions of the Pupil-Teacher Centres 1900–1910', *History of Education* (1999), vol.28, no.1, pp.53–71: 55. See also her chapter, 'Sarah Jane Bannister and Teacher Training in Transition 1870–1918', pp.131–148 in Mary Hilton and Pam Hirsch (eds.), *Practical Visionaries. Women, Education and Social Progress 1790–1930* (Harlow: Longman, 2000).

54. Asher Tropp, *The School Teachers: The Growth of the Teaching Profession in England and Wales from 1800 to the Present Day* (London: Heinemann, 1957), p.171.

55. John Furlong & Trisha Maynard, *Mentoring Student Teachers* (London, 1995), pp.3–4.

56. Mary McHugh, 'The Development of the Catholic Community in the Western Province (Glasgow, Motherwell and Paisley) 1878–1962', PhD, Strathclyde University, 1990, pp.116–117. For Ireland, see Donald Akenson, *The Irish Experiment: The National System of Education in the Nineteenth Century* (London: Routledge & Kegan Paul, 1970), p.354.

57. Sister Martha Skinnider, 'Catholic Elementary Education in Glasgow, 1818–1918', pp.13–65 in T.R. Bone (ed.), *Studies in the History of Scottish Education, 1872–1939* (London: University of London Press, 1967), pp.17–18.

58. For examples see Jane McDermid, 'Catholic Women Teachers and Scottish Education in the Nineteenth and Early Twentieth centuries', *History of Education* (September, 2009), vol.38, no.5, pp.605–620: 610.

59. The Forty-Seventh Annual Report of the Catholic School Committee (1894), Catholic Archdiocese of Glasgow Archive (CAGA), ED9.

60. The Forty-Second Annual Report of the Catholic School Committee (1889), CAGA, ED9/2.

61. Report of the Religious Examinations of Schools for 1880–1881, CAGA, ED7.

62. Frances Widdowson, *Going Up into the Next Class: Women and Elementary Teacher Training, 1840–1914* (London: Hutchinson, 1983), pp.17, 71.

63. David A. Coppock, 'Respectability as a Pre-Requisite of Moral Character: The Social and Occupational Mobility of Pupil Teachers in the Late Nineteenth and Early Twentieth Centuries', *History of Education* (1997), vol.26, no.2, pp.165–186.
64. See Robert D. Anderson, *Education and the Scottish People 1750–1918* (Oxford: Clarendon Press, 1995).
65. Christina S. Bremner, *Education of Girls and Women in Great Britain* (London: Swan Sonnenschein, 1897), p.166.
66. Edinburgh Central Library (ECL), YL353 Edinburgh School Board Minute Book, Seventh Triennial Report of the Proceedings of the Board (1894).
67. Minutes for the Committee of Council on Education, Inspectors Reports for Scotland (1851), p.1085.
68. See Jane McDermid, *The Schooling of Working-Class Girls in Victorian Scotland Gender, Education and Identity* (Abingdon: Routledge, 2005).
69. Wendy Robinson, 'Pupil Teachers: The Achilles Heel of Higher Grade Girls' Schools, 1882–1904', *History of Education* (1993), vol.22, no.3, pp.241–252: 251.
70. Wendy Robinson, *Pupil Teachers and Their Professional Training in Pupil-Teacher Centres* (Lampeter: Edwin Mellen Press, 2003); Meriel Vlaeminke, *The English Higher Grade Schools: A Lost Opportunity* (London: Woburn, 2000).
71. Glasgow City Archives (GCA), D-ED7/96/2, Garnethill High School for Girls Log Book Entry, HMI Report for 1900, p.186. Garnethill seems to have been the only school in Glasgow to offer Greek to girls.
72. Wendy Robinson, '"Less Intelligent and Lacking in Edge"? Female Pupil Teachers and Academic Performance', *Women's History Notebooks* (Winter, 2000), vol.7, no.1, pp.15–20: 18.
73. Coppock, 'Respectability as a Pre-Requisite of Moral Character', p.78.
74. Cross Commission, pp.288–289.
75. *Reports of the Commissioners, Inspectors and Others into Secondary Education* [Bryce] (1895), vol.1, p.110.
76. Ibid., p.75.
77. Ibid., vol.5, p.88.
78. Ibid., vol.1, p.297.
79. Ibid., vol. 6, p.252.
80. Ibid., p.281.
81. Robinson, *Pupil Teachers and Their Professional Training in Pupil-Teacher Centres*, p.189.
82. Ibid.
83. Alec Ellis, *Educating Our Masters: Influences on the Growth of Literacy in Victorian Working-Class Children* (Aldershot: Gower, 1985), p.42.
84. James Greig and Thomas Harvey, *Education Commission (Scotland), Report on the State of Education in Glasgow* (Edinburgh, 1866), p.17.
85. See Joyce Taylor, *Joseph Lancaster: The Poor Child's Friend* (West Wickham: Campanile Press, 1996), p.17. See also John Hassard & Michael Rowlinson, 'Researching Foucault's Research: Organization and Control in Joseph Lancaster's Monitorial Schools', *Organization* (2002), vol.94, no.4, pp.615–639.
86. Barry H. Bergen, 'Only a Schoolmaster: Gender, Class and the Effort to Professionalize Elementary Teaching in England, 1870–1910', *History of Education Quarterly* (Spring, 1983), vol.22, no.1, pp.1–21: 8.
87. Jane Martin & Joyce Goodman, *Women and Education, 1800–1980* (Basingstoke: Palgrave Macmillan, 2004), p.1.

88. George F. Bartle, 'The Role of the Ladies' Committee in the Affairs of the British and Foreign School Society', *Journal of Educational Administration and History* (January, 1995), vol.27, no.1, pp.51–61.

89. Eilis O'Sullivan, 'The Training of Women Teachers in Ireland 1824–1919, with Special Reference to Mary Immaculate College and Limerick', M.A. Dissertation, University of Limerick, 1998, pp.57–61, 65.

90. Maureen Langan-Egan, *Galway Women in the Nineteenth Century* (Dublin: Four Courts Press, 1999), pp.92–93.

91. W. Gareth Evans (ed.), *Fit to Educate? A Century of Teacher Education and Training 1892–1922* (Aberystwyth: University College of Wales, 1992), pp.1, 3.

92. Richard J.W. Selleck, *James Kay-Shuttleworth: Journey of an Outsider* (London, 1994), p.160. Selleck points out that Kay-Shuttleworth spoke exclusively of men and the Battersea training school which he opened in 1840 was for males only.

93. William Fraser, *Memoir of the Life of David Stow, Founder of the Training System of Education* (London: Nisbet, 1868), p.132.

94. David Stow, *The Training System Adopted in the Model Schools of the Glasgow Educational Society; a Manual for Infant and Juvenile Schools, etc.* (Glasgow: W.R. M'Phun, 1827); and *The Training System, the Moral Training School, and the Normal Seminary for Preparing School-Trainers and Governesses* (10th ed., London: Longmans Green, 1854).

95. Asher Tropp, *The School Teachers*, pp.11–12.

96. Jane Martin, *Women and the Politics of Schooling in Victorian and Edwardian England* (London: Leicester University Press, 1999), pp.57–58.

97. See Richard Aldrich, *School and Society in Victorian Britain: Joseph Payne and the New World of Education* (New York: Garland, 1995), p.167.

98. See Martin & Goodman, *Women and Education, 1800–1980*, pp.82–84.

99. See Josephine Kamm, *How Different from Us: A Biography of Miss Buss and Miss Beale* (London: Bodley Head, 1958); Carol Dyhouse, 'Miss Buss and Miss Beale: Gender and Authority in the History of Education', pp.2–39 in Felicity Hunt (ed.), *Lessons for Life: The Schooling of Girls and Women 1850–1950* (Oxford: Basil Blackwell, 1987).

100. See Kevin J. Brehony, 'English Revisionist Froebelians and the Schooling of the Urban Poor', pp.183–200 in Hilton & Hirsch (eds.), *Practical Visionaries*, p.186.

101. Bryce Commission, vol. 1, p.203. See Gillian Sutherland, 'Examinations and the Construction of Professional Identity: A Case Study of England', *Assessment in Education: Principles, Policy & Practice* (2001), vol.8, no.1, pp.51–64.

102. Auberon E.W.M. Herbert (ed.), *The Sacrifice of Education to Examination: Letters from 'All Sorts and Conditions of Men'* (London: Williams & Northgate, 1889), pp.96–97.

103. Lucy H.M. Soulsby, *Stray Thoughts for Mothers and Teachers* (London: Longmans Green, 1893), p.198.

104. Bryce Commission, vol.1, p.205.

105. Ruth Watts, 'Cooper, Alice Jane (1864–1917', *Oxford Dictionary of National Biography*, online ed., October 2005.

106. They did eventually accept public examination, though Cooper thought it unwise to enter before the age of 16 and also offered prizes within their own establishments to those girls who excelled academically. See Joyce Senders Pederson, 'Some Victorian Headmistresses: A Conservative Tradition of Social Reform', *Victorian Studies* (Summer, 1981), vol.24, no.4,

pp.463–488: 469. See also Ruth Watts, 'From Lady Teacher to Professional: A Case Study of Some of the First Headteachers of Girls' Secondary Schools in England', *Educational Management and Administration* (October, 1998), vol.26, no.4, pp.339–351.

107. Alison Prentice & Marjorie Theobald, *Women Who Taught* (Toronto, 1991), p.13.
108. Andrea Jacobs, '"The Girls Have Done Very Decidedly Better Than the Boys": Girls and Examinations, 1860–1902', *Journal of Educational Administration and History* (2001), vol.33, no.2, pp.120–136: 124, 126.
109. Aldrich, *School and Society in Victorian Britain*, pp.162–171. For Beate Doreck, see Jane Read, 'Froebelian Women: Networking to Promote Professional Status and Educational Change in the Nineteenth Century', *History of Education* (2003), vol.32, no.1, pp.17–33: 26–28.
110. Widdowson, *Going Up into the Next Class*, p.23.
111. Frederick W.T. Fuller, 'The Churches Train Teachers: An Historical Survey of the Part Played by the Churches of All Denominations in the Training of Elementary Teachers in England and Wales, from the First Government Grant for Education in 1833 to the Establishment of Day Training Colleges Initiated in 1890', PhD, University of Exeter, 1973.
112. Kim Lowden, 'Spirited Sisters: Anglican and Catholic Contributions to Women's Teacher Training in the Nineteenth Century', PhD, University of Liverpool (2000), pp.123, 144, 176, 316.
113. Skinnider. 'Catholic Elementary Education in Glasgow', p.39.
114. Carmen Mangion, '"Good Teacher" or "Good Religious"? The Professional Identity of Catholic Women Religious in Nineteenth-Century England and Wales', *Women's History Review* (2005), vol.14, no.2, pp.223–242: 230–231. Bernard Aspinwall, 'Catholic Teachers for Scotland: The Liverpool Connection', *The Innes Review* (Spring, 1994), vol.45, no.1, pp.85–108: 87. See also *The Fifty-First Annual Report of the Catholic School Committee* (1898), p.4 and *The Fifty-Third Annual Report of the Catholic School Committee* (1900), pp.2–3, CAGA, ED9/2.
115. Aspinwall 'Catholic Teachers for Scotland', p.87. See also Francis J. O'Hagan, *The Contribution of the Religious Orders to Education in Glasgow During the Period 1847–1918* (Lampeter: Edwin Mellen Press, 2006).
116. Barbara Walsh, *Roman Catholic Nuns in England and Wales 1800–1937* (Dublin: Irish Academic Press, 2002), pp.41–42, 158. A training college for secondary teachers, both lay and religious, was opened in London by the Holy Child Sisters in 1894 and as Carmen Mangion records, two future principals attended Bedford College and attained the Cambridge teaching diploma in the mid 1890s. Such efforts were now encouraged by the Catholic hierarchy: '"Good Teacher" or "Good Religious"?' p.232. For Scotland see Sara Karly Kehoe, 'Special Daughters of Rome: Glasgow and Its Roman Catholic Sisters, 1847–1913', PhD, Glasgow University, 2005; and Sara Karly Kehoe, 'Nursing the Mission. The Franciscan Sisters of the Immaculate Conception and the Sisters of Mercy in Glasgow, 1847–1866', *The Innes Review* (2005), vol. 56, no.1, pp. 46–59.
117. As noted in the previous chapter (Note 199), the first 'L' in 'LLA' is usually taken to mean 'Lady', though this was never entirely clear. See Robert Bell & Malcolm Tight, *Open Universities: A British Tradition* (Buckingham: Open University Press, 1993), p.78. For an example of a woman who was a pupil teacher in Glasgow, became a lecturer in a Church of Scotland training college before being appointed as head teacher of the Higher Grade Central School in Leeds and then as the first woman principal of Homerton College Cambridge in 1903, see Elizabeth Edwards, 'Mary Miller Allan:

The Complexity of Gender Negotiations for a Woman Principal of a Teacher Training College', pp.149–164 in Hilton & Hirsch (eds.), *Practical Visionaries*. Since lower class men and women could take the LLA, the award of one was not always highly regarded: see Carol Dyhouse, *No Distinction of Sex? Women in the British Universities 1870–1939* (London: UCL Press, 1995), p.171.

118. Holy Cross School, Crosshill, GCA, D-ED7/103/1/1, log book entries for 15 August 1898 and summary of HMI Report.

119. *The Forty-Sixth Annual Report of the Catholic School Committee* (1893), CAGA, ED9/2, 13: 'several' was not quantified.

120. Thomas A. Fitzpatrick, 'Scottish Catholic Teacher Education: The Wider Context', *The Innes Review* (Autumn, 1994), vol.45, no.2, pp.147–170: 60.

121. Report of the Committee of Council on Education in Scotland, 1891–1892, p.257.

122. Report of the Committee of Council on Education in Scotland, 1902–1903, p.18.

123. Bremner, *Education of Girls and Women in Great Britain*, p.167.

124. Susan M. Parkes, *Kildare Place: The History of the Church of Ireland Training College, 1811–1969* (Dublin: Church of Ireland College of Education, 1984). There was government support, but grants were limited to 75 per cent of college expenditure and less was given for female trainees. See Akenson, *The Irish Experiment*, pp.356–357.

125. O'Sullivan, 'The Training of Women Teachers in Ireland', pp.113–115.

126. See Alexander Wall, 'The Supply of Certificated Teachers to the Roman Catholic Elementary Schools of Britain 1848–1870', MPhil, Lancaster University, 1983, 289; see also Aspinwall, 'Catholic Teachers for Scotland'.

127. Pamela Horn, 'The Recruitment, Role and Status of the Victorian Country Teacher', *History of Education* (June, 1980), vol.9, no.2, pp.129–142: 136.

128. Helen Corr, 'An Exploration into Scottish Education', pp.290–309 in W. Hamish Fraser & R.J. Morris (eds.), *People and Society in Scotland, Volume 3, 1830–1914* (Edinburgh: John Donald, 1990), p.300; Evans (ed.), *Fit to Educate?* p.5.

129. See, for example, John T. Smith, 'Merely a Growing Dilemma of Etiquette? The Deepening Gulf between the Victorian Clergyman and Victorian Schoolteacher', *History of Education* (March, 2004), vol.33, no.2, pp.157–176; Russell Grigg, *History of Trinity College Carmarthen, 1848–1998* (Cardiff: University of Wales Press, 1998), p.12; Pamela Horn, 'Mid-Victorian Elementary School Teachers', *The Local Historian* (November, 1976), vol.12, nos.3–4, pp.161–166; Christine Heward, 'Men, Women and the Rise of the Professional Society: The Intriguing History of Teacher Educators', *History of Education* (1993), vol.22, no.1, pp.11–32.

130. See W. Gareth Evans, *Education and Female Emancipation: The Welsh Experience* (Cardiff: University of Wales Press, 1990).

131. *The Inverness Courier*, 5 April 1887, p.6.

132. See Victor E. Durkacz, *The Decline of the Celtic Languages* (Edinburgh: John Donald, 1983).

133. Elizabeth Edwards, *Women and Teacher Training Colleges, 1900–1960: A Culture of Femininity* (London: Routledge, 2001), p.16.

134. See, for example, Louisa M. Hubbard, *Work for Ladies in Elementary Schools, with and introduction by an Old Educator (Sir J.P. Kay Shuttleworth)* (London: Longmans, 1872).

135. See Widdowson, *Going Up into the Next Class*, p.61.

136. Linda Mahood, 'Eglantyne Jebb: Remembering, Representing and Writing a Rebel Daughter', *Women's History Review* (February, 2008), vol.17, no.1, pp.1–20.

137. Dina M. Copelman, *London's Women Teachers: Gender, Class and Feminism 1870–1930* (London: Routledge, 1996).
138. Brendan Duffy, 'Late Nineteenth Century Popular Educational Conservatism: The Work of Coalminers on the School Boards of the North-East', *History of Education* (1998), vol.27, no.1, pp.29–38: 36; A.M. Davies, *The Barnsley School Board 1871–1903* (Barnsley: Cheesman, 1965), p.135. For other examples in England, see Peter Gordon, *The Victorian School Manager: A Study in the Management of Education 1800–1902* (London: Woburn, 1974), p.49.
139. GCA, SR10/3/6/7/1, Govan Cross Public School Log Book, entries for 1882, 26 May and 31 July.
140. GCA, SR10/3/6/7/1, Govan Cross Public School Log Book, entries for 1878, 7 June, 14 June and 9 August.
141. See, for example, W. Gareth Evans, 'Gender Stereotyping and the Training of Female Elementary School Teachers: The Experience of Victorian Wales', *History of Education* (1992), vol.21, no.2, pp.189–204.
142. Joyce Collins, 'The Training of Elementary School Teachers in England and Wales, 1840–1890', PhD, Bulmershe College of Higher Education, 1985, pp.4, 65, 70.
143. Cross Commission Report, p.173.
144. Evans, *Education and Female Emancipation*, p.189.
145. Evans, *Fit to Educate?* p.4; John B. Thomas (ed.), *British Universities and Teacher Education: A Century of Change* (London: Falmer, 1990), p.9. See also Marjorie Cruickshank, *A History of the Training of Teachers in Scotland* (London: University of London Press, 1970), p.93; B.K. Hyams, '"Culture" for Elementary Schoolteachers: An Issue in the History of English Education', *Paedagogica Historica* (1981), vol.21, no.1, pp.111–120.
146. Edwards, *Women and Training Colleges*, p.92.
147. Robert E. Bell, 'The Scottish Universities and Educational Studies', p.88 (Chapter 6) in Thomas (ed.) *British Universities and Teacher Education*; Lowden, 'Spirited Sisters', p.256.
148. L.M. Rees, 'A Critical Examination of Teacher Training in Wales, 1846–1898', PhD, University of Wales, 1968, p.368.
149. Tholfsen (ed.), *Sir James Kay-Shuttleworth on Popular Education*, p.167.
150. Bremner, *Education of Girls and Women in Great Britain*, pp.244–245.
151. Elizabeth Bird, '"High Class Cookery": Gender, Status and Domestic Subjects, 1890–1930', *Gender and Education* (1998), vol.10, no.2, pp.117–131: 121.
152. Tom Begg, *The Excellent Women: The Origins and History of Queen Margaret College* (Edinburgh: John Donald, 1994).
153. Cross Commission, p.107; Denis Lawton & Peter Gordon, *HMI* (London: Routledge & Kegan Paul, 1987) p.158; Edward L. Edrmonds, *The School Inspector* (London: Routledge, 1962), pp.154–172. See also Carole Ann Mullins, '"Washtub Women": A Study of Female School Inspectors from the 1890s to the 1920s', M.Ed. Dissertation, University of Liverpool, 1999.
154. Moore, 'Educating for the "Woman's Sphere"', p.25.
155. See Helen Corr, *Changes in Educational Policies in Britain, 1800–1920: How Gender Inequalities Reshaped the Teaching Profession* (Lampeter: Edwin Mellen Press, 2008), pp.186–189.
156. Sarah Stage & Virginia B. Vincenti (eds.), *Rethinking Home Economics. Women and the History of a Profession* (Ithaca: Cornell University Press, 1997), pp.2–3.
157. Ibid., p.7.
158. Copelman, *London's Women Teachers*, p.25.

159. Annemarie Turnbull, 'An Isolated Missionary: The Domestic Subjects Teacher in England, 1870–1914', *Women's History Review* (1994), vol.3, no.1, pp.81–100: 93–94.
160. *The Schoolmaster*, 2 June 1877, p.542.
161. *First Annual Report of the Board of Education for Scotland* (1874), pp.xiv–xv, xvii.
162. Robinson, 'Pupil Teachers: The Achilles Heel of Higher Grade Girls' Schools 1882–1904', p.252.
163. Horn, 'The Recruitment, Role and Status of the Victorian Country Teacher', p.136.
164. June Purvis, 'Women and Teaching in the Nineteenth Century', pp.359–375 in Roger Dale, Geoff Esland, Ross Fergusson & Madeleine MacDonald (eds.), *Education and the State Volume II: Politics, Patriarchy and Practice* (Sussex: Falmer, 1981), pp.366–377.
165. Alison T. McCall, *Aberdeen School Board Female Teachers 1872–1901: A Biographical List* (Aberdeen: Aberdeen & Northeast Scotland Family History Society, 2007), p.52. For Ireland, see Margaret Ó hÓgartaigh, 'A Quiet Revolution: Women and Second-Level Education in Ireland, 1878–1930', *New Hibernian Review* (Summer, 2009), vol.13, no.2, pp.36–51: 39.
166. Janet Nolan, 'The National Schools and Irish Women's Mobility in the Late Nineteenth and Early Twentieth Centuries', *Irish Studies Review* (Spring, 1997), vol.5, no.18, pp.23–28: 26; Copelman, *London's Women Teachers*, p.220.
167. Joyce S. Pederson, 'Schoolmistresses and Headmistresses: Elites and Education in Nineteenth-Century England', *The Journal of British Studies* (November, 1975), vol.15, no.1, pp.135–162: 161.
168. June Purvis, *A History of Women's Education in England* (Milton Keynes, 1991), pp.87, 120; Mary P. Gallant, 'Against the Odds: Anne Jemima Clough and Women's Education in England', *History of Education* (1997), vol.26, no.2, pp.145–164: 161.
169. Dina Copelman, 'Women in the Classroom Struggle: Elementary School Teachers in London, 1870–1914', PhD, Princeton University, 1985, p.280.

NOTES TO CHAPTER 5

1. Harriet Martineau, 'On Female Education (1822)', pp.137–143 in Harriet Jump Devine (ed.), *Women's Writing of the Romantic Period, 1789–1836: An Anthology* (Edinburgh: Edinburgh University Press, 1997), pp. 137–138.
2. Ibid., pp.140–142.
3. Ibid., p.143.
4. Deirdre David, *Intellectual Women and Victorian Patriarchy: Harriet Martineau, Elizabeth Barrett Browning, George Eliot* (Basingstoke: Macmillan, 1987), p.31.
5. See, for example, Sue Morgan, 'The Power of Womanhood: Religion and Sexual Politics in the Writings of Ellice Hopkins', pp.209–224 in Anne Hogan & Andrew Bradstock (eds.), *Women of Faith in Victorian Culture: Reassessing the Angel in the House* (Basingstoke: Macmillan, 1998).
6. See, for example, Pamela Horn, *The Rise and Fall of the Victorian Domestic Servant* (Dublin: Gill & Macmillan, 1975).
7. John Burnett (ed.), *Useful Toil: Autobiographies of Working People from the 1820s to the 1920s* (Harmondsworth: Penguin, 1974), pp.234–235.
8. Jonathan Rose, *The Intellectual Life of the British Working Classes* (New Haven: Yale University Press, 2001), pp.177–181.

9. Robert Anderson, 'In Search of the "Lad of Parts": The Mythical History of Scottish Education', *History Workshop* (Spring, 1985), no.19, pp. 82–104: 84.

10. Stephen Heathorn, '"Let Us Remember That We, Too, Are English": Constructions of Citizenship and National Identity in English Elementary School Reading Books, 1880–1914', *Victorian Studies* (Spring, 1985), vol.38, no.3, pp.395–427. See also J. M. Goldstrom, *The Social Content of Education 1808–1870: A Study of the Working-Class School Reader in England and Ireland* (Shannon: Irish University Press, 1972).

11. See Seosamh Mac Suibhne, *Oblivious to the Dawn: Gender Themes in Nineteenth-Century National School Reading Books, Ireland 1831–1900* (Sligo: F.R.D., 1996).

12. Heathorn, '"Let Us Remember That We, Too, Are English"', pp.407, 411, 414.

13. See Jane McDermid, 'Place the Book in their Hands: Grace Paterson's Contribution to the Health and Welfare Policies of the School Board of Glasgow, 1885–1906', *History of Education* (November, 2007), vol.36, no.6, pp.697–713.

14. Marjorie Cruickshank, *A History of the Training of Teachers in Scotland* (London: University of London Press, 1970), pp.120–123.

15. Jane McDermid, *The Schooling of Working-Class Girls in Victorian Scotland: Gender, Education and Identity* (Abingdon: Routledge, 2005), pp.138–142.

16. See Penelope J. Corfield, *Power and the Professions in Britain 1700–1850* (London: Routledge, 1995).

17. See James Albisetti, 'The Feminization of Teaching in the Nineteenth Century: A Comparative Perspective', *History of Education* (1993), vol.22, no.3, pp.253–263.

18. Jane Lewis, *Women in England, 1870–1950: Sexual Divisions and Social Change* (Brighton: Wheatsheaf, 1984), p.194.

19. Carol Dyhouse, *No Distinction of Sex? Women in British Universities 1870–1939* (London: UCL Press, 1995), pp.18–21.

20. McDermid, *The Schooling of Working-Class Girls in Victorian Scotland*, pp.143–155.

21. Megan Smitley, 'Feminist Anglo-Saxonism? Representations of "Scotch" Women in the English Women's Press in the Late Nineteenth Century', *Cultural and Social History* (2007), vol.4, no.3, pp.341–359: 355; for the quotation from Tod, see p.344. See also Margaret Ward, 'Gendering the Union: Imperial Feminism and the Ladies' Land League', *Women's History Review* (2001), vol.10, no.1, pp.71–92.

22. Martineau, 'On Female Education', p.142.

23. See, for example, Philippa Levine, *Victorian Feminism 1850–1900* (London: Hutchinson, 1987), p.13.

24. Kathryn Gleadle, *British Women in the Nineteenth Century* (Basingstoke: Macmillan, 2001), pp.142–145. See also Jane Robinson, *Bluestockings: The Remarkable Story of the First Women to Fight for an Education* (London: Penguin Viking, 2009).

25. Harriet Martineau, 'Female Industry', *The Edinburgh Review* (April, 1859), no.109, pp.323–336: 336.

26. For a case study see Jane McDermid, 'The Making of a 'Domestic' Life: Memories of a Working Woman', *Labour History Review* (December, 2008), vol.73, no.3, pp.283–268.

27. Patricia Hollis, *Ladies Elect: Women in English Local Government 1865–1914* (Oxford: Oxford University Press, 1987), p.477.

28. See, for example, Meg Gomersall, *Working-Class Girls in Nineteenth-Century England: Life, Work and Schooling* (London: Macmillan, 1997), pp.115–117; McDermid, *The Schooling of Working-Class Girls in Victorian Scotland*, pp.116–117.

Bibliography

Primary Sources

Parliamentary Papers

Reports of the Commissioners of Board of Education in Ireland. First Report [Free Schools], *Second Report* [Schools of Private Foundation], *Third Report* [Protestant Charter Schools] (1809)
Report of the Royal Commission on Irish Education (1825)
Report of the Commission of Inquiry into the State of Education in Wales [Blue Books] (1847)
Report of the Commissioners into the State of Popular Education in England and Wales [Newcastle Commission] (1861)
Education Commission (Scotland) [Argyll Commission]: *Report on the Sate of Education in the Country Districts* by A.C. Sellar and C.F. Maxwell; *Report on the State of Education in Glasgow* by James Grieg and Thomas Harvey; *Report on the State of Education in the Hebrides*, by Alexander Nicolson [Argyll Commission] (1866)
Report of the Schools Inquiry Commission [Taunton Commission] (1868)
Report of the Committee Appointed to Inquire into the Condition of Intermediate and Higher Education in Wales [Aberdare Report] (1881)
Report of the Royal Commission appointed to Inquire into the Working of the Elementary Education Acts, England and Wales [Cross Commission] (1888)
Report of the Commissioners, Inspectors and Others into Secondary Education [Bryce Commission] (1895)
Minutes of the Committee of Council on Education (1851–1858)
Reports of the Committee of Council on Education in Scotland (1859–1860)
Reports of the Board of Education for Scotland (1873–1878)

Archives

Catholic Archdiocese of Glasgow Archive, Reports of the Religious Examinations of Schools, ED7; Reports of the Catholic School Committee (1894), ED9
Edinburgh City Library, Edinburgh School Board Minute Book; Edinburgh School Board Press Cuttings YL353
Glasgow City Archives, Hill & Hogan Bequest, Sederunt Book of Directors of the Glasgow School of Cookery, T-HH4/1/1
National Archives of Scotland (NAS), Records of the Scottish Society for the Propagation of Christian Knowledge, Minutes of General Meetings, GD95/9/1

Publications before 1900

Elizabeth Garrett Anderson, 'Medical Education of Women', *The British Medical Journal* (7 September 1895), vol.2, no.18110, pp.608–609

Elizabeth Garrett Anderson, 'Sex in Mind and Education: A Reply', *Fortnightly Review*, January–June 1874, vol.15, pp.582–594

Anon., *A Word to a Young Governess by an Old One* (Bath: A.W. Bennett, 1860)

[An Anxious Observer], *Hints on Education; or Directions to Mothers in the Selection and Treatment of a Governess* (London: H Rowe, 1821)

George B. Bennett, *The Christian Governess: A Memoir and a Selection of the Correspondence of Miss Sarah Bennett, Late of Melton Mowbray* (London: H. Nisbet & Co., 1862)

Christina S. Bremner, *Education of Girls and Women in Great Britain* (London: Swan Sonnenschein, 1897)

George Combe, *Lectures on Popular Education Delivered to the Edinburgh Philosophical Association in April and November 1833* (3rd ed., Edinburgh: Maclachlan, Stewart & Co., 1848)

The Complete Governess: A Course of Mental Instruction for Ladies: With a Notice of the Principal Female Accomplishments. Intended to Facilitate the Business of Public Establishments, and Abridge the Labour of Private Education, by an Experienced Teacher (London: Ibotson & Palmer, 1826)

Erasmus Darwin, *A Plan for the Conduct of Female Education in Boarding Schools* (London: J. Johnson, 1797)

Emily Davies, 'Some Account of a Proposed New College for Women', *Contemporary Review* (December, 1868), 9, pp.540–557

Maria and Richard Edgeworth, *Practical Education* (2nd ed., 3 vols., London, 1801)

William Fraser, *Memoir of the Life of David Stow, Founder of the Training System of Education* (London: Nisbet, 1868)

Thomas Gisborne, *An Enquiry into the Duties of the Female Sex* (London: T. Cadell jun. & W. Davies, 1797)

John Gregory, *A Father's Legacy to His Daughters* (London: T.Cadell, 1774)

Auberon E.W.M. Herbert (ed.), *The Sacrifice of Education to Examination: Letters from 'All Sorts and Conditions of Men'* (London: Williams & Northgate, 1889)

J.S. Howson, 'On Schools for Girls of the Middle Class', *Transactions of the National Association for the Promotion of Social Science* (London, 1859), pp.308–316

Louisa M. Hubbard, *Work for Ladies in Elementary Schools, with an Introduction by an Old Educator (Sir J.P. Kay Shuttleworth)* (London: Longmans & Co., 1872)

Sophia Jex-Blake, *Medical Women: A Ten Year's Retrospect* (Edinburgh: Oliphant, Anderson & Ferrier, 1886)

[George Lewis], *Scotland A Half-Educated Nation Both in the Quality and Quantity of Her Educational Institutions* (Glasgow: William Collins, 1834)

Harriet Martineau, 'The Governess. Her Health', *Once a Week* (1 September 1860), vol.3, pp.267–272

Harriet Martineau, 'On Female Education (1822)', pp.137–143 in Harriet Jump (ed.), *Women's Writing of the Romantic Period 1789–1836: An Anthology* (Edinburgh, 1997)

Henry Maudsley, 'Sex in Mind and Education', *Fortnightly Review*, January–June 1874, vol.15, pp.466–483

Hannah More, *Strictures on the Modern System of Female Education* (2 vols., 8th ed., London: T. Cadell & W. Davies, 1800)

The New Statistical Account of Scotland (15 vols., Edinburgh: William Black-wood & Sons, 1845)

Bessie Rayner Parkes, *Remarks on the Education of Girls* (London: John Chapman, 1854)

Clara Reeve, *Plans of Education* (London: T. Hookman & J.Carpenter, 1792)

Reflections of an Irish Protestant on the Measure of Roman Catholic Emancipation, Addressed to the Yeomanry of England (Special Collections, Hartley Library Southampton University, WP 946/14)

Some Account of the Life and Writings of Mrs Trimmer (2 vols., London: Rivington, 1816)

Lucy H.M. Soulsby, *Stray Thoughts for Mothers and Teachers* (London: Longmans, Green & Co., 1897)

M.A. Stodart, *Principles of Education, Practically Considered with an essential reference to the present state of female education in England* (London: Seeley, 1844)

David Stow, *The Training System Adopted in the Model Schools of the Glasgow Educational Society; A Manual for Infant and Juvenile schools, etc.* (Glasgow: W.R. M'Phun, 1827)

David Stow, *The Training System, the Moral Training School, and the Normal Seminary for Preparing School-Trainers and Governesses* (10th ed., London: Longmans Green, 1854)

Margaret Thornley, *The True End of Education, and the Means Adapted to It; in a Series of Familiar Letters to a Lady Entering on the Duties of Her Profession as Private Governess* (Edinburgh: T. & T. Clark, 1846)

Priscilla Wakefield, *Reflections on the Present Condition of the Female Sex; with Suggestions for its Improvement* (2nd ed., London: J. Johnson, 1817)

Helena Wells, *Letters on Subjects of Importance to the Happiness of Young Females* (London: L. Peacock, 1799)

Mary Wollstonecraft, *Vindication of the Rights of Woman* (London: J. Johnson, 1792: Norton Critical 2nd ed., New York, 1988)

Secondary Sources

Books Published after 1900

Lynn Abrams, *Myth and Materiality in a Woman's World: Shetland 1800–2000* (Manchester: Manchester University Press, 2005)

Richard Aldrich, *Education for the Nation* (London: Cassell, 1996)

Richard Aldrich (ed.), *Public or Private? Lessons from History* (London: Woburn, 2004)

Richard Aldrich, *School and Society in Victorian Britain: Joseph Payne and the New World of Education* (New York: Garland, 1995)

Lindsay Anderson, *The Autonomy of Modern Scotland* (Edinburgh: Edinburgh University Press, 1994)

Robert D. Anderson, *Education and the Scottish People 1750–1918* (Oxford: Clarendon Press, 1995)

Robert D. Anderson, *Universities and Elites in Britain since 1800* (Basingstoke: Macmillan, 1992)

Donald H. Akenson, *The Irish Education Experiment: The National System of Education in the Nineteenth Century* (London: Routledge & Kegan Paul, 1970)

Ronald G. Asch (ed.), *Three Nations—A Common History? England, Scotland Ireland and British History c.1600–1920* (Bochum: Universitätsverlag N. Brockmeyer, 1993)

Gillian Avery, *'The Best Type of Girl': A History of Girls' Independent Schools* (London: Deutsch, 1991)

John J. Bagley & Alexander J. Bagley, *The State and Education in England and Wales, 1833–1968* (London: Macmillan, 1969)

Andrew Bain, *Ancient and Modern. A Comparison of the Social Composition of the Burgh School Boards of Stirling and Falkirk from 1873 to 1919* (Polmont: Falkirk Council Education Services, 2006)

Thomas W. Bamford, *Rise of the Public Schools: A Study of Boys' Public Boarding Schools in England and Wales from 1837 to the Present Day* (London: Nelson, 1967)

Jane Barnes, *Irish Industrial Schools 1868–1908: Origins and Development* (Dublin: Irish Academic Press, 1980)

Tom Begg, *The Excellent Women: The Origins and History of Queen Margaret College* (Edinburgh: John Donald, 1994)

Enid Moberly Bell, *Storming the Citadel: The Rise of the Woman Doctor* (London: Constable, 1953)

Robert Bell & Malcolm Tight, *Open Universities: A British Tradition* (Buckingham: Open University Press, 1993)

Christine de Bellaigue, *Educating Women: Schooling and Identity in England and France 1800–1867* (Oxford: Oxford University Press, 2007)

Daphne Bennett, *Emily Davies and the Liberation of Women, 1830–1921* (London: André Deutsch, 1990)

Eugenio F. Biagini (ed.), *Citizenship and Community: Liberals, Radicals and Collective Identities in the British Isles 1865–1931* (Cambridge: Cambridge University Press, 1996)

Ida Blom, Karen Hagemann & Catherine Hall (eds.), *Gendered Nations: Nationalism and Gender Order in the Long Nineteenth Century* (Oxford: Berg, 2000)

Mary Cathcart Borer, *Willingly to School: A History of Women's Education* (London: P. Lutterworth, 1976)

Ruth Brandon, *Other People's Daughters: The Life and Times of the Governess* (London: Weidenfeld & Nicolson, 2008)

Helen Brocklehurst & Roger Phillips (eds.), *History, Nationhood and the Question of Britain* (Basingstoke: Palgrave Macmillan, 2004)

Laurence Brockliss & David Eastwood (eds.), *A Union of Multiple Identities: The British Isles, c.1750–c.1850* (Manchester: Manchester University Press, 1997)

Trev Broughton & Ruth Symes (eds.), *The Governess: An Anthology* (Stroud: Sutton, 1997)

Margaret Bryant, *The Unexpected Revolution: A Study in the History of the Education of Women and Girls in the Nineteenth Century* (London: University of London Institute of Education, 1979)

Sarah Burstall, *The Story of Manchester High School for Girls 1871–1911* (Manchester: Manchester University Press, 1911)

Joan Burstyn, *Victorian Education and the Ideal of Womanhood* (London: Croom Helm, 1980)

Linda Colley, *Britons: Forging the Nation 1707–1837* (New Haven: Yale University Press, 1992)

Robert Colls & Philip Dodd (eds.), *Englishness: Politics and Culture 1880–1920* (London: Croom Helm, 1986)

Anthony Cooke, *From Popular Enlightenment to Lifelong Learning: A History of Adult Education in Scotland 1707–2005* (Leicester: NIACE, 2006)

Samuel Cooper, *The 1872 Education Act in Lanarkshire* (Hamilton: Hamilton College of Education, 1973)

Dina Copelman, *Gender, Class and Feminism: Women Teachers in London, 1870–1930* (London: Routledge, 1995)

Penelope J. Corfield, *Power and the Professions in Britain 1700–1850* (London: Routledge, 1995)

Helen Corr, *Changes in Educational Policies in Britain, 1800–1920: How Gender Inequalities Reshaped the Teaching Profession* (Lampeter: Edwin Mellen Press, 2008)

Philip Corrigan & Derek Sayer, *The Great Arch: English State Formation as Cultural Revolution* (Oxford: Blackwell, 1985)

Sir Reginald Coupland, *Welsh and Scottish Nationalism: A Study* (London: Collins, 1954)

Marjorie Cruickshank, *A History of the Training of Teachers in Scotland* (London: University of London Press, 1970)

Mary Cullen (ed.), *Girls Don't Do Honours: Irish Women in Education in the 19th and 20th Centuries* (Dublin: Women's Education Bureau, 1987)

Mary Cullen & Maria Luddy (eds.), *Women, Power and Consciousness in Nineteenth-Century Ireland: Eight Biographical Studies* (Dublin: Attic Press, 1995)

Neil Daglish, *Educational Policy-Making in England and Wales: The Crucible Years, 1895–1911* (London: Woburn, 1996)

Mary Daly, *Social and Economic History of Ireland since 1800* (Dublin: Educational Company, 1981)

A.M. Davies, *The Barnsley School Board 1871–1903* (Barnsley: Cheesman, 1965)

JamesA. Davies, *Education in a Welsh Rural County 1870–1973* (Cardiff: University of Wales Press, 1973)

Sara Delamont & Lorna Duffin (eds.), *The Nineteenth-Century Woman* (London: Croom Helm, 1978)

T.M. Devine, *The Scottish Nation 1700–2000* (London: Allen Lane, 1999)

P.J. Dowling, *The Hedge Schools of Ireland* (Cork: P. Talbot, 1931)

Victor E. Durkacz, *The Decline of the Celtic Languages* (Edinburgh: John Donald, 1983)

Carol Dyhouse, *Girls Growing Up in Victorian and Edwardian England* (London: Routledge, 1981)

Carol Dyhouse, *No Distinction of Sex? Women in the British Universities 1870–1939* (London: UCL Press, 1995)

Edward L. Edmonds , *The School Inspecto*r (London: Routledge & Kegan Paul, 1962)

Elizabeth Edwards, *Women and Teacher Training Colleges, 1900–1960: A Culture of Femininity* (London: Routledge, 2001)

Alec Ellis, *Educating Our Masters: Influences on the Growth of Literacy in Victorian Working-Class Children* (Aldershot: Gower, 1985)

W. Gareth Evans, *Education and Female Emancipation: The Welsh Experience, 1847–1914* (Cardiff: University of Wales Press, 1990)

W. Gareth Evans (ed.), *Fit to Educate? A Century of Teacher Education and Training 1892–1922* (Aberystwyth: University College of Wales, 1992)

W. Gareth Evans, *Perspectives on a Century of Secondary Education in Wales 1889–1999* (Aberystwyth: University College of Wales, 1990)

Leslie Wynne Evans, *Education in Industrial Wales 1700–1900* (Cardiff: Avalon Books, 1971)

Penny Fielding, *Writing and Orality: Nationality, Culture and Nineteenth Century Scottish Fiction* (Oxford: Clarendon Press, 1996)

John Fletcher, *A Technical Triumph: One Hundred Years of Public Further Education in Merthyr Tydfil 1873–1973* (Merthyr Tydfil: Merthyr Tydfil Corporation, 1974)

Sheila Fletcher, *Feminists and Bureaucrats: A Study in the Development of Girls' Education in the Nineteenth Century* (Cambridge: Cambridge University Press, 1980)

Sheila Fletcher, *Women First: The Tradition in English Physical Education 1880–1980* (London: Athlone, 1984)

Margaret Forster, *Significant Sisters: The Grassroots of Active Feminism 1839–1939* (London: Penguin, 1986)

W. Hamish Fraser & Irene Maver (eds.), *Glasgow, Vol.2, 1830–1912* (Manchester: Manchester University Press, 1996)

John Furlong & Trisha Maynard, *Mentoring Student Teachers* (London: Routledge, 1995)

Dorothy Gardiner, *English Girlhood at School: A Study of Women's Education through Twelve Centuries* (London: Oxford University Press, 1929)

Phil Gardner, *The Lost Elementary Schools of Victorian England: The People's Education* (London: Croom Helm, 1984)

Paula Gillett, *Musical Women in England, 1870–1914: 'Encroaching on All Man's Privileges'* (Basingstoke: Macmillan, 2000)

J. M. Goldstrom, *The Social Content of Education 1808–1870: A Study of the Working-Class School Reader in England and Ireland* (Shannon: Irish University Press, 1972)

Meg Gomersall, *Working-Class Girls in Nineteenth-Century England: Life, Work and Schooling* (London: Macmillan, 1997)

Eleanor Gordon, *Women and the Labour Movement in Scotland 1850–1914* (Oxford: Oxford University Press, 1991)

Eleanor Gordon & Esther Breitenbach, *The World Is Ill Divided: Women's Work in Scotland in the Nineteenth and Early Twentieth Centuries* (Edinburgh: Edinburgh University Press, 1990)

Peter Gordon, *The Victorian School Manager: A Study in the Management of Education 1800–1902* (London: Woburn, 1974)

D.M Griffith, *Nationality in the Sunday School Movement: A Comparative Study of the Sunday School Movements in England and Wales* (Bangor: Jarvis & Foster, 1925)

Russell Grigg, *History of Trinity College Carmarthen, 1848–1998* (Cardiff: University of Wales Press, 1998)

Harriet Guest, *Small Change: Women, Learning and Patriotism, 1750–1810* (Chicago: University of Chicago Press, 2000)

Revel Guest & Angela V. John, *Lady Charlotte: An Extraordinary life* (2nd ed., London: Weidenfeld & Nicollson, 2007)

Donald E. Hall, *Muscular Christianity: Embodying the Victorian Age* (Cambridge: Cambridge University Press, 1994)

Edward Hall (ed.), *Miss Weeton: Journal of a Governess, Volume 1, 1807–1811, Volume 2, 1811–1825* (London: Oxford University Press, 1936)

Judith Harford, *The Opening of University Education to Women in Ireland* (Dublin: Irish Academic Press, 2008)

Alan Hayes & Diane Urquhart (eds.), *The Irish Women's History Reader* (London: Routledge, 2001)

P.M. Heath, *The Works of Mrs Trimmer (1741–1810)* (Saarbrücken: Lambert Academic Publishing, 2010)

Stephen Heathorn, *For Home, Country and Race: Constructing Gender, Class and Englishness in the Elementary School, 1880–1914* (Toronto: University of Toronto Press, 2000)

Mary J. Hickman, *Religion, Class and Identity: The State, the Catholic Church and the Education of the Irish in Britain* (Aldershot: Avebury, 1995)

Bridget Hill, *Women Alone: Spinsters in England 1660–1850* (New Haven: Yale University Press, 2001)

Mary Hilton, *Women and the Shaping of the Nation's Young: Education and Public Doctrine in Britain 1750–1850* (Aldershot: Ashgate, 2007)

Mary Hilton & Pam Hirsch (eds.), *Practical Visionaries. Women, Education and Social Progress 1790–1930* (Harlow: Longman, 2000)

Patricia Hollis, *Ladies Elect: Women in English Local Government, 1865–1914* (Oxford: Clarendon Press, 1987)

Heather Holmes (ed.), *Scottish Life and Society. A Compendium of Scottish Ethnology. Volume 11, Institutions of Scotland: Education* (East Linton: Tuckwell Press, 2000)

Robert A. Houston, *Scottish Literacy and Scottish Identity: Illiteracy and Society in Scotland and Northern England 1600–1800* (Cambridge: Cambridge University Press, 1985)

Kathryn Hughes, *The Victorian Governess* (London: Hambledon, 2001)

Jane Humphries, *Childhood and Child labour in the British Industrial Revolution* (Cambridge: Cambridge University Press, 2010)

Felicity Hunt (ed.), *Lessons for Life: The Schooling of Girls and Women 1850–1950* (Oxford: Basil Blackwell, 1987)

Geraint H. Jenkins (ed.), *The Welsh Language and its Social Domains 1801–1911* (Cardiff: University of Wales Press, 2000)

Angela V. John, *Our Mothers' Land: Chapters in Welsh Women's History 1830–1939* (Cardiff: University of Wales Press, 1991)

David Jones, *The Last Rising: The Newport Chartist Insurrection of 1839* (Cardiff: University of Wales Press, 1999)

Gareth Elwyn Jones, *Controls and Conflicts in Welsh Secondary Education 1889–1944* (Cardiff: University of Wales Press, 1982)

Gareth Elwyn Jones, *The Education of a Nation* (Cardiff: University of Wales Press, 1997)

Ellen Jordan, *The Women's Movement and Women's Employment in Nineteenth-Century Britain* (London: Routledge, 1999)

Josephine Kamm, *Hope Deferred: Girls' Education in English History* (London: Methuen, 1965)

Josephine Kamm, *How Different from Us: A Biography of Miss Buss and Miss Beale* (London: Bodley Head, 1958)

Hugh Kearney, *The British Isles: A History of Four Nations* (Cambridge: Cambridge University Press, 1989)

S. Karly Kehoe, *Creating a Scottish Church: Catholicism, Gender and Ethnicity in Nineteenth-Century Scotland* (Manchester: Manchester University Press, 2010)

William W. Knox, *Industrial Nation. Work Culture and Society in Scotland, 1800–Present* (Edinburgh: Edinburgh University Press, 1999)

Maureen Langan-Egan, *Galway Women in the Nineteenth Century* (Dublin: Four Courts Press, 1999)

Paul Langford, *Englishness Identified: Manners and Character 1650–1850* (Oxford: Oxford University Press, 2000)

Roy Lowe (ed.), *History of Education: Major Themes* (4 vols., London: Routledge Falmer, 2000)

Maria Luddy, *Women in Ireland, 1800–1918* (Cork: Cork University Press, 1995)

Maria Luddy, *Women and Philanthropy in Nineteenth-Century Ireland* (Cambridge: Cambridge University Press, 1995)

Louisa Lumsden, *Yellow Leaves: Memories of a Long Life* (Edinburgh: Blackwood, 1933)

Seosamh Mac Suibhne, *Oblivious to the Dawn: Gender Themes in Nineteenth-Century National School Reading Books, Ireland 1831–1900* (Sligo: F.R.D., 1996)

Peter Mandler, *The English National Character: The History of an Idea from Edmund Burke to Tony Blair* (New Haven: Yale University Press, 2006)

J.A. Mangan, *Athleticism in the Victorian and Edwardian Public School: The Emergence and Consolidation of the Educational Ideology* (Cambridge: Cambridge University Press, 1982)

J.A. Mangan, *The Games Ethic and Imperialism: Aspects of the Diffusion of an Ideal* (London: Viking, 1986)

J.A. Mangan & Roberta J. Park (eds.), *From 'Fair Sex' to Feminism: Sport and the Socialization of Women in the Industrial and Post-Industrial Era* (London: Cass, 1987)

William E. Marsden, *Unequal Educational Provision in England and Wales: The Nineteenth-Century Roots* (London: Woburn, 1987)

Jane Martin, *Women and the Politics of Schooling in Victorian and Edwardian England* (London: Leicester University Press, 1999)

Jane Martin & Joyce Goodman, *Women and Education, 1800–1980* (Basingstoke: Palgrave Macmillan, 2004)

Joanna Martin (ed.), *A Governess in the Age of Jane Austen: letters and journals of Miss Agnes Porter dated from 1788–1814* (London: Hambledon Press, 1988)

Colin Matthew (ed.), *The Nineteenth Century: The British Isles, 1815–1901* (Oxford: Oxford University Press, 2000)

Trevor May, *The Victorian Public School* (Oxford: Shire, 2009)

Alison T. McCall, *Aberdeen School Board Female Teachers 1872–1901: A Biographical List* (Aberdeen: Aberdeen & North East Scotland Family History Society, 2007)

Phillip McCann, *Popular Education and Socialization in the Nineteenth Century* (London: Methuen, 1977)

Michael McCram, *Thomas Arnold, Headmaster: A Reassessment* (Oxford: Oxford University Press, 1989)

Kathleen E. McCrone, *Sport and the Physical Emancipation of English Women, 1870–1914* (London: Routledge, 1988)

Jane McDermid, *The Schooling of Working-Class Girls in Victorian Scotland: Gender, Education and Identity* (London: Routledge, 2005)

Antonia McManus, *The Irish Hedge School and Its Books, 1605–1831* (Dublin: Four Courts Press, 2002)

Pavla Miller, *Transformations of Patriarchy in the West, 1500–1900* (Bloomington: Indiana University Press, 1998)

Martin Mitchell, *The Irish in the West of Scotland, 1797–1848* (Edinburgh: John Donald, 1988)

Kenneth O. Morgan, *Rebirth of a Nation: Wales 1880–1980* (Oxford: Clarendon Press, 1981)

Simon Morgan, *A Victorian Woman's Place: Public Culture in the Nineteenth Century* (London: Taurus, 2007)

Sue Morgan & Jacqueline de Vries (eds.), *Women, Gender and Religious Cultures in Britain, 1800–1940* (Abingdon: Routledge, 2010)

Sue Morgan (ed.), *Women, Religion and Feminism in Britain, 1750–1900* (Basingstoke: Palgrave Macmillan, 2002)

Lindy Moore, *Bajanellas and Semilinas: Aberdeen University and the Education of Women, 1860–1920* (Aberdeen: Aberdeen University Press, 1991)

Gerald Newman, *The Rise of English Nationalism: A Cultural History 1740–1830* (London: Weidenfeld & Nicolson 1987)

Francis J. O'Hagan, *The Contribution of the Religious Orders to Education in Glasgow during the Period 1847–1918* (Lampeter: Edwin Mellen Press, 2006)

Paul O'Leary, *Immigration and Integration: The Irish in Wales, 1789–1922* (Cardiff: University of Wales Press, 2000)

Susan M. Parkes (ed.), *A Danger to the Men? A History of Women in Trinity College Dublin, 1904–2004* (Dublin: Lilliput Press, 2004)

Susan M. Parkes, *Kildare Place: The History of the Church of Ireland Training College, 1811–1969* (Dublin: Church of Ireland College of Education, 1984)

Fiona M.S. Paterson & Judith Fewell (eds.), *Girls in Their Prime: Scottish Education Revisited* (Edinburgh: Scottish Academic Press, 1990)

Joyce Senders Pedersen, *The Reform of Girls' Secondary Education in Victorian England: A Study of Elites and Educational Change* (New York: Garland, 1987)

Alison Prentice & Marjorie Theobald, *Women Who Taught* (Toronto: University of Toronto Press, 1991)

June Purvis (ed.), *The Education of Girls and Women: Proceedings of the 1984 Annual Conference of the History of Education Society of Great Britain* (London: History of Education Society, 1985)

June Purvis, *Hard Lessons: The Lives and Education of Working-Class Women in Nineteenth-Century England* (Cambridge: Polity Press, 1989)

June Purvis, *A History of Women's Education in England* (Milton Keynes: Open University Press, 1991)

Deirdre Raftery, *Women and Learning in English Writing 1600–1900* (Dublin: Four Courts Press, 1997)

Marjorie Reeves, *Female Education and Nonconformist Culture 1700–1900* (London: Leicester University Press, 2000)

Kim D. Reynolds, *Aristocratic Women and Political Society in Victorian Britain* (Oxford: Clarendon Press, 1998)

Gwyneth Tyson Roberts, *The Language of the Blue Books: The Perfect Instrument of Empire* (Cardiff: University of Wales Press, 1998)

Wendy Robinson, *Pupil Teachers and Their Professional Training in Pupil-Teacher Centres* (Lampeter: Edwin Mellen Press, 2003)

James Roxburgh, *The School Board of Glasgow 1873–1918* (London: University of London Press, 1971)

Michael Sanderson, *Education, Economic Change and Society in England 1780–1870* (Basingstoke: Macmillan, 1983)

Malcolm Seaborne, *Schools in Wales 1500–1900: A Social and Architectural History* (Denbigh: Gee & Son, 1992)

Peter Searby (ed.), *Educating the Victorian Middle Class* (Leicester: History of Education Society, 1982)

Richard J.W. Selleck, *James Kay-Shuttleworth: Journey of an Outsider* (London: Woburn, 1994)

Robert B. Shoemaker, *Gender in English Society 1650–1850: The Emergence of Separate Spheres?* (Harlow: Longman, 1998)

Colin Shrosbree, *Public Schools and Private Education: The Clarendon Commission, 1861–1864, and the Public School Acts* (Manchester: Manchester University Press, 1988)

Brian Simon & Ian Bradley, (eds.), *The Victorian Public School* (Dublin: Gill & Macmillan, 1975)

Robert Smith, *Schools, Politics and Society: Elementary Education in Wales, 1870–1902* (Cardiff: University of Wales Press, 1999)

Dale Spender (ed.), *The Education Papers: Women's Quest for Equality in Britain 1850–1912* (London: Routledge & Kegan Paul, 1987)

Sarah Stage & Virginia B. Vincenti (eds.), *Rethinking Home Economics. Women and the History of a Profession* (Ithaca & London: Cornell University Press, 1997)

W.B. Stephens, *Education in Britain 1750–1914* (Basingstoke: Macmillan, 1998)

Anne Stott, *Hannah More: The First Victorian* (Oxford: Oxford University Press, 2003)

Gillian Sutherland, *Faith, Duty and the Power of the Mind: The Cloughs and Their Circle 1820–1960* (Cambridge: Cambridge University Press, 2006)

Roger Swift & Sheridan Gilley (eds.), *The Irish in Victorian Britain: The Local Dimension* (Dublin: Four Courts Press, 1999)

Joyce Taylor, *Joseph Lancaster: The Poor Child's Friend* (West Wickham: Campanile Press, 1996)

Marjorie Theobald, *Knowing Women: Origins of Women's Education in Nineteenth-Century Australia* (Cambridge: Cambridge University Press, 1996)

Trygve R. Tholfsen (ed.), *Sir James Kay-Shuttleworth on Popular Education* (New York: Teachers' College Press, 1974)

John B. Thomas (ed.), *British Universities and Teacher Education: A Century of Change* (London: Falmer, 1990)

Isabel Thorne, *Sketch of the Foundation and Development of the London School of Medicine for Women* (London: Women's Printing Society, 1915)

E. Brian Titley, *Church, State and the Control of Schooling in Ireland 1900–1944* (Kingston, Ontario: McGill & Queen's University Press, 1983)

Janet Todd, *Mary Wollstonecraft: A Revolutionary Life* (London: Weidenfeld & Nicolson, 2000)

John Tosh, *A Man's Place: Masculinity and the Middle-Class Home in Victorian England* (London: Yale University Press, 1999)

John Tosh, *Manliness and Masculinities in Nineteenth-Century Britain* (Harlow: Pearson Education, 2005)

Asher Tropp, *The School Teachers: The Growth of the Teaching Profession in England and Wales from 1800 to the Present Day* (London: Heinemann, 1957)

Mabel Tylecote, *The Education of Women at Manchester University, 1883 to 1933* (Manchester: Manchester University Press, 1941)

Norman Vance, *The Sinews of the Spirit: The Ideal of Christian Manliness in Victorian Literature and Religious Thought* (Cambridge: Cambridge University Press, 1985)

Margaret Burney Vickery, *Buildings for Bluestockings: The Architecture and Social History of Women's Colleges in Late Victorian England* (London: Associated University Presses, 1999)

David Vincent, *Bread, Knowledge and Freedom: A Study of Nineteenth-Century Working-Class Autobiographies* (London: Methuen, 1981)

Meriel Vlaeminke, *The English Higher Grade Schools: A Lost Opportunity* (London: Woburn, 2000)

Geoffrey Walford (ed.), *The Private Schooling of Girls Past and Present* (London: Woburn, 1993)

Barbara Walsh, *Roman Catholic Nuns in England and Wales 1800–1937* (Dublin: Irish Academic Press, 2002)

Robert E. Ward, *An Encyclopedia of Irish Schools, 1500–1800* (Lampeter: Edwin Mellen Press, 1995)

Ruth Watts, *Gender, Power and the Unitarians in England, 1760–1860* (London: Longman, 1998)

Ruth Watts, *Women in Science: A Social and Cultural History* (London: Routledge, 2007)

Frances Widdowson, *Going Up into the Next Class: Women and Elementary Teacher Training, 1840–1914* (London: Hutchinson, 1983)

John Williams, *Was Wales Industrialised?* (Llandysul: Gomer, 1995)

John Wolffe, *God and Greater Britain* (London: Routledge,1994)

Nira Yuval-Davis & Floya Anthias (eds.), *Woman-Nation-State* (Basingstoke: Macmillan, 1989)

Chapters in Edited Collections

James R.R. Adams, 'Swine-Tax and Eat-Him-All-Magee: The Hedge Schools and Popular Education in Ireland', pp.97–117 in James S. Donnelly & Kerby A.

Miller (eds.), *Irish Popular Culture 1650–1850* (Dublin: Irish Academic Press, 1998)

Deirdre Beddoe, 'Images of Welsh Women', pp.227–238 in Tony Curtis (ed.), *Wales: The Imagined Nation. Studies in Cultural and National Identity* (Bridgend: Poetry Wales Press, 1986)

Karen Clarke, 'Public and Private Children: Infant Education in the 1820s and 1830s', pp.74–87 in Carolyn Steedman, Cathy Urwin & Valerie Walkerdine (eds.), *Language, Gender and Childhood* (London: Routledge & Kegan Paul, 1985)

Helen Corr, 'An Exploration into Scottish Education', pp.290–309 in W. Hamish Fraser & R.J. Morris (eds.), *People and Society in Scotland, Volume 3, 1830–1914* (Edinburgh: John Donald, 1990)

Helen Corr, 'The Sexual Division of Labour in the Scottish Teaching Profession, 1872–1914', pp.137–151 in W.M. Humes & H.M. Paterson (eds.), *Scottish Culture and Scottish Education 1800–1980* (Edinburgh: John Donald, 1983)

David Fitzpatrick, 'The Modernisation of the Irish Female', pp.162–180 in Patrick O'Flanagan, Paul Ferguson & Kevin Whelan (eds.), *Rural Ireland 1600–1900: Modernisation and Change* (Cork: Cork University Press, 1987)

Janet Howarth, 'The Church of England and Women's Higher Education, c.1840–1914', pp.153–170 in Peter Ghosh & Lawrence Goldman (eds.), *Politics and Culture in Victorian Britain: Essays in Memory of Colin Matthew* (Oxford: Oxford University Press, 2006)

Frank Price Jones, 'The Blue Books of 1847', pp.127–144 in Jac L. Williams & Gwilym Rees Hughes (eds.), *The History of Education in Wales* (Swansea: C. Davies, 1978)

Alison Jordan, '"Opening the Gates of Learning": The Belfast Ladies' Institute, 1867–1897', pp.33–57 in Janice Holmes & Diane Urquhart (eds.), *Coming into the Light: The Work, Politics and Religion of Women in Ulster 1840–1940* (Belfast: Queen's University Belfast, 1994)

Declan Kiberd, 'Irish Literature and Irish History', pp.275–337 in Roy Foster (ed.), *The Oxford History of Ireland* (Oxford: Oxford University Press, 1992)

John Logan, 'The Dimensions of Gender in Nineteenth-Century Schooling', pp.36–49 in Margaret Kelleher & James H. Murphy (eds.), *Gender Perspectives in Nineteenth-Century Ireland* (Dublin: Irish Academic Press, 1997)

Christina Hunt Mahony, 'Women's Education, Edward Dowden and the University Curriculum in English Literature: An Unlikely Progression', pp.195–202 in Margaret Kelleher & James H. Murphy (eds.), *Gender Perspectives in Nineteenth-Century Ireland* (Dublin: Irish Academic Press, 1997)

Lindy Moore, 'Education and Learning', pp.316–343 in Lynn Abrams, Eleanor Gordon, Deborah Simonton & Eileen J. Yeo (eds.), *Gender and Scottish History since 1700* (Edinburgh: Edinburgh University Press, 2006)

Lindy Moore, 'The Scottish Universities and Women Students', pp.138–146 in Jennifer J. Carter & Donald J. Withrington (eds.), *Scottish Universities* (Edinburgh: John Donald, 1990)

Robin Okey, 'Education and Nationhood in Wales, 1850–1940', pp.35–62 in Janusz Tomiak (ed.), *Schooling, Educational Policy and Ethnic Identity: Comparative Studies in Governments and Non-Dominant Ethnic Groups in Europe, 1850–1940* (Aldershot: Dartmouth, 1991), vol.1

Jeanne Peterson, 'The Victorian Governess: Status Incongruence in Family and Society', pp.3–19 in Martha Vicinus (ed.), *Suffer and Be Still: Women in the Victorian Age* (Bloomingon:Indiana Univesity Press, 1972)

June Purvis, 'Women and Teaching in the Nineteenth Century', pp.359–375 in Roger Dale, Geoff Esland, Ross Fergusson & Madeleine MacDonald (eds.),

Education and the State Volume II: Politics, Patriarchy and Practice (Sussex: Falmer, 1981)

Michael Roberts, 'Gender, Work and Socialization in Wales c.1450–c.1850', pp.15–54 in Sandra Betts (ed.), *Our Daughters' Land: Past and Present* (Cardiff: University of Wales Press, 1996)

Rebeca Rogers, 'Learning to Be Good Girls and Women: Education, Training and Schools', pp.93–133 in Deborah Simonton (ed.), *The Routledge History of Women in Europe since 1700* (Abingdon: Routledge, 2006)

Deborah Simonton, 'Women and Education', pp.33–56 in Hannah Barker & Elaine Chalus (eds.), *Women's History: Britain, 1700–1850. An Introduction* (London: Routledge, 2005)

Susan Skedd, 'Women Teachers and the Expansion of Girls' Schooling in England, c.1760–1820', pp.101–125 in Hannah Barker & Elaine Chalus, *Gender in Eighteenth-Century England: Roles, Representations and Responsibilities* (London: Routledge, 1997)

Sister Martha Skinnider, 'Catholic Elementary Education in Glasgow, 1818–1918', pp.17–18 in T.R. Bone (ed.), *Studies in the History of Scottish Education, 1872–1939* (London: University of London Press, 1967)

Robert E. Tyson, 'The Economy of Aberdeen', pp.9–21 in John S. Smith & David Stevenson (eds.), *Aberdeen in the Nineteenth Century* (Aberdeen: Aberdeen University Press, 1988)

Donald J. Withrington, 'Scotland A Half-Educated Nation in 1845? Reliable Critique or Persuasive Polemic?', pp.55–74 in W.M. Humes & H.M. Paterson (eds.), *Scottish Culture and Scottish Education 1800–1980* (Edinburgh: John Donald, 1983)

Journal Articles Published after 1900

James Albisetti, 'The Feminization of Teaching in the Nineteenth Century: A Comparative Perspective', *History of Education* (September, 1993), vol.22, no.3, pp.265–276

Richard Aldrich, 'Educating our Mistresses', *History of Education* (1983), vol.12, no.2, pp.93–102

Robert Anderson, 'Education and Society in Modern Scotland: A Comparative Perspective', *History of Education Quarterly* (Winter, 1985), vol.25, no.4, pp.459–481

Bernard Aspinwall, 'Catholic Teachers for Scotland: The Liverpool Connection', *The Innes Review* (Spring, 1994), vol.45, no.1, pp.85–108

George F. Bartle, 'The Role of the Ladies' Committee in the Affairs of the British and Foreign School Society', *Journal of Educational Administration and History* (January, 1995), vol.27, no.1, pp.51–61

Christine de Bellaigue, 'The Development of Teaching as a Profession for Women before 1870', *The Historical Journal* (2001), vol.44, no.4, pp.963–988

Barry H. Bergen, 'Only a Schoolmaster: Gender, Class and the Effort to Professionalize Elementary Teaching in England, 1870–1910', *History of Education Quarterly* (Spring, 1983), vol.22, no.1, pp.1–21

Elizabeth Bird, '"High Class Cookery": Gender, Status and Domestic Subjects, 1890–1930', *Gender and Education* (1998), vol.10, no.2, pp.117–131

Joanna Bourke, '"The Health Caravan": Domestic Education and Female Labour in Rural Ireland, 1890–1914', *Eire/Ireland* (Winter, 1989), no.24, pp.21–38

Séamas Ó. Buachalla, 'Educational Policy and the Role of the Irish Language 1831–1981', *European Journal of Education* (1984), vol.19, no.1, pp.75–92

Joan N. Burstyn, 'Education and Sex: The Medical Case against Higher Education for Women in England, 1870–1900', *Proceedings of the American Philosophical Society* (April, 1973), vol.117, no.2, pp.79–89

Julia Bush, '"Special Strengths for Their Own Special Duties": Women, Higher Education and Gender Conservatism in Late Victorian Britain', *History of Education* (July, 2005), vol.34, no.4, pp.387–405

Michéle Cohen, 'Gender and "Method" in Eighteenth-Century English Education', *History of Education* (September, 2004), vol.33, no.5, pp.585–595

Michéle Cohen, 'Language and Meaning in a Documentary Source: Girls' Curriculum from the Late Eighteenth Century to the Schools Inquiry Commission, 1868', *History of Education* (January, 2005), vol.34, no.1, pp.77–93

Linda Colley, 'Whose Nation? Class and National Consciousness in Britain 1750–1830', *Past & Present* (November, 1986), no.113, pp.97–117

Paula Coonerty, 'The Presentation Order and the National School system in Limerick, 1837–1870', *North Munster Antiquarian Journal* (1988), vol.30, pp.29–34

David A. Coppock, 'Respectability as a Pre-Requisite of Moral Character: The Social and Occupational Mobility of Pupil Teachers in the Late Nineteenth and Early Twentieth Centuries', *History of Education* (1997), vol.26, no.2, pp.165–186

Marjorie Cruickshank, 'The Argyll Commission Report 1865–1868: A Landmark Review in Scottish Education', *British Journal of Educational Studies* (June, 1967), vol.15, no.2, pp.133–147

Anna Davin, 'Imperialism and Motherhood', *History Workshop Journal* (Spring, 1978), no.5, pp.9–65

Brendan Duffy, 'Late Nineteenth Century Popular Educational Conservatism: The Work of Coalminers on the School Boards of the North-East', *History of Education* (1998), vol.27, no.1, pp.29–38: 36

Carol Dyhouse, 'Good Wives and Little Mothers: Social Anxieties and the Schoolgirl's Curriculum, 1890–1920', *Oxford Review of Education* (1977), vol.3, no.1, pp.21–23

Carol Dyhouse, 'Social Darwinistic Ideas and the Development of Women's Education in England, 1800–1920', *History of Education* (February, 1976), vol.5, no.1, pp.41–58

Adrian Elliott, 'The Bradford School Board and the Department of Education, 1870–1902: Areas of Conflict', *Journal of Educational Administration and History* (July, 1981), vol.13, no.2, pp.18–23

W. Gareth Evans, 'The "Bilingual Difficulty": HMI and the Welsh Language in the Victorian Age', *The Welsh Historical Review* (December, 1993), vol.16, no.4, pp.494–513

W. Gareth Evans, 'Gender Stereotyping and the Training of Female Elementary School Teachers: The Experience of Victorian Wales', *History of Education* (1992), vol.21, no.2, pp.189–204

W. Gareth Evans, 'The Welsh Intermediate and Technical Education Act of 1889: A Centenary Appreciation', *History of Education* (September, 1990), vol.19, no.3, pp.195–210

W. Gareth Evans, 'The Welsh Intermediate and Technical Education Act 1889 and the Education of Girls', *The Welsh History Review* (1991), vol.15, pp.183–217

Maria Yolanda Fernández-Suárez, 'An Essential Picture in a Sketch-book of Ireland: The Last Hedge Schools', *Estudios Irlandeses* (2006), no.1, pp.45–57

David Fitzpatrick, 'A Share of the Honeycomb: Education, Emigration and Irishwomen', *Continuity and Change* (1986), vol.1, no.2, pp.217–234

Thomas A. Fitzpatrick, 'Scottish Catholic Teacher Education: The Wider Context', *The Innes Review* (Autumn, 1994), vol.45, no.2, pp.147–170

Mary P. Gallant, 'Against the Odds: Anne Jemima Clough and Women's Education in England', *History of Education* (1997), vol.26, no.2, pp.145–164

Meg Gomersall, 'Education for Domesticity? A Nineteenth-Century Perspective on Girls' Schooling and Education', *Gender and Education* (1999), vol.6, no.3, pp.235–247

Meg Gomersall, 'Ideas and Realities: The Education of Working-Class Girls, 1800–1870,' *History of Education* (March, 1988), vol.17, no.1, pp.37–54

Joyce Goodman, 'Committee Women: Women School Governors in Early Nineteenth-Century England', *History of Education Society Bulletin* (Autumn, 1995), no.56, pp.48–57

Joyce Goodman, 'Constructing Contradiction: The Power and Powerlessness of Women in the Giving and Taking of Evidence in the Bryce Commission', *History of Education* (September, 1997), vol.26, no.3, pp.287–306

Joyce Goodman, 'Social Investigation and Economic Empowerment: The Women's Industrial Council and the LCC Trade Schools for Girls, 1892–1914', *History of Education* (September, 1998), vol.27, no.3, pp.297–314

Joyce Goodman, 'Undermining or Building Up the Nation? Elizabeth Hamilton (1758–1816), National Identities and an Authoritative Role for Women Educationists', *History of Education* (September, 1999), vol.28, no.3, pp.279–296

Colin Griffin, 'Learning to Labour: Elementary Education in the Leicestershire and South Derbyshire Coalfields c.1840–1870', *History of Education* (2002), vol.31, no.2, pp.95–116

Russell Grigg, 'Educating Criminal and Destitute Children: Reformatory and Industrial Schools in Wales, 1858–1914', *The Welsh History Review* (December, 2002), vol.21, no.2, pp.292–327

Judith Harford, 'The Movement for the Higher Education of Women in Ireland: Gender Equality or Denominational Rivalry?', *History of Education* (September, 2005), vol.34, no.5, pp.497–516

Jennifer A. Hargreaves 'Playing Like Gentlemen While Behaving Like Ladies: Contradictory Features of the Formative Years of Women's Sport', *British Journal of Sports History* (1985), vol.2, no.1, pp.40–52

John Hassard & Michael Rowlinson, 'Researching Foucault's Research: Organization and Control in Joseph Lancaster's Monitorial Schools', *Organization* (2002), vol.94, no.4, pp.615–639

Vanessa Heggie, 'Domestic and Domesticating Education in the Late Victorian City', *History of Education* (May, 2011), vol.40, no.3, pp.273–290

Christine Heward, 'Men, Women and the Rise of the Professional Society: The Intriguing History of Teacher Educators', *History of Education* (1993), vol.22, no.1, pp.11–32

J.H. Higginson, 'Dame Schools', *British Journal of Educational Studies* (1974), vol.22, no.2, pp.166–181

Pamela Horn, 'Child Workers in the Pillow Lace and Straw Plait Trades of Victorian Buckinghamshire and Bedfordshire', *The Historical Journal* (1974), vol.17, no.4, pp.79–96

Pamela Horn, 'The Education and Employment of Working-Class Girls, 1870–1914', *History of Education* (March, 1988), vol.17, no.1, pp.83–99

Pamela Horn, 'Mid-Victorian Elementary School Teachers', *The Local Historian* (November, 1976), vol.12, nos.3–4, pp.161–166

Pamela Horn, 'The Recruitment, Role and Status of the Victorian Country Teacher', *History of Education* (June, 1980), vol.9, no.2, pp.129–142

Pamela Horn, 'The Victorian Governess', *History of Education* (December, 1989), vol.18, no.4, pp.333–344

Janet Howarth, 'Public Schools, Safety-Nets and Educational Ladders: The Classification of Girls' Secondary Schools, 1880–1914', *Oxford Review of Education* (1985), vol.11, no.1, pp.59–71

Maria Hull, 'A Derbyshire Schooling: 1884–1893', *History Workshop Journal* (Spring, 1988), vol.25, no.1, pp.166–170

B.K. Hyams, '"Culture" for Elementary Schoolteachers: An Issue in the History of English Education', *Paedagogica Historica* (1981), vol.21, no.1, pp.111–120

Harold Hislop, 'The Management of the Kildare Place School System, 1811–1831', *Irish Educational Studies* (Spring, 1992), vol.11, no.1, pp.52–71

Andrea Jacobs, '"The Girls Have Done Very Decidedly Better Than the Boys": Girls and Examinations, 1860–1902', *Journal of Educational Administration and History* (2001), vol.33, no.2, pp.120–136

Andrea Jacobs & Joyce Goodman, 'The Music Teacher in English Girls' Secondary Schools before 1939', *Women's History Magazine* (Spring, 2007), no.55, pp.12–20

Deborah James, '"Teaching Girls": intermediate schools and career opportunities for girls in the East Glamorgan valleys of Wales, 1896–1914', *History of Education* (2001), vol.30, no.6, pp.513–526

Gareth Elwyn Jones, 'Education and Nationhood in Wales: An Historiographical Analysis', *Journal of Educational Administration and History* (December, 2006), vol.38, no.3, pp.263–277

Ellen Jordan, '"The Great Principle of English Fair-Play": The Admission of Women to the Pharmaceutical Society of Great Britain', *Women's History Review* (September, 1998), vol.7, no.3, pp.381–409

Sara Karly Kehoe, 'Nursing the Mission. The Franciscan Sisters of the Immaculate Conception and the Sisters of Mercy in Glasgow, 1847–1866', *The Innes Review* (2005), vol. 56, no.1, pp. 46–59

Camilla Leach, 'Religion and Rationality: Quaker Women and Science Education 1790–1850', *History of Education* (2006), vol.35, no.1, pp.69–90

Donald P. Leinster-Mackay, 'Dame Schools: A Need for Review', *British Journal of Educational Studies*, vol.24, no.1 (1976), pp.33–48

John Logan, 'Governesses, Tutors and Parents: Domestic Education in Ireland 1700–1880', *Irish Educational Studies* (1988), vol.7, no.2, pp.1–19

Mary S.T. Logan, 'The Centenary of the Admission of Women Students to the Belfast Medical School', *The Ulster Medical Journal* (October, 1990), vol.59, no.2, pp.200–203

Jane Martin, '"To Blaise the Trail for Women to Follow Along": Sex, Gender and the Politics of Education on the London School Board, 1870–1904', *Gender and Education* (2000), vol.12, no.2, pp.165–81

Jane McDermid, 'Blurring the Boundaries: School Board Women in Scotland, 1873–1919', *Women's History Review* (July, 2010), vol.19, no.3, pp.357–373

Jane McDermid, 'Catholic Working-Class Girls' Education in Lowland Scotland, 1872–1900', *The Innes Review* (Spring, 1996), vol.47, no.1, pp.69–80

Jane McDermid, 'Catholic Women Teachers and Scottish Education in the Nineteenth and Early Twentieth Centuries', *History of Education* (September, 2009), vol.38, no.5, pp.605–620

Jane McDermid, 'Home and Away: A Schoolmistress in Lowland Scotland and Colonial Australia in the Second Half of the Nineteenth Century', *History of Education Quarterly* (February, 2011), vol.51, no.1, pp.28–48

Jane McDermid, 'Place the Book in Their Hands: Grace Paterson's Contribution to the Health and Welfare Policies of the School Board of Glasgow, 1885–1906', *History of Education* (November, 2007), vol.36, no.6, pp.697–713

Jane McDermid, 'School Board Women and Active Citizenship in Scotland, 1873–1919', *History of Education* (May, 2009), vol.38, no.3, pp.333–347

Mary Macdonald with Ann Hope, 'The Scottish Institution: A Pioneer Venture', *History of Education Society Bulletin* (Autumn, 1993), no.52, pp.49–55

Denis McLaughlin, 'The Irish Christian Brothers and the National Board of Education: Challenging the Myths', *History of Education* (January, 2008), vol.37, no.1, pp.43–70

Linda Mahood, 'Eglantyne Jebb: Remembering, Representing and Writing a Rebel Daughter', *Women's History Review* (February, 2008), vol.17, no.1, pp.1–20

J.A. Mangan, 'The Social Construction of Victorian Femininity: Emancipation, Education and Exercise', *International Journal of the History of Sport* (1989), vol.6, no.1, pp.1–9

Carmen Mangion, '"Good Teacher" or "Good Religious"? The Professional Identity of Catholic Women Religious in Nineteenth-Century England and Wales', *Women's History Review* (2005), vol.14, no.2, pp.223–242

Catherine Manthorpe, 'Science or Domestic Science? The Struggle to Define an Appropriate Science for Girls in Early Twentieth-Century England', *History of Education* (1986) vol.15, no.3, pp.195–213

Jane Martin, 'Fighting Down the Idea That the Only Place for Women Was the Home? Gender and Policy in Elementary Education, 1870–1904', *History of Education* (December, 1995), vol.24, no.4, pp.277–292

Jane Martin, '"Hard-Headed and Large-Hearted": Women and the Industrial Schools, 1870–1885', *History of Education* (September, 1991). vol.20, no.3, pp.187–203

Jane Martin, 'To "Blaise the Trail for Women to Follow Along": Sex, Gender and the Politics of Education on the London School Board', *Gender and Education* (2000), vol.12, no.2, pp.165–181

Jane Martin, 'Women Entering the Public Arena: The Female Members of the London School Board', *History of Education* (September, 1993), vol.22, no.3, pp.225–240

David Mich, 'Underinvestment in Literacy? The Potential Contribution of Government Involvement in Elementary Education to Economic Growth in Nineteenth-Century England', *Journal of Economic History* (1984), vol.44, no.2, pp.557–566

Jacob Middleton, 'The Cry for Useless Knowledge', *History of Education Researcher* (November, 2005), no.76, pp.91–99

Lindy Moore, 'Invisible Scholars: Girls Learning Latin and Mathematics in the Elementary Public Schools of Scotland before 1872', *History of Education* (June, 1984), vol.13, no.2, pp.121–137

Lindy Moore, 'Young Ladies' Institutions: The Development of Secondary School for Girls in Scotland, 1833–c.1870', *History of Education* (May, 2003), vol.32, no.3, pp.249–272

Janet Nolan, 'The National Schools and Irish Women's Mobility in the Late Nineteenth and Early Twentieth Centuries', *Irish Studies Review* (Spring, 1997), vol.5, no.18, pp.23–28

Susan O'Brien, 'French Nuns in Nineteenth-Century England', *Past & Present* (February, 1997), no.154, pp.142–180

Susan O'Brien, '"Terra Incognita": The Nun in Nineteenth-Century England', *Past & Present* (1989), no.121, pp.110–140

Anne V. O'Connor, 'Influences Affecting Girls' Secondary Education in Ireland, 1860–1910', *Archivium Hibernicum* (1986), vol.41, pp.83–98

Grainne O'Flynn, 'Some Aspects of the Education of Irish Women through the Years', *Capuchin Annual* (1971), pp.164–179

Margaret Ó hÓgartaigh, 'Emerging from the Educational Cloisters: Educational Influences on the Development of Professional Women', *PaGes* (1996), vol.3, pp.113–123

Margaret Ó hÓgartaigh, 'A Quiet Revolution: Women and Second-Level Education in Ireland, 1878–1930', *New Hibernian Review* (Summer, 2009), vol.13, no.2, pp.36–51

Joan E. Parker, 'Lydia Becker's "School for Science"', *Women's History Review* (2001), vol.10, no.4, pp.629–650

Catriona M. Parrat, 'Athletic "Womanhood": Exploring Sources for Female Sport in Victorian and Edwardian England', *Journal of Sport History* (Summer, 1989), vol.16, no.2, pp.140–157

Joyce S. Pederson, 'Schoolmistresses and Headmistresses: Elites and Education in Nineteenth-Century England', *The Journal of British Studies* (November, 1975), vol.15, no.1, pp.135–162

Joyce Senders Pedersen, 'The Reform of Women's Secondary and Higher Education: Institutional Change and Social Values in Mid and Late Victorian England', *History of Education Quarterly* (Spring, 1979), vol.19, no.1, pp.61–91

Joyce Senders Pederson, 'Some Victorian Headmistresses: A Conservative Tradition of Social Reform', *Victorian Studies* (Summer, 1981), vol.24, no.4, pp.463–488

June Purvis, '"Women's Life Is Essentially Domestic, Public Life Being Confined to Men" (Comte): Separate Spheres and Inequality in the Education of Working-Class Women, 1854–1900', *History of Education* (December, 1981), vol.10, no.4, pp.227–244

June Purvis, 'Working-Class Women and Adult Education in Nineteenth-Century Britain', *History of Education* (September, 1980), vol.8, no.4, pp.193–212

Deirdre Raftery, 'The Academic Formation of the Fin De Siècle Female-Schooling for Girls in Late Nineteenth Century Ireland', *Irish Educational Studies* (Spring, 2001), vol.20, no.1, pp.321–334

Deirdre Raftery, 'Educational Ideologies and Reading for Girls in England 1815–1915', *History of Education Society Bulletin* (Spring, 1997), no.59, pp.4–11

Deirdre Raftery, 'Home Education in Nineteenth-Century Ireland: The Role and Status of the Governess', *Irish Educational Studies* (Spring, 2000), vol.19, no.1, pp.308–317

Deirdre Raftery & Catherine Nowlan-Roebuck, 'Convent Schools and National Education in Nineteenth-Century Ireland: Negotiating a Place within a Non-Denominational System', *History of Education* (May, 2007), vol.36, no.3, pp.353–365

Deirdre Raftery, Jane McDermid & Gareth Elwyn Jones, 'Social Change and Education in Ireland, Scotland and Wales: Historiography on Nineteenth-Century Schooling', *History of Education* (July, 2007) vol.36, no.4, pp.447–463

Jane Read, 'Froebelian Women: Networking to Promote Professional Status and Educational Change in the Nineteenth Century', *History of Education* (2003), vol.32, no.1, pp.17–33

Jane Rendall, 'Women and the Public Sphere', *Gender & History* (November, 1999), vol.11, no.3, pp.475–488

John Roach, 'Boys and Girls at School, 1800–1870', *History of Education* (1986), vol.15, no.3, pp.147–159

A.F.B. Roberts, 'A New View of the Infant School Movement', *British Journal of Educational Studies* (June, 1972), vol.20, no.2, pp.154–164

Wendy Robinson, 'In search of a "Plain Tale": Rediscovering the Champions of the Pupil-Teacher centres 1900–1910', *History of Education* (1999), vol.28, no.1, pp.53–71

Wendy Robinson, '"Less Intelligent and Lacking in Edge"? Female Pupil Teachers and Academic Performance', *Women's History Notebooks* (Winter, 2000), vol.7, no.1, pp.15–20

Wendy Robinson, 'Pupil Teachers: the Achilles Heel of Higher Grade Girls' Schools, 1882–1904', *History of Education* (1993), vol.22, no.3, pp.241–252

Gordon Roderick, 'Social Class, Curriculum and the Concept of Relevance in Secondary Education: Industrial Glamorgan, 1889–1914', *The Welsh History Review* (1998), vol.19, no.2, pp.289–318

Gordon W. Roderick & David Allsobrook, 'Welsh Society and University Funding, 1860–1914', *The Welsh History Review* (June, 2000), vol.20, no.1, pp.34–61

Sheila Rowbotham, 'Travellers in a Strange Country: Responses of Working-Class Students to the University Extension Movement, 1873–1910', *History Workshop Journal* (1981), no.12, pp.62–95

Penny Russell, 'An Improper Education? Jane Griffin's Pursuit of Self-Improvement and "Truth", 1811–1812', *History of Education* (May, 2004), vol.33, no.3, pp.249–265

Richard J. L. Selleck, 'Mary Carpenter: A Confident and Contradictory Reformer', *History of Education* (June, 1985), vol.14, no.2, pp.101–116

J.R. Shackleton, 'Jane Marcet and Harriet Martineau: Pioneers of Economics Education', *History of Education* (December, 1990), pp.283–298

Deborah Simonton, '"Even Some Ladies Talk with Facility about Oxygen . . ." British Women and Higher Education, 1700–1850', *Women's History Magazine* (Autumn, 2007), no.57, pp.11–15

John T. Smith, 'Merely a Growing Dilemma of Etiquette? The Deepening Gulf between the Victorian Clergyman and Victorian Schoolteacher', *History of Education* (March, 2004), vol.33, no.2, pp.157–176

Sarah J. Smith, 'Retaking the Register: Women's Higher Education in Glasgow and Beyond, c.1796–1845, *Gender & History* (July, 2000), vol.12, no.2, pp.310–335

Keith D.M. Snell, 'The Sunday School Movement in England and Wales: Child Labour, Denominational Control and Working-Class Culture', *Past & Present* (August, 1999), no.164, pp.122–168

Gillian Sutherland, 'Examinations and the Construction of Professional Identity: A Case Study of England', *Assessment in Education: Principles, Policy & Practice* (2001), vol.8, no.1, pp.51–64

Marjorie R. Theobald, 'The Accomplished Woman and the Propriety of Intellect: A New Look at Women's Education in Britain and Australia, 1800–1850', *History of Education* (March, 1988), vol.17, no.1, pp.21–35

Else Trangbæk, 'One System, Several Cultures: A Comparative Study of Swedish Gymnastics for Women', *International Sports Studies* (2000), vol.22, no.2, pp.43–56

Annemarie Turnbull, 'An Isolated Missionary: The Domestic Subjects Teacher in England, 1870–1914', *Women's History Review* (1994), vol.3, no.1, pp.81–100

Lorcan Walsh, 'Images of Women in Nineteenth Century Schoolbooks', *Irish Educational Studies* (1984), vol.4, no.1, pp.73–87

Ruth Watts, 'Breaking the Boundaries of Victorian Imperialism or Extending a Reformed "Paternalism"? Mary Carpenter and India', *History of Education* (September, 2000), vol.29, no.5, pp.457–472

Ruth Watts, 'From Lady Teacher to Professional: A Case Study of Some of the First Headteachers of Girls' Secondary Schools in England', *Educational Management and Administration* (October, 1998), vol.26, no.4, pp.339–351

Ruth Watts, 'The Unitarian Contribution to the Development of Female Education, 1790–1850', *History of Education* (December, 1980), vol.9, no.4, pp.273–286

Roger Webster, 'Education in Wales and the Rebirth of a Nation', *History of Education* (September, 1990), vol.19, no.3, pp.183–194

H.G. Williams, '"Learning Suitable to the Situation of the Poorest Classes": The National Society and Wales, 1811–1839', *The Welsh History Review* (June, 1998), vol.19, no.3, pp.425–452

L.J. Williams & Dot Jones, 'Women at Work in Nineteenth-Century Wales', *Llafur: The Journal of the Society of Welsh Labour History* (1983), vol.3, no.3, pp.20–32

Theses and Dissertations

Gerald Ashton Banks, 'The Provision of Elementary Education in Liverpool 1861–1870', M.Ed. Dissertation, University of Liverpool, 1981

Pauline Bell, 'A History of Physical Education in Girls' Public Schools, 1870–1920', M.Ed. Dissertation, University of Manchester, 1978

Andrew Beynon, 'Politics and Religion in Welsh education: A Comparative Study of the School Boards of Caernarfon and Merthyr Tydfil 1870–1880', M.A .Dissertation, Aberystwyth University College, 1985

Eibhlin Breathnach, 'A History of the Movement for Women's Higher Education in Dublin, 1860–1912', M.A. Dissertation, University College Dublin, 1981

Joyce Collins, 'The Training of Elementary School Teachers in England and Wales, 1840–1890', PhD, Bulmershe College of Higher Education, 1985

Dina Copelman, 'Women in the Classroom Struggle: Elementary School Teachers in London, 1870–1914', PhD, Princeton University, 1985

Bryn L. Davies, 'An Assessment of the Contribution of Sir Hugh Owen to Education in Wales', PhD, University of Bangor, 1971

E. John Davies, 'The Origins and Development of Secondary Education in the Rhondda Valleys (1878–1923)', M.A. Dissertation, University of Wales, 1965

Lynn Patricia Edwards, 'Women Students at the University of Liverpool: Their Academic Careers and Postgraduate Lives 1833–1937', PhD, University of Liverpool, 1999

Kenneth David Evans, 'The Development of Secondary Education in South Pembrokeshire, 1889–1939', M.A. Dissertation, University of Wales, 1970

John Fletcher, 'The Influence of the Welsh Intermediate Education Act of 1889 on Technical Education', PhD, University of Wales, 1982

Frederick W.T. Fuller, 'The Churches Train Teachers: An Historical Survey of the Part Played by the Churches of All Denominations in the Training of Elementary Teachers in England and Wales, from the First Government Grant for Education in 1833 to the Establishment of Day Training Colleges Initiated in 1890', PhD, University of Exeter, 1973

Kathryn Jane Gleadle, 'The Early Feminists. Radical Unitarians and the Emergence of the Women's Rights movement c.1831–1851', PhD, University of Warwick, 1993

Joyce Goodman, 'Women and the Management of the Education of Working-Class Girls, 1800–1861', PhD, University of Manchester, 1992

Eirwen Griffiths, 'Monmouthshire and the Education Act, 1902: the "Welsh Revolt" of 1902–1905', MPhil, King's College University of London, 1994

Sheila Hamilton, 'Women and the Scottish Universities circa 1869–1939', PhD, University of Edinburgh, 1987

M.J. Illing, 'Pupil-Teachers and the Emancipation of Women, 1870–1905', MPhil, King's College London, 1978

Catherine Mary Keane (Sr. M. Vincent), 'A History of the Foundation of the Presentation Convents in the Diocese of Kerry and Their Contribution to Education during the Nineteenth Century', M.Ed., Trinity College Dublin, 1976

Sara Karly Kehoe, 'Special Daughters of Rome: Glasgow and its Roman Catholic Sisters, 1847–1913', PhD, University of Glasgow, 2005

Joyce Elizabeth Livingstone, 'Pauper Education in Victorian England: Organization and Administration within the New Poor Law, 1834–1880', PhD, London Guildhall University, 1993

Kim Lowden, 'Spirited Sisters: Anglican and Catholic contributions to Women's Teacher Training in the Nineteenth Century', PhD, University of Liverpool, 2000

Jane McCarthy, 'Contribution of the Sisters of Mercy to West Cork Schooling, 1844–1922', M.Ed. Dissertation, University College Cork, 1979

Lesley Anne Orr Macdonald, 'Women and Presbyterianism in Scotland c.1830 to c.1930', PhD, University of Edinburgh, 1995

Mary McHugh, 'The Development of the Catholic Community in the Western Province (Glasgow, Motherwell and Paisley) 1878–1962', PhD, Strathclyde University, 1990

Mary MacKintosh, 'Education in Lanarkshire: A Historical Survey Up to the Act of 1872, from Original and Contemporary Sources', PhD, Glasgow University, 1968

Jane Martin, 'The Role of Women in the Education of the Working Classes, 1870–1904', PhD, The Open University, 1991

Graeme Morton, 'Unionist Nationalism: The Historical Construction of Scottish National Identity, Edinburgh 1830–1860', PhD, University of Edinburgh, 1993

Carole Ann Mullins, '"Washtub Women": A Study of Female School Inspectors from the 1890s to the 1920s', M.Ed. Dissertation, University of Liverpool, 1999

Eilis O'Sullivan, 'The Training of Women Teachers in Ireland 1824–1919, with Special Reference to Mary Immaculate College and Limerick', M.A. Dissertation, University of Limerick, 1998

James Pressley, 'Childhood, Education and Labour: Moral Pressure and the End of the Half-Time System, PhD, University of Lancaster, 2000

L.M. Rees, 'A Critical Examination of Teacher Training in Wales, 1846–1898', PhD, University of Wales, 1968

Juliet Stevenson, 'A Neglected Issue in the History of Education and Training: Women Students of University College London and the Polytechnic at Regent Street, c.1870–1930', PhD, Thames Valley University London, 1996

Kelvin John Street, 'Female Culture in Physical Training Colleges 1885–1918', PhD, De Montfort University, 1999

Rosemary Annette Thynne, 'The Girls' High Schools 1872–1914 and the Shaping of a New Generation of Middle-Class Girls', PhD, Royal Holloway College London, 2005

Annmarie Turnbull, 'Women, Education and Domesticity: A Study of the Domestic Subjects Movement, 1870–1914', PhD, Polytechnic of the Southbank, 1983

Alexander Wall, 'The Supply of Certificated Teachers to the Roman Catholic Elementary Schools of Britain 1848–1870', MPhil, University of Lancaster, 1983

J. Waugh, 'Aspects of Policy-Making in Teacher-Training and the Teachers' Struggle for Professional Status, 1895–1910', MLitt, Oxford University, 1993

H.G. Williams, 'Elementary Education in Caernarvonshire, 1839–1902', PhD, University of Bangor, 1981

Jenny Zmroczek, 'The Education and Employment of Girls in Norwich, 1870–1939', PhD, University of East Anglia, 2004

Index

fishing 19
fitness 92–97
Fitzpatrick, David 62
Fletcher, Sheila 86

G
Gaelic 38, 131–132
  see language
games 72, 75, 84, 94–97
Garrett, Elizabeth 26
  see Anderson
gender roles 41
Girls' Friendly Society 94
Girls' Public Day School Company
  (GPDSC) 81, 83, 86, 87, 88, 125
Girton College 88, 101
Gisborne, Thomas 107
Glasgow Association for the Higher
  Education of Women 101
Glasgow Infant School Society 124
Goodman, Joyce 87, 90, 123
Gordon, Peter 26
governess 69–71, 89, 105, 106–111,
  112
  training 110–111
  salary 112–113
Governesses' Benevolent Institution
  (GBI) 113, 114
Gregory, Sir John 107
Grey, Maria 81, 86, 125
  training college 126
Griffin, Colin 55
Guest, Lady Charlotte 44
  Sir John 51
gymnastics 96

H
half-time education 15, 54, 55, 59
Harford, Judith 98
Haslam, Anna 82
health 26
Heathorn, Stephen 144
higher education 97–103
Hilton, Mary 13
Homan, Ruth 61
Home Arts and Industries Association
  90
Home and Colonial Institute 126
Home Rule for Women 4, 23
Home Rule for Ireland 4
Honourable Society of Cymmrodorion
  83
Horn, Pamela 59, 131, 139
Hume, David 12

Highlands (Scottish) 18, 37
Hollis, Patricia 24, 28, 147
housewifery 23, 46, 61, 109, 147
  see domestic
Hughes, Kathryn 110
Hughes, Thomas 72
Humphries, Jane 15

I
illiteracy 36, 38
inspectors 14
  Her Majesty's Inspectorate (HMI)
  28
Intermediate Education (Ireland) Act
  82
Intermediate and Technical Education
  (Wales) Act 85
Irish National Society for Promoting
  the Education of the Poor 34
Irish University Act 100

J
Jacobs, Andrea 127
James, Deborah 64, 85
Jebb, Eglantyne 132
Jellicoe, Anne 81, 82
Jones, Gareth Elwyn 1, 63
Jordan, Ellen 98

K
Kamm, Josephine 87
Kay-Shuttleworth, James 37, 116, 117,
  124
Kildare Place Society 34, 123
King's College Ladies' Department 99
knitting 3, 19, 20, 33, 42, 44

L
lace 16, 59, 62
lad of parts 1, 27
Ladies' Collegiate School 81
Ladies' Institute (Belfast) 63
Lady Superintendent 81, 114–115,
  133
Lancaster, Joseph 123, 124
Langham Circle 81
language 6, 39
  and schooling 32–33
  Welsh 6, 37–38, 56, 64, 83, 131–132
  see Gaelic
laundry 20, 22, 23, 28, 45, 57, 64, 67,
  91, 92
Lingen, Ralph 37, 40, 47
literacy 55

#0050 - 280417 - C0 - 229/152/12 [14] - CB - 9780415181969